PRINTMAKER'S DAUGHTER,
PAINTER'S WIFE

GUERNICA WORLD EDITIONS 47

PRINTMAKER'S DAUGHTER PAINTER'S WIFE

Nina Barragan

GUERNICA
World
EDITIONS

TORONTO—CHICAGO—BUFFALO—LANCASTER (U.K.)
2022

Guernica Founder: Antonio D'Alfonso

Michael Mirolla, editor
Interior design: Jill Ronsley, suneditwrite.com
Cover design: Allen Jomoc Jr.
Cover Images: *Nina, at one year*
Left: Mauricio Lasansky, *Aitana* [detail] intaglio, 1948
Right: Alan Weinstein, *Nina* [detail] ink drawing, 1991

Guernica Editions Inc.
287 Templemead Drive, Hamilton (ON), Canada L8W 2W4
2250 Military Road, Tonawanda, N.Y. 14150-6000 U.S.A.
www.guernicaeditions.com

Distributors:
Independent Publishers Group (IPG)
600 North Pulaski Road, Chicago IL 60624
University of Toronto Press Distribution (UTP)
5201 Dufferin Street, Toronto (ON), Canada M3H 5T8
Gazelle Book Services, White Cross Mills
High Town, Lancaster LA1 4XS U.K.

First edition.

Legal Deposit—First Quarter
Library of Congress Catalog Card Number: 2021947562
Library and Archives Canada Cataloguing in Publication
Title: Printmaker's daughter, painter's wife / Nina Barragan.
Names: Barragan, Nina, author.
Series: Guernica world editions ; 47.
Description: Series statement: Guernica world editions ; 47
Identifiers: Canadiana (print) 20210337214 | Canadiana (ebook)
20210337370 | ISBN 9781771837293 (softcover) | ISBN 9781771837309 (EPUB)
Classification: LCC PS3552.A72 P75 2022 | DDC 813/.54—dc23

Foreword

M Y PLAN WAS TO WRITE about one year on Ibiza—exhilarating, serene, memorable for its lasting impact. Alan and I stepped onto an island where ties to the natural environment, to history, to self-knowledge and dignity, became ours. Where the people, their dwellings, and the rhythm of life, became ours. That remarkable encounter ushered me from a protected youth toward maturity. Like flakes of glistening mica, the essences of Ibiza marked our future paths.

One year swiftly evolved into decades, effortlessly linking me from ancestors to grandchildren. The constancy of a shared life, and my good fortune of having known more love than pain, has accompanied this exploration through genetics, experiences and destiny.

Regardless of how much we remember, it is never everything, and for me, frequently not enough. Because memories are often formed from our needs and eventually feed those needs, some truths are left behind; others, enhanced. Events from my childhood regularly appear in my writing and I've occasionally checked with my siblings for confirmation. Just as we see in our own ways, we recall differently. The bigger the family, the more diverse the encounters, the more difficult to recognize the reality that was.

For the most part, I've deferred to my own versions and imaginings. The interspersed pieces of fiction—from various decades of my writing—are intended as spotlights on the fusion of life and work. This may not be a perfectly accurate, linear or complete recording of events and circumstances, but it is my story's truths, and I believe, some of my family's.

Murder in the Patagonia

A LOT HAS BEEN SAID ABOUT memory and the importance of not forgetting. Recalling and retrieving are at my core—in my house, in my head—truths and fabrications, chipped crockery, body language, smiles that never surface. Remembering less and forgetting more might be useful for someone like me. My 'good recall' has probably wasted much of my time, but it hasn't compromised my grasp of the present. I've never felt entangled by sentimentality because of memories. That was my father's fear. So much so, he often reminded my mother not to talk about the past, not to dwell on their previous lives—their childhoods, their people, the country they left behind.

My knowledge of family history came in response to my curiosity, an ongoing and fitting springboard for both my parents. Their verbal reflecting occurred one-on-one with me, out of earshot of each other, hoping to prevent emotional meltdowns. Opening windows to her happy youth, my mother, Emilia, whispered of things that had not seen the light of day for so long, they'd become secrets. My father, Mauricio, navigated the landscapes of his past, managing his facts to avoid the landmines of his heart. He was conscious of my mother's reticence adjusting to their American life, and perhaps that was why he dreaded the tug of memory, that frontier that would not, could not be erased.

Recollecting is not a source of trepidation for me. On the contrary, I welcome its contribution to who I am. Not a hoarder, I understand the importance of cleaning house. I've learned to throw out the damaged crockery, and, at last, those negative accumulations that contribute nothing beyond pain and impairment.

Summer, 1946. I was three and a half, standing alone and very still in the garden at the Green Farm, one of my earliest memories. That first scent of warm tomato plants and parsley has never left me. I still gravitate to the serenity of vegetables growing in the earth. Contentment surrounded me. The hot, Iowa sun on my face and arms, the tall, stalky foliage, the dove's mourning call. Even the large yellow and black creatures in their translucent webs were a curiosity, rather than the terror spiders became. Alone and happy at that tiny age, I listened to the sounds of a tractor churning in a nearby field, closer, the baby crying. Pushing my way out of the jungle I stepped onto the mowed yard. My mother and Roberta sat on the wooden steps of the back porch, laughing and bathing my unhappy little brother in a large tub. Ma was wearing her red and white polka dot halter top, Roberta, that turban scarf. Smiling, beckoning, they patted the spot between them as my little brother continued whimpering. I remember he cried a lot, even before the accident.

My mother was beautiful. She had the looks of a 1940's movie star with her white complexion and arched eyebrows, red lips and swept up black hair. She was happy. Bad things still hadn't happened and a return visit to her family in Argentina was a viable possibility.

Timid about her English, she was soft-spoken next to Roberta's outgoing personality. Blond, tall and attractive, Berta had a big American heart, a boisterous laugh, and a cigarette perpetually dangling from the corner of her mouth. A milliner by profession, amazing colors of felt and tulle, grosgrain ribbon, feathers and buttons, all boogied their way out of her magical bag. Hand stitching occupied her days. With cigarettes and ashtray beside her, she could sew anywhere. The kitchen table, couch, or cross-legged on the grass.

Best friends, they were together one season to the next. Emilia made *empanadas* while Roberta helped her with the English language. That summer at the Green Farm, we ate lots of Jell-O and tuna salad enhanced with sweet pickle juice. The following winter at Grand Avenue, it was meringues and macaroons. Stepping onto the cold, back porch in wooly cardigans, Roberta taught my mother how to whisk egg whites on a turkey platter. 308 Grand Avenue— our first Iowa home. A university rental on the north side of the street, it was halfway up the climb toward the Field House arena, one of two houses on that hill. Eventually they were both demolished and the sites became dormitory parking lots.

When my sister, María Jimena, was born, my dad bought my mom an Argus twin lens reflex camera and a featherweight Singer sewing machine. While we kids played outside in the Iowa sunshine, Ma kept busy with the camera. Her spirits were buoyant on bright days and nothing seemed a chore. A large front porch wrapped the front of the house and as sun poured in through the screens, Ma happily hung laundered diapers. Having grown up with Buenos Aires' damp winters and overcast skies, she was content observing the changes in luminosity as the day progressed, as she looked after us and continued her household tasks. A series of 3" x 3" photos survive her fascination with Iowa's sunlight. My older brother, William, posing beside snow drifts, his serge aviator's cap lined with curly fleece, the goat-like earflaps dangling. In an interior porch scene, my baby frown is illuminated as I attempt to unbutton a minuscule doll's dress, an impossible task for my tiny fingers.

Before taking up the camera that morning, Ma playfully released my braids. A memory from the Prado? She'd been taken many times as a small girl and always to Velázquez's salon, to the *Infanta Margarita*, with bow, blondness and bodice resplendent. I was my mother's *infanta*, with ribbon and petulant pout. My rivulets of fair hair flowed over summer pinafores, over autumn herringbone and winter's houndstooth. Years later, skilled with a needle and a lover of wool, I would covet the fabric in those cold weather photographs—my father's discarded greatcoats, repurposed as tiny jackets to keep me warm.

The ghost of Velázquez must have kept Mauricio company in the studio as he toiled on 'Little Girl,' his first grandchild, my niece,

Diana. More granddaughters would follow. My girls, Rachel and Anna, bouncing like clones from that portrait.

The sewing machine was pulled out when needed and Emilia managed without patterns. She sewed because it was necessary, not because the Singer sang to her. It was the same with cooking. The camera was her companion, her diary, and she had an instinctive sense of composition. By recording our lives and sending images back to Buenos Aires, she kept her distant family within her world. Despite the sadness of separation, she wanted them to know the brightness of Iowa.

Winter melted away. In the spring of that first year, William discovered the fun in sending our empty baby carriage careening down the hill's sidewalk. Coming to a stop in the middle of traffic, the pram caused a mayhem of screeching, breaking cars. Quickly the caper ended and we found other ways to amuse ourselves.

As word got around about our presence in Iowa City, Argentine grad students began visiting Grand Avenue, eager compatriots for my parents. Despite their cheerful company and Spanish conversations, Roberta remained my mom's closest friend, and in those first years of the University's printmaking program, Malcolm, Roberta's husband, was Mauricio's teaching assistant. I don't know whether Roberta and Malcolm were childless by choice, but they loved kids, and their steady presence and good humor were central to our lives. Roberta's companionship was a ballast for Emilia, especially in those early days when homesickness and isolation struck.

I was an adult before I figured out that for some people, birthright is an assumed comfort: identity and values, history and relatives, all escorted by a family's specific happiness and misery, humor and heartbreak. Facts may not always be neatly laid out, but they're available, at least enough to understand that more information might be in order, maybe even desirable. My legacy came to me in an imaginary satchel like Roberta's magical bag of boogying surprises. I've carried it with me like Garcia Marques' little girl in *One Hundred Years of Solitude*, the child destined to drag around the sack of her ancestors' bones. Always close so I could rummage and retrieve necessary information, bits and pieces of the known and the imagined—fragments, to create a whole. I resented having to 'discover' what I felt should have been given to me. What does it say about me that I was so interested in what my parents did not reveal, knowingly, or unknowingly? And why didn't they? I'm not talking about deep secrets, just facts of their lives, and quite possibly, mundane facts of ordinary lives. Both my parents would be appalled at the suggestion that 'ordinary', in any sense, might describe their spheres.

In my essay, *Doing Archaeology in My America*, I wrote that learning about my heritage was like an archaeological dig. Some of my siblings may have questioned this obsessive concern with the past. I heard their silence, their indifference to what came before them. I've remained as unresponsive to their need for not knowing, as they to my need for knowing. When the future no longer seems hopeful, no longer full of new possibilities, history, like an old acquaintance, steps forward. The past came to me in photographs, shoe boxes full, bursting in closets. Despite this plethora, photos were never displayed in our home, neither of places, nor of family. It was not for lack, and considering the quantity, precious few exist of my immediate family all together.

One is a 1953 snapshot taken on the Saturnia ocean liner as we traveled to Spain (before my youngest two siblings were born), and there are pictures of my wedding a decade later. We never posed together as a family during holidays, squeezing in close, smiling out '*cheese*'. If we had, it would've been either Thanksgiving or New Year's Eve, the only holiday celebrations my father permitted in our home, because, as he said, 'They were not religious.' Yet the occasional Christmas slipped in, under the wire. Our relationship to the holiday was complicated, fraught with indecision. As a young child I understood there was a problem, but religion was never discussed or explained. My first memory is of kindergarten at Roosevelt Elementary, when we lived on Grand Avenue. The day my teacher wished the class a Merry Christmas with their families around the tree, I told her we didn't have one.

She gently suggested that if my father came to the school on the last day of class before the holiday break, he could take the class tree for our home. When I told Pa, he hit the ceiling and immediately went out and bought a tree.

Years later, my mother was such a loyal customer at Whiteway Super Market in downtown Iowa City, the owner made sure a tall tree was delivered every holiday season. It used to sit on our back porch for days, ignored, until my sister and I dragged it in, set it up in the living room, and proceeded to decorate with paper chains and anything we could find around the house. Then, the waiting game.

So Pa, are we having Christmas?

On more than one December 24th, my father hurried to the Paper Place across from the campus and bought books for everyone, and William hit the hardware store and did the same. If the 'yes' decision happened with time, my mother could drop into Younkers on one of her Saturday morning shopping trips, happily taking the bus while I stayed home and babysat. Jimena and I had our gifts ready: store bought cookies and candies I'd made during my Brownie Troop meetings, all wrapped in hand decorated paper napkins. The candies were a delicious combination of dried fruits and nuts, ground together and rolled in powdered sugar. If my parents had been able, I believe they would have eradicated the holiday—my father, eager to dodge the pervasive attitude that it was 'just an American celebration' (as though American and Christian were one and the same), and my mother, so as to avoid my father's anxious vacillation.

Back to my family and photographs. In September of 1976, there was an awkward occasion when we were unexpectedly caught together in an elevator. Rushing to the dedication of the Lasansky Room in the New Carver Wing at the University of Iowa Museum of Art, all of us, Ma, Pa and my siblings, found ourselves inadvertently together and alone. In the confusion of exiting our parents' condominium, we were temporarily separated from our mates and children. Stunned by the realization of 'together and alone', our mute embarrassment morphed into raucous laughter as the elevator reached the lobby.

That event was marked by another family shoot later that evening. University photographers were ready and waiting at the Museum dedication.

I was the first to marry and my ceremonial wedding images survive, still in glassine sleeves. Neatly stacked under those shoeboxes, they keep company with over-size certificates and awards, documents of one kind and another. There are snaps of my older brother's wedding and my sister's, but none with the family posing formally as we had for mine. Given the palpable resistance to 'posed' photos, who arranged for my wedding photographer? Probably my mother.

My father's uncle, *El Tío David*, was a professional photographer in Buenos Aires, so we have a substantial record of the Lasansky side, both formal and informal. My maternal grandparents, Luis and Pilar Barragán, had traditional portraits taken for special occasions. Dressed in their finery they sat and stood, with props and without, Emilia with that large white bow in her hair and her six-year-old moping mouth. So, no, it was not for lack of images. When my parents moved from our old home on South Summit to their condominium at Quail Creek, then on to their final dwelling—the renovated 1880's building in downtown Iowa City, originally a paint, varnish and wallpaper business—the shoe boxes of history accompanied them, only to end up on more closet shelves.

As an adolescent visiting my friends' homes, I wondered about my family's habit. Why didn't we display photographs? In answer to my question, my mother's proud response was swift and final. Mauricio, an artist, a printmaker, considered the custom *bourgeois*.

My maternal grandparents' lives had not gone against the grain, other than being anti-clergy, so most likely family photos had a presence in their home. Since Ma did not have a history of rejecting her parents' values, on the contrary, she always seemed at peace with her upbringing, I figured she had trouble with the *bourgeois* decree. Was there a more visceral explanation? Did the displaying of family, specifically Pa's parents and siblings, cause him more pain than pleasure, taking him to some murky place where his burdens and superstitions gained the upper hand, paralyzing him in the process? Conceivably. *La Bobeh* Ana, our paternal grandmother, came from Buenos Aries to Iowa for an extended visit when I was 15. It was hard to ignore my dad's anxiety about his mother. They had a tense relationship and he was always short on patience, whether communication was long-distance or in person.

Pa had the final word in our family, but to be fair, after my last trip to Argentina, I've questioned the 'photograph thing'. Was it truly his ruling or did it have more to do with a partial story I'd heard from my mother? A devastating account so blurred by time, the facts were lost to those who once knew them. Unguarded truths, melting like icicles in the sun, are apt to be lifted by winds and turned to vapor in the sky.

There was no reason to question my mother's version until I learned more. When my parents were newlyweds and living in Villa María, Córdoba, Pa's father, Abram, and his eldest son, Guillermo, were tragically killed in a car accident while on a job excursion in the Patagonia. The catastrophe occurred just as they were returning home. Only days before their departure from the south, Guillermo mailed off a post card to his mother and siblings with the good news that it had been a productive trip. They had saved their wages and would soon be home. Before they'd left for the Patagonia, Abram told his sons it would be his last journey south. In the future, he would find work in the city. Soon to be a grandfather, he wanted to stay near his family.

They were in the back seat of a taxi traveling to a train station for the return trip to Buenos Aires. It was raining and the road, mountainous. The cab was following a large lumber truck carrying heavy logs. The truck came to an abrupt stop but the taxi did not. A huge log smashed through the taxi's front window, missed the driver but instantly killed my grandfather and uncle, smashing their heads against the sides of the car.

When the telegram reached Buenos Aires, my uncle, Bernardo, contacted Mauricio in Córdoba, and they hurriedly left to claim the bodies. Before arranging to have the bodies shipped north, they had the coffins closed. The disfigurement was extensive. That's how it happened, end of story.

My mother knew nothing more. Questions were pointless.

The second version came from my father's youngest brother, Marcos, when I was last in Buenos Aires decades later. After serving coffee in the living room of their condominium on *Avenida Corrientes*, my aunt Perla disappeared into the kitchen. She understood her husband's desire for privacy. He was old and preoccupied by then, anxious to get things off his chest, including details about the deaths. I related what I knew and he said yes, that was the story told to my grandmother. Surprised it was Emilia's account, he concluded she might not have been told the whole truth. Marcos reminded me that she was expecting their first child, my brother, William, when the accident occurred. It had not been an easy pregnancy and perhaps after the birth, Mauricio chose not to re-visit the subject.

The fact was, Marcos said, they were murdered. The postmortem examination concluded the head trauma did not kill them. After the accident, the taxi driver apparently slit their throats as they lay unconscious. Their money and papers were stolen, their bodies left on the road in pools of blood, the wrecked taxi abandoned, and a trail of blood (the driver's?) led into the woods.

From skid marks on the road, there was evidence of a collision and it was apparent the driver had been seriously injured. The police were involved, but strangely, no report was filed. The taxicab was not registered and the driver was never found. Charges were never pressed. The only source of identification was a card found in the lining of Guillermo's shoe. Having just graduated as an accountant, he had been accepted as a member of a professional bookkeeping organization. The card listed his name, address and the association's information.

Marcos was 12 when he answered the door for the Western Union boy. The telegram came from a rural police station in the Patagonia. Bernardo relayed the information to Mauricio. From that point on, the two versions of the story mesh—how the two brothers traveled to Patagonia to retrieve the bodies, how they closed the coffins, not wanting *La Bobeh* and the family to see what had happened.

Marcos agreed with me that too much remained unclear. Putting down his coffee he began pacing the floor. Why didn't the driver of the log truck stop? Was it possible he hadn't felt the impact and continued driving? Couldn't police dogs have followed the trail of blood into the woods? Marcos believed that because there was no family present to insist on pursuing the investigation (it took a couple days for Bernardo and Mauricio to get down to the Patagonia by train), the police dismissed the case.

When I asked Marcos how he knew the details, he said both his brothers told him, on separate occasions. Standing beside the window, staring distractedly at the activity on *Corrientes* street, my uncle's voice was hushed. He told me there was no closure for his brothers—two distraught young men who felt they were doing right by closing the coffins, who thought they were protecting their mother. But Ana did not believe her husband and eldest son were dead. When their deaths finally became a reality for her, she never forgave her younger sons for depriving her of a final viewing. Marcos said that after the funeral, his brothers were never able to please her, regardless of how hard they tried. Her bitterness and anger nearly destroyed the family.

On that same visit to Buenos Aires, I spoke with my mother's brother, Julio. Annoyed that Marcos had told me, he confirmed and quickly dismissed the story, saying it was long ago and no longer mattered. They were dead. I needn't concern myself. He too was in the business of protection. On a couple occasions I heard my dad mention the deaths in passing. It had been a car accident somewhere in the Patagonia. No details. I haven't any idea if he ever spoke beyond that to any of his other children.

Where do these two versions end? Crashing into the plaster wall of my parents' first, Córdoba bedroom.

'Before, it was such a happy room …' My mother's quiet voice described the bed and washstand, the armoire, the sun landing on the balcony with geraniums and the ornate wrought iron railing. She made it sound like a Matisse. After the funeral, Mauricio hammered nails into that wall and hung pictures of his deceased family.

She wept telling me it was like living with ghosts. Retiring at night or waking in the morning, she had to confront their faces staring at her, faces she knew to be dead. She was so distressed and unable to calm herself, Mauricio finally took down the photographs and put them away, somewhere with his books.

Did they talk about it, or was it a flash of unspoken understanding? Maybe neither. Possibly, 'too *bourgeois*,' simply ended up the default exit for both my parents.

During my youth, only if I suggested were the photo boxes pulled out of the closet. It was more for me than my mother, times I needed her spontaneous joy. Laughing lightly, explaining details of relationships, she was in her element. The bundles of photos were quickly put away before my dad came up from the studio for lunch. She might have liked organizing and keeping albums, but such an idea probably never surfaced. While visual memories remained rubber-banded and tucked away in boxes, while they were not permitted the light of day, the past could not encroach, could not become the throbbing threat he feared.

Did she know the other truth, the postmortem revelation of murder? Was she ever able to acknowledge why our home did not include the reassurance of her parents' portraits? Images she could pass on the way to make school lunches, to make beds and do laundry, faces she could glance at or touch, the family she had so reluctantly left. Regardless of how it started, the problem of photographs developed into a constant ache. It was what it was.

Emilia became an expert at converting her husband's negative 'markers' into noble ideals she could believe in. Not endowed with strengths of full passion or ambition, her modest personality and quiet beauty were the figurehead of her ship, Mauricio, its mast.

She went along with his attitudes and decisions, at least to us, their children. With the rest of the world, she learned to smile and remain silent, allowing him the attention, permitting her own near diminishment.

When I returned from that last Argentine trip, I brought back old photographs. Ma as a young woman standing as tall as she could, her little brother, Julio, beside her, both wearing the embroidered peasant shirts their mother, Pilar, had sewn. *El Abuelo Luis*, handsome with his black hair and mustache, still not bald. My paternal grandparents, Ana and Abram, early in their marriage. Family photos finally joined the shelves' clutter of art books and the ephemera of a collecting life: a grandchild's drawing, a miniature pre-Columbian jade face, a vintage wooden mannequin sitting politely, two strands of African beads hanging from his neck. Pa positioned the images so they were easily visible. Supposedly, adjusting family photographs was something he'd been doing all along.

The final decade was sweeping in, hovering over mannequin, books and my parents sitting on the worn, leather couch. Those old pictures I brought back from Argentina were not conscious of time, neither the first decade nor the last. Still shiny and eager, out of breath from hurrying, they were sorry to be so late.

Yes, I display photos. Those who've crossed over, our parents and grandparents, and those who live—my husband, my children, my children's children. They've all made my world what it is and me who I am. My past, my present, my future.

As I approached the porch steps at the Green Farm, my brother, Leonardo, snuggled in Ma's lap, wrapped in a towel. Roberta tipped over the enamel tub and flicked a grasshopper off her knee. William explored the barn. My sister, Jimena, would be born the following year. In that suspended moment, my world was perfect as those two, gorgeous women patted the wooden step, my little spot between them. The sun's warmth and the garden's delight followed me, then and still, momentous smidgeons of good fortune.

Iowa, *April 4, 2009*

Opening the sliding glass door at the top of the staircase, I move toward the kitchen counter with my parcels and boxed cake. It's been rainy all day and the warmth feels good. My 94-year-old father is asleep in his chair beside the television. My mother stands in the dining area mesmerized by a luminous grid on the floorboards. She doesn't realize I'm here. Despite the drizzle, western sunlight stretches from the deck's French door to her slippered feet.

I wait to hear that an old woman is getting married. *'Si llueve con sol se casa una vieja,'* but Ma is silent.

Lifting one foot, toes pointing down, she pauses like a small bird. With her left hand still on the Colima dog, she shifts her weight. Hopscotch on the pattern of light?

Raising her eyes to the windows and wooden deck, she caresses the dog on his stand. The bathrobe droops from her tiny shoulders, her white hair wilts in disarray.

I tend to her hair during my visits. She dutifully holds the silver U-shaped pins while I gently lift and arrange the wisps of whiteness. It's no longer possible to recreate her trademark wave of magnificent hair, but my efforts make me think of cherry pies.

When we first moved to Summit Street, a row of six cherry trees lined the right side of our driveway. As Pa and Roy climbed ladders and shook branches, the rest of us collected. White sheets were spread under the trees and half-filled bushel baskets held down the corners. For days, Ma and Sophie sat at the picnic table pitting yellow cherries with those U hairpins. Newlyweds, the Siebers occupied the upstairs of our house. While Roy worked on his PhD thesis in African art, Sophie taught in a country schoolhouse. The cherry harvests went on for a few years before windstorms took the old trees, one after the other. When I learned that, in Japanese culture, the cherry tree is a symbol of *life's fragility and beauty*, I was reminded of my mother's sadness over the loss, as if it had been family rather than trees.

Ma made the fanciest cherry pies in the world, crimping the excess pastry into curly undulations around the pan, like that wave on her forehead. I'd watched other mothers, their paring knives moving deftly around pie tins balanced on palms, the extra strips of dough landing on floured rolling pins like sensibly shorn locks.

She still hasn't turned. What beckons from the deck? Does she remember there is earth to turn and seeds to plant? Perhaps, but somewhere between thought and action, desire and fulfillment, the path to the French door has vanished. Someone once brought her a potted Sweet William because of the name, her eldest son's. She still harvests its descendant seeds every fall, working her way along the flower boxes Pa built for her. By summer, mobs of pygmy carnations rise to torment the blue blossoms of succulent, lone weeds, trembling in fear. *Strength in numbers, survival of the fittest*, they shriek, those pinks, reds and purples, box after box.

She can never say he's still her sweet William, her first born. There would be nervous snickering from her other sons, followed by resentful silence. But where are they, the Sweet William seeds? Is that what she seeks, not words about old women marrying in rain and sun. Her hand won't lift off the Colima dog, nor will her feet move forward.

I step past the bookshelves toward the dining table, hoping not to startle her, hoping she'll feel my presence and turn.

There are no signs that my brothers have come by—no reason they would have. Alan and I were married on April 4th, but after that first occasion, it was never a date to recognize.

When we were young, birthdays, Thanksgiving and New Year's Eve were all events to 'festihate', Pa's merger of *festejar* and cele-brate. Thinking of the ties he created between Spanish and English,

I still see a suspended, Amazonian footbridge. The new lingo swayed side to side as it moved across to the other shore, melding into the vernacular of our private world. Colorful and graphic, even musical, those words and phrases became like homeless urchins with whom we shared a bond, though they bewildered outsiders. Pa had an instinct for fusion. Concoctions with a nice ring or beat, or on occasions of forgetfulness or linguistic uncertainty. It was one of the habits enabling his alluring, maverick personality. It's not that he tried to be defiant, it's that he rarely wanted to conform. I vividly remember being seven years old and walking with my family from our house on Grand Avenue, across the Burlington Street bridge, heading into town. It was a Saturday and we were bucking an enormous sports crowd moving in the opposite direction, toward the Field House and a University of Iowa basketball game. A student stopped my father to tell him we were walking the wrong way. Pausing on the bridge, my father cheerfully assured the young man we were not.

As the years passed April 4th by, more and more family events went unnoticed, until our once verdant familial landscape became a fallow field. It's hard to identify when and why we stopped celebrating. There was the time Pa became capriciously angry while a couple of my siblings and I discussed our parents' important, impending wedding anniversary—party suggestions, food, venues. Disgruntled about something, he declared the date a private matter and none of our business.

A pall fell over the plans. After that, reviving family milestones became too risky, although the occasional opportunity presented. One April 4th, Alan and I took a bottle of champagne over to my parents so they could join us in marking our anniversary. It quickly became uncomfortable. The truth is, my parents were not celebratory by nature, at least not in the years we were growing up. Something held them back.

Pa rarely hid his feelings, and the impact of his emotional surges never concerned him. Accustomed to his outbursts, we understood his discontent probably had nothing to do with their wedding date, just as we understood it was not always possible to leave behind the studio's frustrations. Good days, however, followed him home like a purring cat. Regardless of what we comprehended, my brothers took him at his word about minding their business. And why not? It would simplify their lives, this new circumvention.

Not a peep from my mother about their anniversary—her habit was to follow his lead—and I'd learned to dodge his volatility. Her silence and my self-protection were not unusual, just as Pa's flare-ups were not surprising. In those years, it took little to set him off, little to calm him.

On this April 4, I bring my parents candies and an anniversary cake, not because it's their wedding date, but mine. I'm hoping to ignite a flame in my mother's memory, at least a candle's worth.

Last week, I arrived to find Ma giggling with abandon. My brother, Tomas, was poised behind her, gently creating a thin braid. Seeing me approach, he flashed a shy smile—insomniac eyes, layers of disheveled garments because he's never warm enough, the mess of his own black mane. By times, there's so much white dust on his hair and clothes, he looks like a ghost. Plaster from renovations in his studio, gesso from a new undertaking?

His early childhood tumbles forth. The drawings and art projects, the construction of miniature cities at dawn. I would find him on the landing at the top of the back staircase, still in pajamas, the house deep in sleep. In the serenity of dawn, he maneuvered wooden blocks, empty cigar boxes and tins of Campbell soup, alone and happy. Even at the age of six or seven, he required little sleep.

So last week when he left his studio—undoubtedly something had to dry or set—this middle-aged man hurried to visit his mother, to braid her hair. Dementia had briefly withdrawn, granting her a rare flash of pleasure with her last born. She had the reassurance of his presence, and he, her tranquility.

Balearic Islands, April 3, 1965

IT SEEMED LOGICAL THAT, IF Ibiza island was as inexpensive as Dr. and Mia Potts said, then Formentera, the smallest of the Balearic archipelago, would be even more economical. After the three months of fall visiting museums in England and France, and the winter in Holland with trips to Belgium's national collections, Alan and I were ready to find a place in the countryside and settle down. We weren't particular, as long as it was in Spain.

My younger brother, Leonardo, who had traveled with us from Holland, accompanied as we boarded a motorboat ferry for the short, gusty crossing. In dazzling sunlight, the old Formentera houses called to us with their whitewashed walls and simplicity of design. Their interiors, however, dark and claustrophobic with tiny windows and low ceilings, made Alan seem like a giant. An exhausting April wind swept across the small island, and the high pitch of female voices shrieking out in the clipped dialect of Catalan was relentless and disconcerting. It was hard to ignore the women's sparse hair and visible scalps, the rough hands continually adjusting black scarves. Evidently the island was so inbred, congenital deafness and female baldness were rampant.

There was more. On the ferry, we met an American couple from San Francisco. They weren't exactly hippie-wannabes, but they wanted something, maybe to reinvent themselves, as we say now. Quitting their jobs and relinquishing their middle-class possessions (house, cars, cottage and boat), they'd taken off to experience the world. They spoke casually about the children they'd left behind— something told me not to ask with whom or the kids' ages—their gestalt group, and finally, their approval of 'open' marriages.

Fortunately, the Americans were not staying at our *pensión*. Enough was enough.

We remained on Formentera for two days hoping to find a house. The evening before we left we had dinner in the restaurant next door to the *pensión,* and the three of us fell into a discussion about family. Since our wedding, I had not spoken to any of my siblings about banishment, my banishment. Besides the emotional topic, the day's surreal qualities may have contributed to my weeping and vulnerable state: The San Franciscans, the constant wind, the screeching voices. Many years would pass before I returned to that early theme of expulsion—willing and able to spread it out, dissect, and attempt to leave it behind.

It must have been a very dramatic dialog in the restaurant. Not long ago I came across a letter from Leonardo mailed more than a decade after Formentera. The typed message came in response to a phone conversation that had not gone well. He'd called to cancel a planned visit to us. Alan and I were living on our farm in Ontario with our first three kids. I was hurt Leo had changed his plans and he became perturbed that I was hurt. We both lost it over the phone.

His letter addressed that Formentera evening rather than our phone call. He wrote of being so moved hearing and seeing my distress, he pledged to always be an attentive, loving brother, from that moment forward. Years have passed since that letter. Regrettably, the circumstances of our lives neither permitted Leonardo to fulfill that promise, nor enabled me to reach out a hand, generous and steady enough, to bridge the chasms in our family. We'd come from a home advocating manual dexterity and the rewarding ability to create and fix the tangible—Pa's championing, not Ma's. (While always supportive of his wishes and beliefs, Ma neither valued physical labor the way he did, nor was she eager to paint her own walls.) We were taught and encouraged to use our hands, but learning to care for and nurture emotions—rather than abandoning them along the journey—was another language we would have to pick up on our own, as adults. Some of us are still learning that vocabulary.

About our wedding. After the dancing and champagne, as the others happily threw rice on the veranda of my Summit Street family home, Pa seized my arm in panic, powerless to give up. We were not a touchy-feely family. Silent withdrawal was our fallback. There were things we didn't do, things we didn't say, or I might have blown him a kiss and told him I loved him. Instead, laughing and ducking under flying rice, I held hands with my husband as we moved toward the waiting taxi. Had I been older and wiser I might have understood my father's panic, his inability to let me go. I might have understood that he saw the union as a realignment of my loyalties. His loss, Alan's gain. Neither older nor wiser, I was unprepared for the open wounds that can form around debilitating silences, unprepared for the consequences of unyielding possessiveness. My mother's inability to intervene did not surprise me.

My father behaved appropriately at our wedding ceremony, but his initial response to our marriage was incredibly damaging. When we returned from our honeymoon a week later, I learned of my new status. My shell-shocked, younger siblings rushed to our apartment with the report. I was no longer part of the family. The long arm of Pa's explosive anger—the selfishness of word and action, the infliction of pain, knowingly or unknowingly—would call for ongoing, steadfast battling to mitigate. Certainly on my part, and I like to think his as well.

The next day, Alan, Leonardo and I said goodbye to Formentera. Giving up our house search, we boarded the ferry, leaving behind screeching voices, wind and wannabes.

Ibiza, the third of the Balearic Islands. We knew only what our friends, the Potts, told us while we were living in Holland. Well informed and helpful, they came for dinner and we discussed our plans to live in Spain. Ibiza was the place to go, they said, if you want to live economically. We did.

Before the wedding, we told Alan's parents of our plans for Europe, explaining we'd like cash as presents. No silver, china or linen. Alan's mother conveyed the message to friends and relatives. The $2,000 we were gifted financed our two years in Europe, but we were incredibly frugal. When we heard about the Potts' acquaintance, a painter who'd rented a farmhouse, a *finca*, for one thousand *pesetas* a month—in 1965, the equivalent of $16—we were sold. The Potts said we might have to manage without electricity or running water, and quite possibly on an Ibizan mountain. Could we?

Probably.

The 'probably' quickly changed to 'for sure'. We were enthusiastic. There were paintings to paint, tales to write and reasons for Spain.

Just as I held onto stories of my Spanish heritage, a vivid collage of maternal family and ancestors, so too I carried 1953. It was the year of Pa's Guggenheim to study Goya at the Prado, the year my parents took their children to Spain. During those pivotal 12 months, we were presented with the magnificence of Spain—her poverty and suffering always close at hand. I turned 11 in Madrid. My experiences became a virtual snow globe to carry into my future. I had only to shake my captured Spain to reconnect with all that had made me a wiser version of the Iowa girl I'd been.

Fast forward to the pier on Ibiza and the three of us leaving the Formentera ferry, blinking in the sun, shaking off the crossing's chill. Leo stood guard with the luggage while Alan and I headed for the tourist kiosk. 'Old Town,' or *Dalt Vila* in Ibicenco, had the inexpensive *Pensión Oliver*, the attendant told us, gesturing to the white town rising behind us. Ibiza, wrapping the mountain in structures and ramparts and terraces of windows, like countless eyes keeping guard over the sea.

With its walls of bougainvillea and balconies of geraniums, *Dalt Vila* basked in memories of past civilizations. In 650 BC, Phoenicians established Ibiza Town and the island's first major port. Next came the Carthaginians, followed by Romans, Vandals, Arabs and a Norwegian King who invaded most of the Balearic Islands on his Crusade to Jerusalem. Finally, in 1235, the Catalans conquered the island under the leadership of James I, King of Aragon.

Since the 1920's, Ibicenco farmers and fishermen had been peacefully sharing their quiet island. Artists and writers came,

Bauhaus architects, fugitives from society, survivors from the Spanish Civil War, from the Second World War, from the persecution of Nazi Germany. Seeking tranquility they often made their homes beyond the port, deep in the interior, where Ibiza remained much as it had for generations, where the man-made meshed organically with nature. Old *fincas* became one with the rugged terrain. Arrangements of white-washed cubes and surrounding parapet walls, snuggling on mountain plateaus, stretched to meet terraces of olive trees and orange groves. Unassuming, small-windowed churches waited patiently, their white, courtyard stones extending to village doors. Monumental edifices were few—the cone shaped 16th century watch towers dotting the coasts, the ramparts of Old Town climbing to protect their citadel and Cathedral. In earlier times Ibiza had been an important outpost for conflicting nations. No longer. For epochs, peace had embraced the humble island.

By 1965, our year, Ibiza was awakening from her sleep of centuries. Poised between ancient history and the present, old rural patterns and contemporary values, she was suddenly a 'destination' in the azure Mediterranean. Modern-day *conquistadores* were arriving in hordes from across Europe—the *extranjeros,* foreigners. Tourists, for vacations of partying in the sun, hippies, for the *finca* communes, and expats, hunting for anonymity, cheap wine and the famous, inexpensive lifestyle. The construction industry boomed, the scramble was on—more and more hotels, cafés and bars to satisfy the throngs. Halfway between North Africa and the Spanish mainland, Ibiza ended up a stop on the drug route.

Alan and I fit somewhere in that *extranjeros* category, though we didn't frequent beaches and stayed longer than tourists, had no interest in drugs or the hippie movement, and we were basically non-drinkers and too youthful to be expatriates. I don't mean to sound smug or aloof. We were just young and fortunate—well matched, happy loners, lucky in love. The independent, self-directed chunk of our personalities was always the same for both of us, before marriage, before and after Europe. Obstinately committed to our work—Alan's painting, my writing—our habit was to avoid extraneous distractions. A lifetime later, I'm still pondering our stubbornness and all we missed.

Until Ibiza, I hadn't realized my personal longing for Spain was more than the sum of ancestral connections and the memory of a transformative, childhood year. My desire to replicate my parents' youthful joy, a need that first made its appearance when I understood my mother had been happier before, was now primed and moving off on its own trajectory.

Córdoba, Argentina, and the first years of married life. Villa María and the birth of my parents' first child, William, followed by the idyllic village of Villa Rivera Indarte with the large country house and mountain air. I'd heard the stories about teaching in art schools and children's camps, about their interactions with other artists and writers, about sharing their house with the British poet, Hugo Manning, and later, with Ma's brother, Luis, and his wife, Isabel. It was a golden moment and my mother happily remembered everything, small details and important events.

I've wondered if the fixation with my parents' early happiness was the incentive for finding my own rural experience, a mutual connection that would bring me closer to a time when all was good in their lives. A link that would help me reap their uncomplicated bliss. But children are not meant to know their parents without the complex layers of parental love, responsibilities and apprehensions. That knowledge is not part of the grand scheme.

'Stefan Zweig in Córdoba', 2019
from a story collection in progress,
This I Can Tell You

Like so much about the psychiatrist, Alexander Shulmann, Sunday meals at his Córdoba home have become legendary. Soup followed by beef or fish, pasta, fruit, and sometimes, Alexander's mistress, the Russian diva, Isa Kremer, sings for dessert. Those in attendance, including the young printmaker, Isaac and his bride, Clara, are aware that conversation is to remain calm and civilized, regardless of their own apprehensions, the war, the world's turmoil. Shulmann's luncheons are considered a respite, and that early November day, 1940, is no exception. The guest of honor is the Austrian writer, Stefan Zweig, recently arrived in Argentina on a lecture tour.

Clara is seated in the middle of the long table directly across from Zweig, a horizontal arrangement of eucalyptus and cedar boughs stretching between them. She doesn't understand why Dr. Shulmann would separate her from Isaac, knowing they've only been married a few months. Feeling uneasy before the celebrated author, she breathes in the calming eucalyptus. Isaac is seated at the end of the table squeezed in between Dr. Roberto Hernán, the tuberculosis expert, and the lady correspondent for the society page of *La Voz del Interior*. Makeup cakes the pores of her coarse features, but the young woman has presence, Clara decides, taking in the stylish bolero jacket, high shoulder pads and military style cap cheerfully angled on her forehead. Red felt nestles in a mass of bleached curls and a single feather shimmies alone. Ignored since they sat down, the girl smiles bravely, unaware lipstick has stained her teeth. Clara feels for her. There's no reason she would know that the artist beside her has little patience for lady reporters.

Nevertheless, she should know that everything hangs in the balance for all of them, especially the guest of honor, and they don't need a lady's hat to remind them of war.

Deep in conversation with Dr. Hernán, Isaac is looking particularly handsome with that lock of black hair falling across his forehead and right eye. He takes her breath away, and after a hundred days of marriage, she would still follow him to the end of the earth. So why does she want to cry? Why does she worry, constantly, every day? Glancing beyond the patio to the garden, Clara watches the green parrot on his green perch, staring wistfully at the sky.

Two days ago, she noticed a new preoccupation casting Isaac's face in shadow. It's not the fixation of work. She's become accustomed to that. For over a month he's been bringing home his copper plate, burin, and the latest proof from the studio. He sits at the kitchen table eagerly marking up the paper image with chalk and a stubby pencil, smearing lead lines with his thumb. Leaning back, squinting at the proof, he returns to the plate, digging out copper curls with his burin, brushing them away. He says he wants her near him when he works, but why? The plate absorbs him.

Clara turns from the parrot back to Isaac. Why does he ignore her? It feels like hours since he's looked in her direction. Hernán is speaking. They must be discussing education, possibly Isaac's teaching experiment at the school, something about the children's instinctive use of color. He tells her about it in the evenings, but she feels so sleepy after dinner, she can hardly focus. His hand moves up and down, side to side, accompanying his words as he answers Hernán. There, now he turns, now he sees her, now he flashes a grin.

Nothing is wrong. Clara breathes deeply, straightening her fork and knife. The worrying has to stop—she's making herself crazy. Looking up, Clara focuses on the author as he nervously wipes his forehead. He's just as uncomfortable. What is she to say? What is she to ask this unhappy man? The bread has gone to her head, jamming her brain with wet crumbs and the smell of cannelloni drifting in from the kitchen makes her nauseous. She watches

Zweig stare distractedly at the greenery between them. Finally, his elegant fingers lift the handkerchief back to his breast pocket.

Alfredo Cahn, Zweig's Spanish translator, is seated beside Isa Kramer at the other end of the table. Dazzling Isa, with her black hair and heavy-lidded dark eyes, that slinky emerald dress. Clara remembers Isaac's recent comment that Shulmann and Isa aren't married. He mentioned it in passing, as though talking about the weather. She understood he needed to tell her, but she wasn't to ask questions. Clara reaches for her napkin and focuses on Cahn. Last Sunday he spoke about the author's impending tour and recent writing—the autobiography, the book on Brazil, the Balzac manuscript left behind when the Zweigs fled England. Was it like leaving behind a child? Cahn cautioned that the lecture tour would be incredibly paced: Buenos Aires, Córdoba, Santa Fé, back to Buenos Aires, on to Rosario and possibly Uruguay, all in a matter of days. He assured them Zweig thrives under pressure. Still, he warned, there's a good chance of despondency. She watches Zweig's attention shift from the eucalyptus to his garlic soup.

Isaac is always pleased to speak with Hernán about teaching, and that afternoon he's especially grateful for the distraction. It isn't like him to feel so nervous. His habit is full steam ahead, let the worries roll and don't look back. His father warned him that marriage takes getting used to. Isaac glances at Clara, watching as she folds and re-folds her napkin, ignoring her soup. Looking at her makes him ache with love—her exquisiteness, her heart, the way she's struggling to engage the Austrian writer.

Earlier, on the walk over, she was in high spirits as they strolled along the boulevard under the plane trees. She hasn't been herself in the last few days—the constant tears and lack of appetite—so her chatter about their 95-year-old neighbor was a welcomed change. But Isaac was too preoccupied to listen. He wanted to explain before they arrived at Shulmann's home, before it came up at lunch. It's possible that Alexander Shulmann might mention something about the American State Department—he'd been the one to recommend Isaac. When Clara stopped walking and turned to him, asking what the trouble was, why so far away, she caught him off guard. He'd told her about last week's visit with the Americans—how impressed they were seeing the school and his studio—but not a word about the possibility of a fellowship.

He was surprised seeing a woman in the group of men, and even more surprised that they let her do most of the talking. After speaking knowledgeably about the New School in New York City, she made observations about his work, and finally asked if there would be a problem leaving his family and his country for so long. He was embarrassed by his quick response. Nine months to study with master printmakers in America. Would any artist hesitate at such an offer?

Crossing Shulmann's front patio with the mosaic fountain and lion-legged benches, Isaac watched Clara pause under the persimmon tree. Turning toward him, she held out her hand, smiling, her face dappled by sunlight. He wanted to tell her, but before he realized, they were standing in the vestibule exchanging greetings with Isa Kremer.

At least time is on his side, Isaac realizes. It'll take months for the Guggenheim's paperwork to come through. He finishes his soup and turns back to Clara. Why would Shulmann place Clara opposite Stefan Zweig? It makes no sense. Isaac is suddenly annoyed. Can't Alexander see that she's too shy and inexperienced to handle such a man? And why isn't she eating? Doesn't he have enough to worry about?

He, Isaac, is the one who should be sitting closer to Zweig. He's the one to hear about the collections of prints and Rembrandt drawings. He's the one to ask about the famous encounter with Rodin. He's the one to invite the author to his own studio to see his prints.

What was Shulmann thinking?

Ibiza, April 1965

B EFORE IBIZA, HOLLAND. WE'D SPENT the winter months
in the village of Bergen aan Zee so Alan could have train
access to Amsterdam's Rijksmuseum and Rembrandt. On a
first visit to the city we looked up one of Alan's graduate school
classmates, John W., a printmaker on a Fulbright in Holland. In
the town of Bergen, John introduced us to the Bolkesteins, with
whom he'd been billeted upon arriving in Holland. The Bolkesteins
in turn, presented us to their friends, Dr. Potts and his wife, Mia.
Both families spoke excellent English. My brother, Leonardo, a
new Iowa high school graduate embarking on a tour of Europe
before college, joined us for our last month in Holland. We were
grateful to converse in our language.

While Alan's high school German was helpful, the Dutch people, polyglots fluent in the language, refused to speak it. Memories
of war were still vivid, despite the twenty years that had passed
since the German occupation of Holland. Though I found Dutch
completely impenetrable, occasionally I managed to communicate.

It was the Christmas season and we were invited to dinner at
the Bolkesteins. With the assistance of *Mrs. Beeton's Cookery Book*,
purchased in London along with the many Virginia Woolf penguin
classics, I decided to make a fruitcake. It was a short bus ride from
Bergen aan Zee to Alkmaar—an ancient, peaceful city with pealing
church bells, children skating on the canals, and the iconic cheese
market in progress. I was excited by shopping—the falling snow,
popping in and out of warm, well-lit shops searching for the best
nuts, the plumpest glazed fruits. But where to go for red and green
food coloring, the final, essential ingredients? At last someone

understood my request and pointed out an apothecary down the street. Though the fellow behind the counter spoke no English, we managed a lively exchange and I left the establishment with two small vials of *kleur, rood en groen.*

The cake was declared a huge success as Mrs. Bolkestein held a very thin slice to the winter light, marveling at the luminosity of the jeweled fruit, fascinated by the snowy icing's red and green yuletide decorations. When it came to American frosting, Betty Crocker, with me in spirit, had outdistanced Mrs. Beeton.

Our rented Bergen aan Zee flat was in a multistory apartment building constructed for the tourist industry. Germans flocked to the village during the hot months to enjoy the North Sea. In cold weather, the only warmth was from an electric radiator in the living room, so we purchased a portable kerosene unit to get us through those months. There were enough roll up cots to sleep eight, but the place was not intended for winter habitation. The tiled shower stall was the size of a sauna, and we'd take in the portable to warm it before our joint showers. Every morning, thick ice greeted us on the inside of windowpanes. The weather was a constant, damp cold and before long, I had chilblains on my toes. Once we learned to carry the heater around the apartment, we were quite comfortable. It accompanied us from the kitchen and the preparation of meals to the living room to eat and read, then on to the bedroom at night.

The train ride to Amsterdam and the Rijksmuseum was under an hour, a bit longer to Leiden. We visited museums once a week, sometimes twice. The other days, we remained in our village by the sea. Alan painted in one of the empty, dormitory style bedrooms while I huddled by the electric radiator—typed, edited pages spread on the floor around me. My professor at the University of Iowa Writers Workshop, Eugene Garber, had agreed to let me register for the advanced, second semester course. Sending him stories from Europe I was able to complete my requirements for a minor in creative writing. There were a few remaining classes to fulfill for my major in English literature, as well as a couple courses in science and sociology. Because the core science classes had to be attended on campus, finishing my degree would have to wait until we were back in Iowa. For the moment, I had the freedom to write.

When the North Sea wind calmed and the afternoons weren't bitterly cold, we went for walks along the sand dunes. Our Dutch days were frequently overcast with a muted panorama of sand, water and sky stretching before us. In the Rijksmuseum, I learned to slow my pace in the rooms of 19th century Dutch landscapes. Those unassuming gray-blue scenes with sky taking up more than half the canvas, were not so distant in time or place. In university, I'd become immersed in my art history courses, and in Europe, encountering paintings in person proved as gratifying as reading literature.

With winter over, we were ready to depart Holland. Toward the end of March we packed our belongings, crated Alan's paintings and boarded the train for Spain. Though our stay in Madrid was brief, we managed a reunion with my mother's cousin, Paquita, in between trips to the Prado. And because we'd promised the Potts to look up the daughter of friends, we met the Molezuns. Joos de Wolff was a Dutch painter married to a Spanish painter, Manual Molezun. We visited their contemporary Madrid residence built in in the style of an old country *finca, estilo antiguo*—very much the home of painters. Surrounded by open living spaces, simple furnishings and the Molezuns' quiet presence, I felt a sudden connection as my past entered the present. When Alan introduced himself as a printmaker—he spoke in French, the Molezuns preferred it to English—Manuel said that ten years before he had met a printmaker by the name of Lasansky from Iowa. He came to Spain on a Guggenheim fellowship with his wife and children, and one of the girls had long, blond braids. I remember the overcast day in 1954 when my family visited a model village designed for Spanish workers. We were taken to the site by the architect, José Luis Fernández del Amo. I'm not aware of how or why my parents connected with Fernández del Amo, but I recall several people were part of the architect's entourage, and it seems Manuel Molezun was one.

Before we left Madrid, I wrote my parents of the serendipitous encounter. As usual, my letter was full of news—our visit with Paquita, the Molezuns' beautiful collection of ceramics and the odd feeling of *déjà vu,* and finally, my assurances that Leo was fine and traveling with us to Ibiza. Ibiza, where hopefully, a *finca* for $16 a month awaited us.

On April 4th, we celebrated our second wedding anniversary on the island. Settling in at the *Pensión Oliver,* our housing search took on a focused urgency. Restaurants and bars lined Ibiza's main boulevard, *Paseo Vara de Rey*, with its eucalyptus trees and flowering shrubs, the statue of General Rey, the park benches. Realizing the side streets might be best for inquiring about rental properties, we stopped at hardware suppliers, bicycle repair shops, spice vendors and green grocers.

Ibicenco, a dialect of Catalan, was closer to French than Spanish and a far cry from the Spanglish I'd grown up speaking at home. Alan spent his junior year of university in Paris, so he had no trouble adjusting to this new vernacular. We pooled our strengths. For native islanders not accustomed to speaking Spanish, the language presented challenges, especially conjugating verbs. Nevertheless, friendly shopkeepers eagerly chatted in their dialect, answering our questions and expressing their opinions.

Foreigners and their activities were fair game: the wizened, bikini clad older women at outdoor cafes, the arrest of a threesome fornicating on the pier in broad daylight, the regular sightings of stoned, barefoot hippies strolling obliviously on the *Paseo*. With draggling skirts and flowered shirts, they attracted a cursory curiosity. The shop proprietor standing at his door, the dull-eyed foreigner ordering his first drink of the day, the observant *campesino* hitching up his horse-and-cart. Almonds, dried figs or a piglet for market—how many trips to town before the Ibicenco farmer acclimatized to all he saw?

We were told we didn't seem like tourists, the Americans, British, French and Germans. It was a compliment. Our Spanish language skills helped, as well as our wardrobe—boring, tidy nylon, easily managed in all the bathroom sinks we encountered in *pensión* rooms across Europe. The widow of an Ibicenco merchant, a tall, elegant matron with an aristocratic face and starched, white blouse, was quite taken with our wrinkle-free garments. Sitting next to the cash register—firmly in charge of the business since her husband's passing, and quite possibly before—she never hesitated to reveal her mainland pedigree.

Having learned to conceal flesh and eyes in the presence of Spanish men, my skirt was black and loosely pleated, my white blouse long-sleeved, my cardigan and sunglasses, dark. A headscarf often concealed my fair braids, coiled and arranged 'Swedish style', as in the Ingmar Bergman films I'd seen the year before in college. Eye makeup was out. I looked like a clown. Antique, gold earrings, in. I'd already started a modest collection. Alan's attire was a pair of beige polyester pants and a white nylon shirt. We both wore Dr. Scholl's leather sandals, precursors to those 'earth' shoes that became so stylishly popular in the 70's. Designed as 'orthopedic' for flat feet—not a problem I've ever had to deal with—they were exceedingly comfortable. In Israel, I was stopped on the street by fascinated Israelis wanting to know where they might be acquired. Evidently the land of the bible was not yet accustomed to all manner of sandals.

Leo was still with us on April 5th, so he came along to see a mountain property available for rent. We were given directions to Vicente's house, a neighboring *campesino* who could lead us up the craggy paths. Vicente was talkative and willing, but cautioned it had been abandoned for years. The old people had died—blind, deaf and decrepit, like their *finca*. They'd never had children. Their siblings were gone, but there was a *sinvergüenza sobrino*, a shameless nephew, who'd fled the island years back and was hiding out somewhere on the mainland. That was it, no other family. If we were interested in renting, we'd have to go back to the shopkeeper who told us about it, Vicente said, adding that he didn't know who was in charge, probably one of those *abogats*, lawyers, in Ibiza Town. He wasn't surprised there'd been no interest in renting since the old people had passed.

The higher we climbed, the more difficult and overgrown the trails. I wasn't feeling as adventuresome as we'd indicated to the Potts, but I maintained a brave front, struggling to keep up. Vicente led the spirited hike, chatting cheerfully in the half Spanish/half Ibicenco we'd already accepted as our new language.

After nearly an hour of strenuous walking we arrived at a clearing on the side of the mountain. Weeds and wild shrubbery had overtaken the patio of the primitive little *finca*, unsettling in its misery. Inside, total disorder—cooking pots on the wood stove, rags strewn on the bed, birds flying about. After a polite but absurd inspection of the crumbling out buildings (hunting for possible studio space was an ingrained habit), I explained to Vicente that it wouldn't do, in view of the general conditions he'd warned us about. I wanted to tell him he wasn't just whistling Dixie, but even if I knew how to translate the expression, he probably wouldn't understand it.

Momentarily subdued, he pulled himself together and insisted we follow him back to his place. It was his Saint's Day, San Vicente, and we could not return to the city without having a celebratory glass of wine and a chunk of cake. We happily left that sorrowful place, following him down the mountain.

Hot and tired, we waited on the patio as he called to his wife, Asunción, in his 'master-of-the-manor' voice. Drawing aside the beaded door curtain, she stepped out hesitantly, a slow-moving woman dressed in black. Her faded apron was pulled up and fastened behind as we'd seen among the island women wearing the traditional costume—long full skirt and petticoats, fringed shawl, straw hat over a head scarf. She wasn't accustomed to seeing strangers, and certainly not foreigners. He mumbled a command and she returned to the kitchen, soon reemerging with a tray of refreshments.

I was already familiar with women in black. Bereavement never ended in Spain. Mourning for one parent moved into years for the other, followed by more black for the deaths of aunts, uncles, siblings or children. There were rules. Like Queen Victoria, a widow remained in full mourning for the rest of her life. After so many years of full mourning for a close relative, half mourning was permissible. The skirt still black, the blouse white with black trim, stripes or polka dots.

Smiling shyly, Asunción offered us glasses of cool water from the cistern. We drank, admiring the landscape, majestic and peaceful. Alan asked about the plantings of grain stretching beyond the animal pens, the terraces of grape arbors and ancient olive trees. Vicente explained his family had lived there for generations and that Asunción came from the other side of the mountain. Learning our names, he said he knew of Santa Rocío and San Leonardo, but he'd never heard of San Alan. On cue, Alan jumped into the conversation, '*todavía no!*', not yet!

Our guide laughed enthusiastically, scratching his head as he translated for his wife who understood only their dialect. A refreshing breeze moved through. I would have liked asking about their lives, about family and children, but something told me that would be as inappropriate as asking to see the inside of their *casa*.

Barrenness on Ibiza, like the problems of deafness and female baldness on Formentera, were all due to inbreeding, so we were told. We rarely saw children among our mountain friends. As in Garcia Lorca's *Yerma,* the mute longing for a child took on a life of its own; *Si Dios quiere,* God willing, the default hope and hushed response. After we left the island and were living in Saskatchewan, our own familiarity with infertility would echo back to Ibiza.

Regina, fall, 1966

ALAN'S FIRST TEACHING JOB, SEPTEMBER 1966 to June 1969: assistant professor of drawing and printmaking, department of art, Regina campus, the University of Saskatchewan. A leap of faith took us from our Mediterranean island to that far away land—one whiteness to another, almond blossoms to snow. We soon learned about the challenges of weather, hurling their way across our new arctic landscape.

Our abrupt introduction to university volatility came the autumn morning of the dean's phone call. Alan was asked to immediately take over a colleague's classes, in addition to his own. How long? No one could say for sure. The colleague had abruptly and unexpectedly departed for India. Later, we heard he'd traded his wife for an Indian professor's Visa card, and that he'd gone for the hashish.

Then the snow. From the middle of October it continued relentlessly until April, when the streets became rivers of melting slush and Wellingtons, a natural extension of feet. As the months progressed and the cold intensified, alcohol consumption at university functions ratcheted expeditiously, culminating in visits to the psych ward by the beginning of January.

In that place of unforgiving winters, we were surrounded by new friends clinging to what they could: partner swapping and the resulting children, Hoya leaves cut into tossed salads, pot, LSD, more niacin for depression. In the decade before our arrival, The Weyburn Mental Hospital, an hour and a half south of Regina, became the hub of hallucinogenic research in Canada. LSD was being used to treat disorders from schizophrenia to alcoholism, and the term 'psychedelic' was coined by the British psychiatrist, Dr. Humphry Osmond, one of the researchers at Weyburn. Members of the Regina art faculty had been recruited as test subjects, and for some, the experience proved disastrous. Regardless, LSD remained, so we were told, the drug of choice, despite 'bad trips' and nearly fried brains.

EXCERPT
'Auction', 1985
from a story collection in progress,
This I Can Tell You

IT DIDN'T SURPRISE ROSE TO hear the flour grinder was missing a screw or bolt. Her cousin could never keep track of anything. Last night over the phone, Melinda said she was searching for it. Her voice sounded as though it was coming from under the table. No, the boys couldn't help because they were at the cottage with Richard, and as for Toby, she was out again with her new boyfriend.

When Melinda finally stood up—Rose could tell from her breathing and the sound of the chair scraping the floor—she spoke at length about the kids' activities, the garden, the stupid cat jumping into the last bucket of ground wheat berries. For Melinda it was 'at length', but really, it was so she wouldn't have to talk about her other problem.

Nathaniel Simpson.

Exactly what is he to Melinda? Partner, lover, soulmate? The one thing Rose knows for sure is that she's never liked him, and yes, she's been jealous of his power over her cousin. Self-involved and entitled, he's struggled with addiction and depression all his life, but until recently, his phenomenal constitution has repeatedly pulled him through. Nathaniel Simpson—a gifted painter, so they say. A big, sexy guy with an easy, charming smile, Nathaniel storms through life on his own manic terms, drugs and alcohol trailing behind. Melinda follows blindly, believing in his artistic genius, believing enough to never find him culpable.

How has this man managed to invade her cousin's soul, stealing her away to one of his dark caves?

As for Richard, Melinda's husband, where is he in all this? Despite certain flaws of character, Rose has always considered him an adequate spouse—occasionally loving, mostly caring, and certainly a good father.

The entire, tangled up business is beyond Rose, completely beyond her. On top of this mess of their personal lives, the university had just suspended Nathaniel. One too many drug and alcohol parties with his painting students, and recently, that crazy escapade attempting to scale the Computer Science building with two co-eds from the women's hockey team.

Regina, 1966 continues

THE LATE 60's—DRAFT DODGERS, ANTIWAR rallies and turmoil on American campuses. The University of Saskatchewan at Regina was not spared. Like protests across North America, demonstrations were influenced by issues of democracy, notably the Civil Rights Movement. Students opposed the Board of Governors' censorship of the Regina student newspaper—openly critical of the provincial government—and demanded representation on University decision making boards. Though discontent was not about war, Vietnam was the backdrop during that era of rebellion.

In retrospect, I've wondered if my disengagement was youthful apathy, or if it said more about the normalcy of turbulent times and a contentious war. I remained untouched, no brothers or friends in harm's way. It seems remarkable now, but I personally knew no one who went to Vietnam, and like so many around me, I did not follow the battles or discuss the news. I was free to empathize with those American families who'd pulled up roots and moved to Canada so their sons would not go into combat.

I found it hard to identify with Saskatchewan. In warm months, walking to the last crescent street of our residential neighborhood, we'd gaze out at a dizzying ocean of rippling wheat, the sleepy flatness broken only by a lone silo. Winter's descent to 45 degrees below was never surprising: car motors left running during dinner parties, instant frostbite to exposed flesh between boot top and mini-skirt, eyelashes turned to icicles. Grateful for our purring furnace, I stood at the kitchen window in awe of hoarfrost mornings, their beauty and stillness. But it was a world too harsh and distant from everything I knew. Running parallel to these extremes, our inability to conceive in those three years trapped us in a web of concern. We had our circle of faculty friends. Alan was busy with teaching and his own printmaking and painting; I was writing and taking pottery courses at the university. But we wanted a baby.

Our worrying increased. In the second year, we made plans to return to the University of Iowa for the summer. I had those remaining core courses to complete on campus for my BA, and we were anxious to consult with doctors at the University Hospitals. When we were first married and still living in Iowa City, I participated in the gynecology department's study on the new 'Pill', in exchange for medical attention and free contraption. Informing the doctors that we were leaving for Europe, I was given a year's supply of pills for our European travels. When we decided to stay longer on Ibiza, I was sent an additional stash. My only requirement was to fill out a questionnaire every few months and return it to the hospital.

That July, we were back at the UIHC, off the pill for nearly two years and still unable to conceive. After a series of tests, it was determined that pregnancy might never happen. We should plan to adopt. The doctors said we could certainly attempt intrauterine insemination, known as IUI, but any procedure involving the manual injection of a foreign substance into the body carried a risk of infection. Furthermore, success was unproven. I was bewildered. The instruments of injection might be considered foreign, but surely not the 'substance'.

Returning to Regina in the fall, we'd decided, though why we chose to subject ourselves to three tries, I have no idea. The whole thing was incredibly casual, almost sloppy, but we lived in hope.

Our doctor, a friendly, absentminded Brit, was challenged by multi-tasking. During our initial infertility appointment, while filling out forms and attempting small talk, he asked if we had a good babysitter. Despite his distracted flakiness and my hesitation, I let it pass and returned for the next appointment and our first IUI attempt. Waiting nervously on the examination table, I watched the doctor fussing over a small enamel cart. Abruptly turning toward the door, he announced that a piece of equipment was missing.

The turkey baster? A friend mockingly asked when I told her the story.

"I would feel more comfortable if that doesn't leave this room." I pointed to the specimen, the vial of 'substance' in his hand. It was a given he'd put it down and inadvertently pick up someone else's.

The strain accompanying those IUI sessions was awful. We tried to be optimistic, trudging through snow from our row house to the bus stop and a ride into town. Following the procedure at the clinic, there were days of endless waiting to see if it took. Negative times three. That winter, I practically lived in the floor length fur cape I'd made from two muskrat coats, thanks to the *Regina Chapter Hadassah* fall sale.

People wore real fur in those days, and the annual fundraiser attracted spectacular donations and dazzling excitement. Early in the morning, we purchased a flawless russet muskrat for $25. By the end of the day, all furs were slashed to $5. Alan returned. We ended up with another three coats—a luscious black muskrat I transformed into the cape's trim, hood and muff, a brown mouton, and something I can't remember. My husband said they were so inexpensive, you could throw them on a car as an engine warmer, but we didn't have a car. Dynamic enthusiasm and sensible restraint— what a winning combination for a young marriage.

In addition to muskrat, our closet housed the enormous buffalo coat Alan acquired from the RCMP—Royal Canadian Mounted Police—when they upgraded to nylon parkas. Saskatchewan in the age of Dr. Zhivago. Big mouton hats, bulky scarves, and the precious flask tucked deep in the buffalo pocket's warmth. Turkey baster, prepare thyself.

The things we do for children—yet to be and those begotten.

When Alan was given tenure at the end of his third year of teaching, he requested and was granted a temporary leave of absence. We were eager to return to Ontario and find a property that could become our summer place. Teaching in Saskatchewan and summering in Ontario—a good plan, especially with Alan's extended family living in Toronto. In June, shortly before leaving Regina, our friendly fertility doctor made us aware of an interesting link between our inability to conceive and Britain's low birth rate during the Second World War. He was cheerily confident about the correlation: England's high intake of canned corned beef preserved with nitrates, and Alan's use of nitric acid in printmaking. We listened closely to this final revelation. Wanting to believe, we decided he was a sweetheart.

A month later we'd found our farm in Teeswater, Ontario. A hundred acres of scenic, rolling land with a river running through it. Classified as non-farmable (only a horse and plow could manage the hilly acreage), it was referred to as a 'hobby' property, and thus its price of $14,500. Negotiations went smoothly: a down payment and two small mortgages. We'd saved $6,000 from three years of teaching—it helped not having the expenses of a car, even a fur covered one—and Alan's grandfather made a timely disbursement to all his grandchildren. We recruited friends from Regina, a print student and her husband, and the four of us began pitching veneer dressers and moldy mattresses from the second floor veranda, stripping multiple layers of wallpaper, sanding and varnishing pine floors. For six weeks it was camp-like living, especially after our dug well went dry and we had to drive to Lake Huron in the evenings with our shampoo and bars of Ivory soap. The nearest laundromat was in Walkerton, a town 15 miles north. In July, we were told the well drilling company was very busy and would not be able to come until September, and in July, we were told I was pregnant. But I'm jumping ahead.

Back to Vicente, Asunción, and that mountain on Ibiza. It was an extraordinary moment. The allure of the unknown accompanied by the reassurance of my husband's jubilant personality and steady self-confidence, both making an appearance amongst a people and language we were just getting to know. We were opposites, Alan comfortable in almost any situation, I so hesitant. When he was optimistic, I saw the other side. I had already come to rely on his positive world view in contrast to my caution. His charisma, in contrast to my reticence.

Vicente's wine, the odor of ink and color of eggplants, was nearly impossible to swallow. In the years that followed, Alan and I never learned to drink more than a half a glass of white or rosé, and it took a divorce and lots of water under the bridge for Leo to befriend scotch. Out of respect to Vicente and his Saint's Day, we consumed the purple wine and Asunción's heavy, whole wheat cake. Wobbling our way down the mountain we managed to locate the highway.

A few days later, after putting Leonardo on the mainland ferry so he could resume his travels, we found our house—a small bungalow on the road to San José, beside the *Tienda Can Chocolate*. Fifteen minutes out of the city with several stops along the way, the bus came to an abrupt halt. A group of straggly bushes near the road marked the spot. The driver pointed out the modest *tienda* about 50 yards down the highway. Descending the bus, we were surrounded by a landscape of country fields and goats and *campesinas* in long skirts and shawls, the April sky bright, the air invigorating.

A one-story stone cottage awaited our inspection. Well-constructed and tidy, its two squared columns and whitewashed walls beamed in the sun. Standing at the waist-high, stone parapet, we saw a purple bougainvillea towering at the end of the patio, persimmon, flowering shrubs and a fig tree that would produce black fruit. A huge daisy bush grew beside the walkway to the house. Orange trees had been planted along the west wall.

In the distance, an iron-red mountain, olive, almond and carob trees. In the arid, rocky soil of the foreground, *Frígola*, an aromatic low brush of wild thyme, accompanied tangles of wild sweet peas, blue and mauve, swaying in the breeze.

Breathing calm relief, we turned to the *tienda* to begin our inquiries. An Ibiza merchant had given us the landlord's name—José Ribas Palerm.

Iowa, April 4, 2009

I DON'T EXPECT MY FATHER OR brothers to tend to Ma's hair, but I expect it of the caregiver. She doesn't bother. Some of us call her *La Jefa*, or just *Jefa*, the boss woman. She laughs at my request, insisting my mother doesn't know if it's up or down, combed or not. I've told her the rest of us know, but she ignores me. A few minutes ago, standing my dripping umbrella against the front door in the entrance and rearranging the parcels in my arms, I found her wiping down the front staircase. *La Jefa* doubles as my parents' cleaning lady.

"Look what your Mami did this morning." She lifted her arm, feigning pain. "I can't believe how strong she is. It still hurts."

"What?" I saw nothing.

"She pinched me again … I know she wants to bite me." *Jefa* complained. "Don't I take care of her? Don't I love her like my own Mami?"

"My mother forgets," I answered quickly, starting up the stairs.

"I can't get near her with the hairbrush, all the crying and screaming!" She raised her voice defensively, trying to engage me from the bottom of the stairs.

I didn't take the bait.

"She's such a mean *vieja*. Face it, your Mami is out to lunch!"

Halfway up the staircase I turned, about to say something. Seeing her adjust the varicose bandage on her leg before returning to work, I refrained.

We're engaged in a power struggle, absurd as it sounds. In her position as head caregiver, *La Jefa* is in charge, *punto final*, period. My parents are her domain, her fiefdom. Mistress of all she can see, she wields her authority and lords it over her underlings, devoted women who assist with caregiving on a rotating, 24-hour schedule. Leaving behind families of young children, they've come from Mexico, Honduras, El Salvador. They have no money, little English, and more often than not, no work papers, but they're kind and speak gentle Spanish to my parents. I'm grateful to them. *La Jefa* need not answer to me. I am not the final voice in my parents' care, but they are my parents and I am their daughter. The task of managing all aspects of my parents' lives, a job that becomes more difficult and thankless as they age, was entrusted to my brother, Phillip.

Thus far I haven't attacked *La Jefa*. My parents haven't tripped on the Navajo rugs. The Colima dog hasn't fallen and shattered. Maybe everyone is doing the best they can, as Alan has recently taken to saying.

It seems incredible now, but as kids, when the six of us had the run of our old house on Summit Street, art was rarely, if ever, damaged. African pieces remained on their pedestals and rubber balls missed the Kunisada actors hanging on the dining room walls. Our Spanish Romanesque Christ from Burgos, mounted between floor length windows in the living room, never once opened his eyes in consternation at our commotion. Over life-size, arms gone, his head remained bent in sleep as it had for centuries.

Raising kids and collecting art held similarities for my parents—the commitment to protect, the patience with vulnerability, the respect for individuality. When new pieces joined our household, the sighs of relief were almost audible: from wood, from clay, even stone. They would have restoration and sanctuary. Goya prints were matted and framed, African and Pre-Columbian sculptures, carefully cleaned. Their new homes became the Plexiglas cases Pa constructed with epoxy glue.

We took in stride the constant activity accompanying and accommodating an expanding collection: the rearranging, re-hanging. As the years progressed and more objects entered our home, the fellow from Burgos remained my favorite. He spoke to me. I have no idea if he had the same effect on any of my siblings, but from the beginning, his riveting presence was integral to my visual well-being—the swag on graceful hips, the tranquil harmony. I loved him for what he was: damaged, worn, softened by time. His genesis might not have been so likeable: the sharp edges and distinct planes of the creator's chisel, the polychrome, the reality of religious purpose.

In high school, while writing my senior paper on the Gutenberg press, I audited a history of typography course taught by Professor Harry Duncan at the University of Iowa. The next year, my first semester of college, my schedule included his 'hands-on' typography class, an elective amid the string of boring requirements. When Professor Duncan learned of my poetry, he encouraged me to handset a booklet of poems. 'Christ from Burgos', one of four in the collection, was written in my mid-teens.

It's been years since I read the poem. Now, I'm shocked. As a young person writing, I had neither religious knowledge nor the associated vocabulary. The inferences within the naïveté of that poem are astonishing: the decline of faith, corruption, resurrection and hope. It goes without saying I knew little of these concepts if anything at all.

—◦•◦—

'Christ from Burgos', 1959
from the handset pamphlet,
Four Poems, 1961

Slain by man, carved by man, his home was
once the church altar,
Many, many years ago.
Your church was destroyed, you were buried.
The bugs and the worms ate their way into man,
Many, many years ago.
Uprooted from his grave, golden as the dirt
herself,
Man Came.
Many, many years later.
Once again you hang on a wall, old and pained,
your arms gone, your eyes closed heavy with sleep,
your ribs eaten by worms and aged by time.
Now.
Lost in his quiet face is the grief yet hope of
all man.
Still.
May I rub my fingers through your dusty ribs?
Yes.
You, you with your peacefully quiet face, why,
why don't you cry out once in your dreams!
Open your ancient eyes, just once … to me.
When?

Iowa, *April 4, 2009 continues*

A T THE AGE OF 16, I was describing what I saw in that piece
of wood—fragility caused by the passage of time. Those
'inferences' were accidental by-products of youthful writing. That's all.

But why so many worm holes? Why so much dust? As a
child, I'd seen similar crucifixions in our travels across Castilla and
Cataluña, Romanesque pieces in near perfect condition, still shiny
with paint. To this day, our Christ's physical deterioration remains
entangled with my poem, the Prado Museum, and my youthful fascination with the painters Pieter Bruegel and Hieronymus Bosch.

That winter in Madrid, when Pa picked us up from *Colegio
Británico*, the English grammar school Leonardo and I attended, if
time permitted, he'd circle back to the museum for another quick
look before returning home for the mid-day meal.

Wearing our coats and hats, we'd follow him across the ro-
tunda, through the long, chilly gallery of Spanish painting, and
finally, salon XII—Velázquez. We knew the drill. Standing before
the portrait of Queen Mariana of Austria that Pa had abruptly
left—realizing the late hour, realizing we'd be waiting at the school
entrance playing hopscotch—Leo and I watched as he resumed his
observation.

With his left eye squeezed closed, the index and third finger
of his right hand moved horizontally through space, blocking the
mass of drapery in the top quarter of the canvas before dropping
assertively to the tower shaped clock in the background. But it had
to be there, the velvet covered table, the miniature brass spire, picking up golden highlights of her coiffure and bodice, forcing the

eye to not ignore the right side of the room. Turning vertically, his fingers concealed the perpendicular alignment of the skirt's edge against the hint of a chair—leather-backed, tasseled—just a hint. By removing it, how much would change? In a final question, a bold challenge, Pa's fingers obscured that luminous white kerchief on the black skirt. Finally, stepping back, smiling, he shook his head in silent amazement.

After, as promised, he took us downstairs. Leo and I were so drawn to the Dutch painters, especially Bosch, with typical, child-like curiosity we moved in as close as possible. The old guard, with his missing teeth and mended gray uniform, straightened up to his full height. As he approached, his voice serious and smelling of garlic, we pulled back, our cold noses nearly touching those fascinating scenes.

A leaking church roof and dripping water was the obvious explanation for our Christ's crumbling wood, but why not interment? Even feisty Faustina, my family's household help while we lived in Madrid, even she would not have come up with such a wild possibility. Maybe Hieronymus Bosch wouldn't have either.

The scenario emerged spontaneously, pulling forward from the distant past, from an unknown, remote corner of Burgos province. A rural churchyard gathering of baying animals and devout, frenzied peasants. A Technicolor display of religious fervor: strange musical instruments and passionate dance around ladders and shovels, flamboyant garments and elaborate knitted caps (the kind Flagstaff hippies would kill for), a swarming mass, teetering at the brink of lunacy. Moving across the cobblestones and into the ancient church—ladders with which to lower, shovels with which to inter—the crowd approached. He, still in the prime of youth, wept, knowing there was more to come.

My father found the Christ in an antiquities shop in the vicinity of *El Rastro*, Madrid's flea market. William and Leonardo, who both speak of accompanying Pa to art dealers that winter, have clear recollections of all the art purchased during the year. I do not. Remembering pieces that were passed up, they tell the story of how, at the end of our stay, Pa wanted to trade the English Ford—acquired in Paris for our time in Spain—for a group of small, polychromed Romanesque virgins he could not afford. The dealer would have liked to complete the transaction, but it was out of the question. He was not allowed to own a car because he'd fought on the wrong side of the Spanish Civil War and was still under many constraints. I never saw those Romanesque sculptures and only recently heard the story—though one brother places the dealer in Segovia and the other in Madrid.

It no longer matters why I wasn't involved, as my brothers were. Being a girl in my patriarchal family is another story, for another moment. But the certainty is that I wasn't included in the process— visits to dealers and hearing discussions of origins and aesthetics. If I had been, would my visual memory be more complete? Would I have taken an interest in the details of procurement?

Perhaps not. *Provenance, seller* and *cost versus value* are preoccupations I've come to associate with the male artist/collector.

Despite not having my brothers' visual recall, I was instinctively drawn to three pieces besides the Romanesque Christ. My favorite was an early Spanish panel painting of the Flagellation of Christ at the Column. The weeping saint's teal garment felt accessible enough to repurpose for the sewing projects that occupied me, and the sixth digit on Christ's left hand called for regular inspection. I vividly remember when the 15th century Madonna and Child entered our home, missing her crown. The wooden statue was so covered with grime, our outspoken Faustina declared she'd never seen a Madonna *tan cubierta de mierda*, so covered in shit. We all watched as Pa spent days carefully cleaning her with a toothbrush.

The most unusual piece joining us at 77 Francisco Silvela was the African harp. Many things caught my father's eye, but he was stopped in his tracks by the harp. Though he hadn't yet begun to collect, he was familiar with African art. One of his first print students was Roy Sieber.

We all knew Roy and Sophie from the early days on Summit Street, picking cherries and waiting for Roy to complete his PhD thesis. Sieber received the first doctorate in African art history from the University of Iowa, made trips to Africa, and was ultimately considered a foremost authority in the field. Our families became lifelong friends. In addition to the rapport with Sieber and their ongoing exchange of knowledge and visual experiences, Mauricio knew that Matisse, Lipchitz and Picasso had been discovering and acquiring tribal art since the first decade of the century. It seems reasonable that he would have seen images of non-western art in their collections.

Facts of attribution were secondary for him. He was an artist, not a scholar; he would leave that to his friend, Sieber. The harp's tribe was the Fang people of Northern Gabon, and its purpose of creation? An instrument of communication with the spirit world of Fang ancestors. When Mauricio found the harp, it's unlikely he knew any of these details, or that it would prove to be extraordinarily valuable, or that it would become iconic in the world of Fang art.

But he knew aesthetic uniqueness, and instinctively recognized what he needed: the maker's emotive candor, his humility, his humanity. With future purchases of tribal art, this winning combination could make my father tune-out the world, and make him 'want'.

My siblings speak of a purchase price of $15. Amazing now, but it couldn't have been trivial in 1953, especially for an American university professor with a wife, four children and his Guggenheim Fellowship's fixed amount. The harp, my parents' first African piece, formed the nucleus of their collection. The assemblage of art eventually stretched beyond paintings by graduate students, Pre-Columbian sculpture, Japanese, Piranesi and Goya prints, to concentrate solely on the numerous tribes of Africa. The years changed my father's collecting habits and purpose. What began as diversion grew into passion, passion that morphed into need, need that became the mania of possession escorting him to the end of his life.

Iowa, 1954

AFTER LENGTHY DEALINGS AND PREPARATIONS, the Christ was crated and shipped to Iowa along with the other acquired pieces. On the chance our containers would be opened and inspected by Spanish customs officials, household items and William's black bomber jacket were packed in among the works of art. Though oblivious to the difficulties involved in exporting historic art from Franco's Spain, and unaware of the complications that surfaced before our Christ arrived in the new world, I never questioned that he belonged with us. I knew he would fare better in Iowa than collecting dust in the backroom of an antiquities shop in the *Rastro*. When those wooden boxes were finally dismantled in our Iowa home, we all breathed a sigh of relief. William's jacket and the Christ had both survived their journey.

404 South Summit in Iowa City had to have been more peaceful than our Christ's beginning, possibly in that church with the leaky roof. I was familiar with Spanish women in black, their cloth slippers shuffling across cold stones of churches and cathedrals. Approaching in prayer, they must have pleaded for so many things, so many cures, so many miracles he could not fulfill. In our home, there were no expectations. We felt his gratitude, his serenity.

Countless came to see our Romanesque friend: those who could see and those who couldn't, the knowledgeable and those who weren't, the art faculty, students, curious neighborhood kids, and finally, our caring family doctor, Pauline Moore, a devout Catholic. She'd stop by our home whenever one of us was sick. It was a bonus that Christ was present. In response to my mother's calls—a fever, possible strep throat, flu, general malaise—she'd show up at the end of the day on her way home. It was the 'polio scare' era: public swimming pools and young, stiff necks that would not bend to touch chests. Tired and hoarse after long days, our patient doctor would amble into the living room to write out prescriptions. Sinking into one of the Eames' style plywood chairs, she'd kick off her shoes and settle back for a few minutes of reflection in the company of our ancient friend. I was fascinated by her empathy, her acquiescence. More than once we saw her leave our house moist-eyed and remarkably refreshed.

Our parents' protective, evasive tendencies prolonged our innocence and ignorance. Barely conscious of world religions, I knew little of the traditions we came from, what would have been our birthrights. I was aware that my maternal grandparents had been non-practicing and ardently 'anti-clergy', despite their Spanish Catholic backgrounds. Since my father rarely mentioned his Jewish upbringing, my assumption was that it was no longer relevant, or had simply vanished. That was the extent of my knowledge, so I clung to the hereditary trivia that delighted my mother—lavender had been my grandmother, Pilar's, scent of choice, like mine. Sewing had been her pleasure, like mine. Solitude her companion, like mine.

Eventually I understood why the subject of religion was banned in my family. Mauricio had been disowned by his mother for marrying a non-Jew. After my parent's marriage, *La Bobeh* Ana entered bereavement and cut buttons off her garments. This act of threatening finality deeply distressed my mother. I was 15 or 16 before she told me the story, and it took the advent of maturity before I grasped its full meaning.

A spin on the Jewish mourning custom of tearing one's garments, right? That's what I assumed, but I've found no reference to the practice. It's easy to imagine the hinterlands of 19th century Lithuania, where grieving but practical women might have opposed the slashing of perfectly good clothing. I certainly would have. Buttons could be sewn on again. The young Ana Kahn lived in a village near Kovno before her emigration to Argentina. Though quick and clever, she had not been taught to read and her name was all she could write. It's unclear how cognizant she was of Jewish traditions, or in actuality, if she cared. Known for being obstinate and with a mind of her own, the 'button thing' may have been her own *mishigas.*

When *La Bobeh* came to stay with us in Iowa, she brought an assortment of ancient, dark garments smelling of mothballs. The long evening gown was unforgettable with its hip to hem bias-cut godets and an ample bodice of black sequins and tiny pleats—the slippery, black crepe, a seamstress' worst nightmare as she labored at night in bad light. Mindful and proud of the important status of her son, 'The Professor', *La Bobeh* may have imagined sparkling, festive events requiring evening attire. Her disappointment must have been immense. On the few occasions she wore the dress, it was my job to tend to the row of tiny, satin covered snaps running down the back. In those moments, still not conscious of the menacing power of *La Bobeh's* buttons, I could not know Ma's bewilderment as a bride. And while I could feel the vibrations of anxiety, I could not know their origins, years before and a continent away.

There it was, plain and straightforward: the explanation for 'no religion'. A mother goes into mourning for a son who is very much alive. The overwhelmed newlyweds must come to terms with a new reality.

My curiosity continued its course. Alice Turner, my high school girlfriend, enticed me to join the Unitarian Youth Group with stories of interesting discussions on creativity. Nothing to do with religion, she assured me. Her family was Unitarian. Since parental permission was necessary, I figured that was the end. Wrong. My parents consented. They deserve credit for that generosity of spirit. Their repudiation of *Religion*—the mere mention of the word—was a gold standard they adhered to. I was drawn to conversations about poetry at the Unitarian Youth Group meetings, but had no interest in spirituality. My attendance was brief. Even after learning something in university classes, Western Civilization, World Religions, the Bible as Literature, a huge piece of puzzle was missing. It was troubling not being able to complete my personal picture.

A rabbi married us. After our wedding, I began the cautious, tightrope walk over Alan's Jewish terrain. My dad at one end, exasperated by the resurfacing of his submerged albatross, and my husband at the other, pained by his father-in-law's abdication. Abandonment as the only solution, was not part of Alan's well-lit world. This conflict of two giant personalities would continue for the equivalent of a generation. Their difficult relationship had not begun well, but ultimately ended gently.

One day, long after our children had completed their B'nai Mitzvahs, Pa told me that none of his other children had given him 'trouble about religion'. He was genuinely puzzled. I'm not sure if 'trouble' meant my innocent curiosity and the Unitarian Youth Group, or the more portentous subject of his own heritage. None of my siblings had resuscitated Judaism. None of them had pulled it to the forefront, making it, once again, a presence in his world. The years hadn't lessened his bewilderment, but by then he'd gotten over the angry belief that I'd dredged up that unmentionable from his past and thrown it in his face.

There was no dredging. Judaism came to me riding my husband's carefree coattails. Together, we invigorated it for our children.

Eventually, Pa and I we were able to move beyond the 'trouble about religion', arriving at a point of easy communication that was often about the past and Buenos Aires. Our conversations were reinforced by my ongoing interest in the experiences that shaped my parents' formative years.

When speaking of his youth, my father habitually referred to the hardships of the Depression, but rarely to anything pleasurable. The positive reminiscences he did reveal were a treat, a sprinkling of contentment and normalcy. His rabbi grandfather disappearing up to the attic with a candle and crust of bread—fleeing to study Torah, fleeing to avoid his daunting wife. The drudgeries of *cheder* lessons. Memories of *La Bobeh's* Rosh Hashanah cooking, especially teiglach candy and the specific copper pot used in its preparation. The combination of emotion and serenity felt good. I wanted more.

In the early 80's I made several trips to Argentina. While happily re-connecting with extended family, I was able to pursue my growing interest in the Jewish agricultural colony of Moisés Ville, in Santa Fé. The village became the focus of my second book of fiction, *Losers and Keepers in Argentina*. Settled by Russian Jews in 1889, Moisés Ville was sponsored by the Austrian born French philanthropist, Baron Maurice de Hirsch. Convinced the answer for Russian Jews escaping pogroms was 'a return to the land', specifically in Argentina, he created The Jewish Colonization Association to purchase acreage and manage the influx of refugees. Following the example of Moisés Ville, Hirsch went on to establish a number of colonies in other provinces.

During the months of research at the University of Iowa Library, pre-internet, I brought my father old books languishing in the stacks' '*oversize*' sections. Some had never been checked out. Reading aloud captions as we studied pages of images, the shared moments carried me back to summers in Maine when he'd have me read aloud in the studio while he worked on prints—*Madame Bovary, The Red and The Black*, segments from *Anna Karenina*, from *The Jungle*.

We exchanged information about Baron Hirsch's colonies and their influence on Argentine society: medicine, law, philosophy and education. It was fascinating to learn of my parents' ties to people connected to the colonies, especially Moisés Ville. And in a Buenos Aires conversation with my Aunt Perla, my uncle Marcos's wife, she told me that her grandfather was Noe Cosiovich—the founder of Moisés Ville. This exciting discovery, too good to be true, added enormous momentum to my project.

The conversations with my father were kept private. We both understood there was too much discomfort about religion in the family and zero tolerance for 'Jewish talk'. When I told Pa I was reading about Jewish names in pre-Inquisition Spain, and that Ma's family names, Medina, Fernández and Barragán, were all included on the list, the information mischievously delighted him. He'd known it all along. After all, 'doesn't Emilia look like El Greco's wife, Doña Jerónima de las Cuevas, the Jewess from Toledo?' One day he tried to involve my mother in a cheerful discussion about the Jewish origin of old Spanish names. She could not be persuaded, and was certainly not amused.

As kids, sharing the house with our Christ from Burgos, conceivably there was no need for extended knowledge. For us, he was not about belief, as he was for our family doctor. He was another piece of art, another opportunity to exercise our visual curiosity and appreciation. If Pa had spoken about birthright, if he'd used the word—which I never heard him do—I believe he would have considered art to be our heritage, our inheritance. Did any of us give thought to how completely we were raised in its embrace, how comfortably and easily we moved in the visual world? I certainly took it for granted.

When presented with art he admired, it had already been filtered through his lenses, yet he refrained from intruding when it came to our individual pursuits and interests. True in my case, but I became a writer, not an artist. My artist siblings might have different thoughts on the subject. As with most parents and children, my dad and I had joint experiences. The same landscapes, the same familial and societal concerns, the same positive and negative poles, waiting for our winds to point us during dilemmas and under duress. On some occasions he spoke about our joint encounters, other times he did not. He moved quickly. There was always more beyond, more to see, more to do. He did not dwell, especially if he felt the experience irrelevant to him.

Pa wasn't concerned with my imaginative explorations. My inclination to literature and writing presented him neither vested interest nor threat. This reality was, knowingly or unknowingly, a wand's wave of genius on his part, a stroke of luck for me.

When my parents moved from Summit Street, they gifted the Christ to the Cedar Rapids Museum of Art, where it was displayed for years. Wanting an image for this writing, I reached out to the museum director and to my brother, Phillip. Before Phillip located the one I used, five photos arrived by email from the director. The individual shots of the head, torso and thighs lying on a white sheet, looked like something from a postmortem, rather than a museum's storeroom. Missing were the tagged toes. What a way to end.

EXCERPTS
'Reyna and Max'
from *ONE APRIL AFTERNOON*
in the time of Silberman and Gould
unpublished novel, 2010

ONE DAY, SHORTLY AFTER EMMA and Max's wedding, Emma convinced her mother to pull out her box of keepsakes. Max had a keen interest in old jewelry and he'd searched long and hard for Emma's engagement ring, a gold band with the striking arrangement of antique garnets and seed pearls. Reyna chatted happily about the origin of every piece in her box: her mother's Spanish earrings and brooches, her father's gold watch, the Mexican jade and strands of fine, African beads that Abe bought in Paris, long before they became common. She pointed out the silver scarab Emma's brother created in one of his casting classes, as well as a tiny, granite man he carved for her last birthday. Finally, after a moment's hesitation, Reyna pulled the last item out of its muslin bag.

Like a moth to flame or a bee to blossom, Max was riveted by the gold medallion with the embossed image of a sad-eyed Virgin. He immediately asked about it.

"What?! Who said anything about the Virgin?" Reyna's voice suddenly became haughty, her posture erect. "This is a family trinket, a memento from my grandmother." Indignant, she quickly slipped it back into the bag. "It has nothing to do with religion ... nothing."

Max was stunned. What had he said to offend his new mother-in-law?

Emma hadn't yet explained her family's taboos and bad words. Nor had she spoken of the private fiefdom where her mother, the tiny Queen Reyna, ruled. Her isolated domain was so closed to the world, much like Shangri-La, few souls had ever entered, and fewer still had questioned its realities.

She often thought that was the moment, that was the turning point in Max and her mother's relationship. They hadn't known each other long or well, but when Max had the nerve to refer to the medallion's image as the Virgin, things changed forever, or at least, for a very long time, until Reyna's memory seriously failed her. As far as Emma knew, no one had ever caught her mother in one of her denials. Could the rift have been prevented? Probably not, Reyna's obstinacy and Max's candor would have surely collided on another occasion. Only when Emma and Max's children were born did Reyna forget, forgive, at least for a while. Otherwise, her clandestine need to attack her son-in-law has remained constant over the years.

It's goes beyond the Virgin medallion. Emma knows Max's kindness has always annoyed her mother. It's ironic. Considerate and gentle, Max buys roses for Mother's Day and if Emma mentions that Reyna's birthday is approaching, he happily assumes the task of shopping. He's purchased sweaters, hats, all manner of clothing for his mother-in-law, his artist's eye tuned to her delicate stature and fine coloring. His gifts always make her look beautiful.

It hasn't helped. Reyna's assaults on Max appear out of nowhere and without reason. She slides them nimbly into routine conversations, and Emma is left bewildered. It's like a repeat performance of Reyna's mother, Isabella, and her relationship with her own mother, Inés. Reyna loved telling the stories. Inés never liked her son-in-law, Aurelio Ribera, neither his goodness, nor his adoration of her daughter.

The last time Reyna was still able to attack was after Noah's first visit to the psychiatrist. She made that comment about Max's possible neglect, how it might be the cause of Noah's problems. 'Maybe Max hadn't been as attentive as he was with the other kids. It's not uncommon with last children,' Reyna assured Emma, 'especially if they're smart and independent, like Noah.' Emma learned long ago not to respond when her mother makes angry statements. Recently, she tried talking to her parents about addiction and chemical imbalances in the brain, about mental illness, but it may have been too late for Reyna. Was she able to understand? Abe always appears to know about the other side of life's mountains, but he's rarely willing to admit he's been.

[Excerpt]

Reyna no longer attacks. Her communication has become disconnected utterances, desperate for memory and articulation. Perhaps her fragmented mind loosened underlying truths that have lost their resistance to denial. The thing about Reyna's discomfort with Max involved more than his goodness of character. She resented his ease with Judaism. A solace her sons neither had, nor would want or need, she once stated proudly, as though Judaism was an extra pillow, only for spoiled boys.

Max, a most secular, private Jew, quickly became a verbal activist when he met Emma's family, much to their embarrassment and resentment. Any chance, any occasion, and he'd spin out the vocabulary—*Bubbe, ganef, Ladino, meschuga, mench, mishpocha, Mitzvah (Bar, Bat and plain), Rabbi, Rebbitzin, schlemazel, schlemiel, Semitic (and anti), Sephardic, Synagogue, yarmulke, Yiddish*—anything to make a point, until it became a badge of honor for him, a dreaded malaise for her family.

In the past, Emma's visits to her parents were generally Sunday afternoons, now they're more frequent. Not long ago, they were sitting in the living room chatting about Marcus Silberman, 'the relative', from Cuernavaca. Reyna seemed especially alert as she happily poured the *maté* and passed it to Abe. It was calm and quiet. Only days before they had received a letter from Marcus.

Emma met Marcus and his wife, Belle, on a visit to her parents, years ago, while they were still wintering in Mexico—before Reyna got paratyphoid, before they sold their property. Her parents became acquainted with the other Silbermans at the home of mutual friends. After a few months of friendship and the exchange of information, it was decided that Abe and Marcus were related. Marcus insisted the evidence was indisputable: the exact spelling of their surname, the 'uncle' who had immigrated to Cape Town from

Poland, the crazy relatives in both families. The so-called evidence never convinced Emma, but clearly, there was mutual rapport and the desire for a familial relationship. Fine. Now, according to the letter, Marcus and Belle were moving back to the States, for health reasons.

"He's a good person," Abe said, putting on his glasses and reaching across the coffee table for the envelope. "Both of them, they believe in helping people, really helping. Did you ever see the sign they had on their door?"

Emma was surprised by her father's positive comments.

"They had the same thing on their door that you have. You know what I mean. Anyway, below it, they'd hung a sign: '*If You're Hungry, come in and Eat*'."

"Naturally it wasn't the main door," Reyna interrupted knowledgeably. "There was a special entrance at the back of the house for deliveries and service people."

"They meant it, too," Abe added.

"They fed a lot of people." Reyna nodded, pouring herself another *maté*. She stopped and looked up. "What thing on the door? What are you talking about, Abe? I've never seen anything on Emma's door."

"Yes, Reyna, it's there," Abe said. "It's there. Anyway, what do you call it?" He looked at Emma.

"You mean the *mezuzah*?"

"Right, doesn't it have something to do with money?" he taunted, smiling.

"I don't think so." Emma forced back a smile. "Come on, you remember. How many times have you told me your grandfather was a rabbi?"

"I don't know what you're talking about," Reyna said. "Abe, what does your grandfather have to do with all this? I've never seen anything on the door!" Confused, she looked from Abe to Emma. "What did you say it is?"

"A *mezuzah*," Emma said. "You don't notice because I've painted over it a few times."

Not true. Emma carefully removes their *mezuzah* when re-painting the entranceway. The 'painting over' happens in one of her stories, her fiction, not in her life. It's a story about New York Jews who live in an apartment. They've become so distanced from Judaism, so disconnected, they don't seem to care that their *mezuzah* is painted over whenever the painters come, whenever the halls and doors are given a fresh coat. She supposes it hardly matters; her fiction or her life, it's probably all related, and besides, who really cares? Emma wanted to end the conversation. It's never good to be talking *Jewish stuff* with her father in front of her mother. She didn't even start the discussion, but it was already too late.

Her mother was upset because she didn't know what that 'thing' was. At least, that's what she said. Was it true that she's never noticed the *mezuzah* on her daughter's door? Or had she purposely ignored it, Emma wondered? In any case, Reyna was convinced she'd never seen it.

"What about Amy and her violin?"

"What?" Emma asked, turning to her mother.

"Amy, your daughter, when she was young. Amy and her violin, I remember. I was sitting right here," Reyna said, patting the couch, "right here when Max said Amy didn't need to be a professional violinist, that it was enough to enjoy playing for herself." Reyna sat back against the couch, arms folded across her chest in defiance.

"You misunderstood," Emma said calmly.

Reyna turned to Abe. "Didn't you always say the girl could play professionally, that she had what it took?"

"Sure, you bet she had what it took!"

"See, there you are!"

Abraham Silberman had spoken—his word was the word.

"You misunderstood …" Emma repeated, quietly.

"Wasn't that the way it was, Abe?"

Emma knew her father could not deny his Queenie. She wanted to hit on her son-in-law; she wanted to cut him down at the knees. That's all.

"Now just a minute," Abe said, "let me think how it was—"

"Amy never wanted to be a soloist." Emma looked at her mother.

"Her professor wanted her to perform, and she didn't want any part of it. She refused. So when Max said that, about playing for herself ..."

Reyna turned away.

The next day, her mother would be cool and distant on the phone because Emma hadn't let her win. Is she, Emma Gould, learning something? She too has daughters and sons, sons-in-law.

Religion continues to be a problem for the Silberman family, especially Max's Judaism. It's been hard for Reyna to accept that a Jew could *want* to be a Jew. Really hard, because her own husband had chosen to ignore, had even tried to forget that truth. Abe and Reyna managed to raise six children ignorant of their parents' birthrights, and their own. To that, Emma's sister, Apple, would probably say that Emma has an unhealthy preoccupation with the things their parents chose to ignore while raising children. Could be. And Abe? He would insist that birthright has nothing to do with religion. Nothing! Birthright is about culture and art.

When Abe Silberman pulls heritage forward, it becomes his own creation, free from the reality of the past, free of baggage. Apparently, his personal history offered him no legacy. The mountains and valleys of ancestral traditions never figure in the terrain of his idealized land. Emma knows that to understand Abe Silberman, it is necessary to comprehend his sense of self-preservation and the role that voracity played in his life. If he wanted something, and it could be had for the taking, he took it, especially a heritage.

From the very beginning, he coveted Reyna's Spanish legacy. He took it on, much the way women take their husband's surnames. Had he convinced himself that it was more to do with Spain than him? How could a man proud of his own tradition want another? Emma often heard her father's disparaging words about the Polish ghettos of his ancestors, their mud streets and wooden slums, their poverty and orthodoxy, binding and restrictive. For him, they held nothing redeeming. He saw Reyna's heritage as Greco, Velázquez and Goya, all those Spanish painters he had loved since childhood. He saw the Spanish, as a heroic, noble race.

[Excerpt]

Emma remembers her parents in a rare moment of matrimonial candor. They were sitting at the table going through boxes of photographs when she came across the few existing snapshots of their honeymoon. Wedding portraits were never taken. Although they'd known for years they would marry, the ceremony happened without fanfare because of Sonia Silberman's disapproval. Reyna looked tranquil, lounging back against the warm stones of the Córdoba stream Emma had heard so much about. She wore a red dress printed with tiny, blue fleur-de-lis and red sling-back shoes. Abe stood behind Reyna, slim and lanky in his wool trousers, shirt and tie. They looked so young, so in love.

"Despite the circumstances, everything came together," Reyna said cheerfully, pointing to her red dress.

Her mother, Isabella, made the dress in one afternoon, and together they'd shopped for shoes the day before the wedding. For the few days of their honeymoon, a good friend lent them the small cottage on his family's property in the mountains of Córdoba. They were dressed up, Reyna added, because they'd just lunched at his home, *Casa Totoral*, where the excitement of the moment was the recent purchase of a camera. Abe moved his thumb across the image, recalling the stone landscape with the simple cottage on the hill above the stream.

"Abe, should we tell Emma? Should we tell her what we used to read in the evenings, down at the stream?" Reyna asked spontaneously, her eyes luminous.

"The Ten Commandments," Abe said quietly.

The revelation—joyful innocence, willing trust—came and left, and Emma was grateful for the moment. It was good to meet this young, hopeful couple in the fading photograph. It was good to know their peace, their devotion, their need to surmount disparate backgrounds.

In the meantime, Sonia Silberman sat *shiva* for her son, Abraham. *Shiva?* But why? Because he'd married a *shiksa.* She wept and cut the buttons off her black, crepe dress. Returning to the city, Abraham Silberman was cautiously told of this event by his brothers. Abe never forgave his mother for performing such an appalling act while he and Reyna were on their honeymoon.

Despite the perfection of the Ten Commandments and the optimism of that honeymoon moment, insecurity set in. Abraham and Reyna must have decided that the business of religion was too confusing and painful and they would not pass it on to their children.

Ibiza, April 1965

THE DAY ALAN AND I stood in the door of *Tienda Can Chocolate*, inquiring about the house next door and asking directions to the Ribas Palerm farm, we were about to embark on an adventure that would last from April 4, 1965, to the beginning of July 1966. Not long, yet the essence of Ibiza added dimensions to our lives that continue today.

I did not keep journals while we lived on Ibiza, but I regularly wrote to my family in Iowa. My mother saved my correspondence, approximately 40 aerograms and letters, and a stack of postcards, more than half written in English, the rest in Spanish. After Ma's death in November of 2009, I retrieved the Ibiza letters, in addition to writings from our travels in England, France and that winter in Holland. Everything had been neatly stored in her documents and sewing cupboard.

The narratives have been a valuable resource—seasons and weather, dates, names and revelations of character. In the beginning of our Ibiza stay we made several crossings to Barcelona. There were leads to pursue about an intaglio printing press or a collection of Goya prints, purchases to make for necessities not available on the island, the train to board for a week of museums in Paris, and toward the end of our stay, visits to a doctor for my nagging hip pain. The diligently recorded adventures filled gaps in my memory.

When Alan recently saw me handling the greenish Spanish aerograms, their edges striped with diagonal red and yellow, he declared them 'a gift'. Ma was a keeper of such things. The rubber-banded-piles of piano and dance performances, report cards and exhibition announcements, all stashed with odds and ends of sewing notions and bits of carefully coiled darning wool. She hung on to stuff, so I didn't think anything of it. It wasn't until Alan and I wondered what might have prompted her to keep my letters, carefully gathered together and organized by date, that I was reminded of something my mother may never have forgotten.

In 1954 when my family returned to the States from Spain, I was 11. We traveled on the ocean liner Saturnia, going and coming—New York, our port of departure and arrival. On both occasions we visited the city for several days, staying with my parents' good friends, Sergio and Clari Bagú, also Argentines. Their apartment in Jackson Heights, Queens, was small, and we were six guests. I don't recall where my siblings slept, but I was accommodated on two armchairs pushed together—a novel experience, like the deliciously creamy, New York milk. During our return stay, Ma asked Sergio to read my Spanish diary. A Marxist historian, sociologist and political philosopher, Bagú had taught at Middlebury in Vermont and at the time of our visits, he worked for the UN. Eventually, he would be exiled from his homeland after the military coup of 1966 and the fall of the Argentine government. A renowned scholar, he graciously agreed to read my oeuvre, and upon completion, declared: 'Esta chica será escritora'. This girl will be a writer.

Bagú's words may have been what my mother never forgot.

A decade later, if she heard the discussion between Pa and Alan's father on the day before my wedding, she probably forgot it immediately. Ma tended to do that when she didn't like what she was hearing.

As they sat in the living room chatting over a drink, I heard Pa assure my future father-in-law that I'd been 'groomed' to be the wife of an artist, so he needn't worry. It's hard to imagine what Alan's dad thought of the declaration. A kind, easy-going man, my father-in-law, Moe, didn't appear worried about anything on that exciting, prenuptial day, including the concept of his son being an artist. If he had concerns about how an artist makes a living, they would have been eased knowing that Alan, soon to receive an MFA degree, could become a professor, like Mauricio. That day before our wedding, the 'artist' part of Alan's equation was secondary to my father-in-law—and would remain so—the word 'professor' easier understood than 'artist'.

It seems Emilia may have had other ideas for her 'groomed' daughter. Regardless of my parents' spoken and unspoken thoughts, the challenge of printmaker's daughter, painter's wife, was mine alone to embrace and deconstruct.

Tienda Can Chocolate on the *Carretera de San José*, was owned by Juan and María, brother and sister. Juan was 70 and María (a.k.a. María Chocolate, to distinguish her from the other Marías in our midst), was 65, but she could have been 80—her short, stocky figure encased in layers of faded, dark cloth, the tied, black scarf, the shocking baldness. Juan, who spoke a crisp, formal Spanish, told us the *casa* belonged to the older Palerm brother and suggested we make ourselves comfortable on the bench under the fig tree while he climbed the mountain to fetch José. Bending to tie his *alpargatas* before departing, he assured us José and María were excellent landlords. The stone walls were regularly painted with *cal* (whitewash), the shrubs and trees maintained, and the orderly, empty house, swept and aired.

José appeared in his work clothes and straw hat, smiling amiably, eager to make our acquaintance. Speaking in a mixture of Spanish and Ibicenco, he showed us about the house, explaining that his brother and sister-in-law lived in Santa Eulalia, a city north of Ibiza, also on the eastern coast of the island. They were employed as butler and housekeeper for *unos Señores Alemanes*, a German couple. Financially comfortable after years of work, they no longer had the inclination to look after the property.

We stood with José on the veranda happily agreeing to one month's rent in advance and the same amount down. No need for a lease. It appeared $16 a month was indeed the going rate for a *finca* on Ibiza. Our only condition was the enlargement of a north facing window in the room Alan would use as a studio. José had no problem with the request.

Eager to move in with our two suitcases, we immediately went out to buy needed items while José began on the window. A mattress from a furniture shop in Ibiza Town, an old table and chairs from a farmer José knew, a propane gas tank, two-burner cooktop and a few kitchen supplies from the hardware store. The stone walls of our *casa* were over a foot thick and the labor-intensive window project continued for several days. From that first encounter working together, José with his pickaxe and Alan collecting debris, a new lingo lifted from the rubble. In their blend of Spanish, French, Ibicenco and the occasional English word, the *pintor* and the *campesino* spoke of many things, including the significance of north light.

Until the hardware store was able to deliver our cooking supplies, María lent us their old, portable cookstove. The smell of kerosene brought back a childhood visit to an isolated place in Castilla and having to eat *bacalao*, codfish stew, cooked over kerosene. I don't remember who was on that trip, one of several my family took that winter, nor the city, but it was a small, damp place that I associate with a train station, or the vestry of an ancient church. I stood in my gabardine coat with the faux fur collar, knit cap and mitts, watching as the caretaker's wife hunched over the stove, stirring our dinner. It smelled awful and I refused to eat.

Ibiza's sunlight quickly rolled the recollection back into my crater of incomplete memories.

The afternoon our gas tank arrived, we could hardly wait to fry our evening eggs. Not having electricity, we managed with candles until Anna Wachsmann lent us her English kerosene Aladdin lamp. We'd befriended Anna only days before. On the first excursion to Barcelona, we purchased a gas Coleman lantern, and eventually, a second one to keep in the kitchen.

Our water supply was a cistern under the patio, accessible from a wooden door beside the purple bougainvillea (visible beside Alan), and a small holding tank on the roof that stored sun-warmed water. The recent addition of a bathroom was a huge plus, definitely rare for an old Ibicenco farmhouse without running water. The cement block construction added to the east side of the existing house, proudly displayed a brand-new sink and flush toilet. The entire room, tiled in white porcelain with a drain in the slightly sloped floor, functioned as the shower. The key to flushing the toilet and a warm shower was *la bomba,* the hand pump that forced water from the cistern up to the roof reservoir. Gravity brought the water down to the toilet tank, sink and shower pipes. By taking joint showers at the end of the day, we conserved the limited supply of water in the reservoir.

My brother, Leo, back in Madrid after visiting the south, was charged with the onerous task of shipping our remaining Dutch belongings to Ibiza. Weeks earlier when we'd first arrived in Spain, it had not been easy claiming our shipment at Madrid customs. After a stifling trek on subways and buses, waiting and delays to speak with officials and sign papers, further confusion awaited us. No one knew the whereabouts of our freight and it wasn't located for over an hour. More bureaucratic Spanish blundering followed. The inspectors in charge did not have a simple screwdriver to open the crates of canvases. Impatient and annoyed because of the heat, the brutes used a hammer. Fortunately, only two small paintings were damaged. The boxes and compromised crates were put into storage until we had a permanent address.

After negotiations with customs, Leo managed their release and shipment. Placing a call from the American Express in Madrid to the *Pensión Oliver,* he left word that our belongings were on their way. Within a week, retrieving our messages from the *Oliver,* we met the shipment at the Ibiza pier and were finally reunited with our belongings. Alan's paintings, my mint green Dutch typewriter, books purchased in England, an embroidered Afghan carpet from the department store, Libertys of London, and the small household items we'd acquired in Holland. By April 15, 1965, Alan and I were enjoying our sparsely furnished Ibiza dwelling, reading by the glow of Anna's Aladdin lamp and composing aerograms home to our families.

Our friendship with the Palerms spontaneously crossed borders of geography, knowledge, and cultures—the similarities greater than differences. José, outgoing and talkative, learned some Spanish in the army but had never gone to school. Nor had María or Antonia. We were assured the law had changed since their youth and children were required to attend school.

The women were shy about speaking, but Antonia laughed easily and seemed content and calm. When we met, she was still wearing the traditional Ibicenco attire. A long skirt and petticoats, apron, shawl and scarf. Shortly after our arrival, she abandoned the old garments and followed her newly 'modernized' sister-in-law into the 20th century. María was reticent and it took several encounters before she felt comfortable with us. She smiles in the photograph, but her personality was stamped by residual sadness. I believe their inability to conceive a child was the cause. While we lived on Ibiza, we counted only one child among the Palerm's neighbors and relatives, a small, impish boy of five or six, a sibling-less Prince of princes.

The Palerm's farmstead, José's original family home, was spread out on a plateau halfway up the mountain. For generations, the small hilly patches of barley and wheat fields had been worked with a horse and plow. Flour was still ground on the grist stone and grapes from their vineyards still stomped into wine. They kept chickens, rabbits, goats, sheep, honeybees and a couple hogs, one to market and the other for their own butchering needs. Sausage, bread, and cheese were all *casera*, made at home. Carob bean (St. John's Bread) was harvested from the *algarroba* trees to feed the hogs, and almonds and figs were collected for the family's use. If there was an abundance, the nuts and fruit were sold at the *mercado* in town, along with the extra hog. They collected mushrooms in the surrounding woods, and their gardens included some vegetables and herbs, but many farmers rented garden plots in the flats of Sant Jordi near the ocean. Those *huertas*, vegetable farms, equipped with watering systems and sprinklers, accommodated the planting of potatoes, beans and leafy greens.

Caretakers of their rugged terrain, the land was their life. Like most Ibicenco *campesinos*, José, María and Antonia lived on what they grew and raised, and they grew and raised what they needed. It was a lifestyle that moved beyond primitive survival to encompass good health, self-reliance and satisfaction—a centuries-old existence that would not last, intact, beyond the next generation.

Iowa, April 2009

W HAT HOLDS MY MOTHER'S INTEREST—THE deck, the sunlight on the floor? She still hasn't turned, still doesn't realize I'm here. Intentionally rustling the plastic bag, I pull out the pair of pajamas and move a chair away from the table, allowing it to scrape the floor, hoping she hears. Does she miss natural light? There's so little here in the condo. The elongated windows of our Summit Street house kept the rooms bathed in daylight. First floor and second, even the attic. She knew which hour in which space was best for the sun. When my youngest siblings were babies, she kept the bassinet in the small music room facing south. Like her mother, who endured Buenos Aires' damp, gray winters, Ma required luminosity. Connecting the dots, I too gravitate to the bubbly old glass of sash openings, to double-paned new—east, south, west. Preferring the variations of daylight as the day progresses, the constancy of reflected north light has never been an attraction, but I'm not a painter. Appreciating southern exposure can't be unusual, yet there are people who buy a house and never know the direction it faces.

"Hi, how are you?" I whisper, approaching.

She turns, lifting her hand off the Colima pup.

Does she know me?

She glances up, trying to focus.

"Ma, your pajamas are fixed. I shortened them and put in new elastic. The waist should be more comfortable."

Reaching to touch the garment in my hands, her fingers gently trace the woven sprigs of buds and ivy.

"How do you know, where did you learn?" She looks up, amazement striking her face like a child's.

When I was young, whatever project I was involved with, my mother's praise let me know I'd accomplished something incredible, something she couldn't imagine doing herself.

"I had a good teacher."

The fall we returned from Spain, I decided to lengthen the gray skirt from my *Colegio Británico* uniform. I had grown and the skirt was short. Letting out the hem was not difficult, but in the re-doing, my stitches were a mess. Exasperated, it was relegated to the closet. A week later, I retrieved the skirt, determined to finish the job. My mother had taken out all my untidy sewing and replaced it with neat crisscross stitching, making sure to do only as much as I had. She pressed the hem and hung the skirt back in the closet. I was able to finish by copying her stitches.

I know the incident was a typical example of her unspoken lessons, but I find it troubling that neither of us felt it necessary to acknowledge and speak about what had occurred. We both knew, and both acted as if it hadn't happened.

Maybe that's the bad part of silence, its involuntary trail to denial. Regardless, I was fortunate. One of my best friends suffered horribly under her mother—a professional woman with a PhD and serious career, an accomplished cook and superb seamstress. Yet she could only relate to her daughter by criticizing. Nothing my friend ever did was good enough, not her cooking, not her sewing. My companion's self-esteem was rattled and attacked, over and over.

When I attempted to hem my pleated skirt, I was 11. Within a few years I had learned to sew and was making skirts, blouses, dresses, even purses. No big deal in my family. Pa encouraged and expected us to 'work with our hands', and we understood that manual labor was the panacea. Carpentry, painting walls or furniture, they were all instinctive and never considered beyond our abilities. With the freedom to be self-reliant came willingness and ingenuity.

My father's relationship to manual labor was central to his autonomy. Whatever it was, he could do it. He could fix and he could build. He took pride in being from Iowa and from Maine, where people worked long and hard until they got it right. The egalitarian spirit of 'do-it-yourself' was a fundamental value that Pa loved about America. It was a defining feature of his character to break rules, whether it was ingrained expectations of class, or artistic establishments. When my father lived in Córdoba, printmaking was not a discipline favored by the art community. Yet his serious work in the field of drypoint gave a new prominence to *Grabados*, prints.

On my first visit to Argentina in 1983, my Uncle Julio became my guide, leading me through the neighborhoods of my parents' youth and to gatherings with artists who had been my father's companions in art school. Everyone I met had opinions and stories to tell about Pa. From a young age he was considered a rebel who bucked the prescribed course. An example I was given was his refusal to copy the work of old masters in his classes at the Superior School of Fine Arts in Buenos Aires. He did things his way. According to Ernesto Farina, a painter and contemporary, 'Mauricio was always sniffing out situations to see what he could learn, what he could pick up, the quickest way possible. He believed the bad things that happened to him were because of his *race*.' Farina shook his head. 'Your *viejo*, your old man, was paranoid.' Ernesto Farina followed that statement by informing me that Argentina neither was, nor had ever been, an anti-Semitic country, even during the late 30's and early 40's.

I'd heard that refrain more than once during my visit. Why were they still repeating it, 40 years after my father?

Julio, younger than my parents by more than a decade, used to spend summer holidays with them in Córdoba. He described occasions when Pa would point out a kid to be avoided, because his father was a Fascist or because he hated Jews. Julio thought his reaction understandable. When Mauricio was teaching during those years, *El Pampero*, an Argentine Nazi newspaper, condemned the province of Córdoba for permitting a Jew to teach.

'Paranoid or not,' Farina went on to say, 'Mauricio, whose interests were more poetic and literary than plastic, was always positive and certain about what he wanted, when all around him were confused and losing their heads.' Farina asked me, 'Does he still get mad? Do his eyes squint in anger? Is he still so sure of himself?'

After my conversations with Pa's companions, I was struck by the fact that in Argentina, my father was considered a Jewish artist. I've wondered how he felt about that truth. Did he take it in stride? It was after all, a fact. (A fact perhaps, but it was a startling reality for me, given his resistance to 'labeling' while we were growing up, especially any attempt to tie him to Judaism.) The painter and writer, Luis Waisman, a Córdoba friend, told me he 'felt it was important to nurture and protect Lasansky, because at that time in Córdoba, there were no other serious, Jewish artists.' Emilio Sosa Lopez, another poet and novelist, referred to my father as '*nervioso y neurótico*', nervous and neurotic, and that his saving grace was that he found an incredible woman who understood him. 'He was a serious artist,' Sosa Lopez continued, '*una luz*, a light, compared to everyone else.' On my last day in Córdoba, I attended a luncheon with a couple of Pa's old friends. Victor Manuel Infante, an art collector and director of the *Museo de Arte Religioso Juan de Tejeda*, showed me a catalog of one of Pa's first Argentine shows. The cover had been desecrated with swastikas and anti-Semitic insults. Perhaps my father was paranoid, but not about that. Argentina's rampant anti-Semitism was not his imagination.

I was profoundly moved by all those encounters, and I left Argentina with a better sense of the obstacles and complications Pa experienced, because of his personality, and because of the times in the country he deeply loved. I saw his need to leave, to make a new life for himself and his family in America. He used to say he left because of Perón. That was only one reason. Certainly an important motive was his understanding that the States could offer a more expansive opportunity to grow and develop as an artist. But more than anything, I believe my father needed freedom, freedom from everything.

Back to my sewing skills. As a teenager complaining of not having enough outfits, my father told me I could have all the clothes

I wanted, as long as I made them. He would buy me all the fabric I needed, and he did, including a white, nylon parachute. It was during a summer in Maine that he placed the order from a military surplus catalog. When the men in my family weren't using the machetes in the woods, they hung above our Franklin stove. When I became exasperated by the pervasive French seams of the parachute yardage, my mother helped me finish the dress.

Sophie Sieber once said: 'When I look out and see Leonardo playing in the yard, I know the temperature is the opposite of what he's wearing'. As a youngster of five or six, he was already doing his thing. So did we all, intuitively ignoring the outside from the safety of our private domain. In our family, resourcefulness negated dependence, the unusual valued over conventional, seclusion prized above society. If Pa were alive in today's reality of the COVID-19 virus, he would probably declare he'd prepared his children for *sheltering in place*. Could be. In any case, like ducks to water, we took to the strengths that shaped our environment. We were an island onto ourselves with precious few ties to the outside world, including the realm of kin. Except for the brief encounter with my maternal family in Spain, and *La Bobeh's* visit to Iowa, we were not raised to feel connected to extended family. Like other things, they had been left behind in the old country. Mauricio felt put-upon by familial demands, complications and problems. They were too great a hindrance. The value of 'relatives' was not something he taught us and Emilia could not do it alone. The relationships some of us formed with ours aunts, uncles and cousins were achieved on our own, and not until we were adults.

Occasionally, our natural order collapsed under the weight of its isolation, and the most ordinary of American experiences could push my parents into what I considered irrational immigrant anxiety. I was never permitted to climb onto Alice Turner's horse because I might fall off. Period. Nothing to discuss.

What? As far as I knew, no one on either side of the family had ever been kicked in the head by a horse, or died from a fall—the only explanations I could think of for such unwarranted fear. If my parents had exited their privacy long enough to come and watch—as invited—they would have found Alice's dad, Dan Turner, professor and composer, happy to walk alongside their particularly gentle horse, ensuring my safety, willing and serious about teaching me to ride.

Ma lifts her hand off the pajama and smiles. She still makes me feel gifted, though now she hardly knows who I am, or who she is.

"I brought you a cake. Who has an anniversary today?"

Shaking her head, my mother inches in closer, closer, attempting to erase the distance between us. She raises her hand and gently caresses my cheek.

"Do you know me?" I ask. "Do you know who I am?"

"No," she murmurs, leaning in to rest her head on my chest. She looks up, her eyes happy. "No ... but I know you're a beautiful girl ..." she whispers, as if telling one of her secrets.

I laugh, astonished. "You think so?"

She wants to say more. I watch her gather up what she can, what remains in the rubble of memories—fragments of words, flickers of emotion. Slowly and with significant effort, she forms the question.

"Are you the one I love?"

"Oh," I gasp, "I hope so ..."

Ibiza, Anna Wachsmann, 1965

S HE WAS 65 WHEN WE met on the bus to San José. It was the April day Alan and I were on our way to *Tienda Can Chocolate* in search of the Palerms and a house to rent. By then, Leonardo had left the island, eager for more independence, more traveling. I remember thinking if only my brother had met Anna, he could report to my family.

The feeling that my parents might be worried, that they would be reassured knowing there were other Americans living on Ibiza, was my preoccupation. They never expressed concerns to me. Operating from a position of my 'needs' if the tables were turned, if my child had retreated to a distant island, I was ill-equipped to accept what my parents didn't need.

Powerless to oust her inherent bitterness, Anna was attracted to happiness, envious of tranquility. I suspect she would have brushed off my brother because of his youth and budding inclination toward melancholia. Yet surely his name might have attracted her curiosity. Besides her first husband, the German-born French painter, Leo Marchutz, there had been other important Leos in her life.

Anna liked men. They brought out her coquetry, even at 65. Young women were tolerated, older ones, dismissed as tiresome and meddling. She had retired to Ibiza after a full, adventurous life— from bookstore clerk in 1919 Berlin, to running a boarding house in the south of France during the war, to chief cook and bottle washer for a children's camp in upstate New York, and finally, to a photography career with Abrams Art Books.

That day on the bus, she insisted on speaking English. Her command of Spanish was passable—her accent, terrible. German was her native language, French her second, English her third. She had a smattering of Italian. We became instant friends.

We communicated by post to arrange our frequent rendezvous. Ibiza Town had plenty of cafés, but it wasn't easy finding tables away from the curbside sewer grates. I found the stinky air hard to take, but it never seemed to bother Anna. After bringing us up to date on the small house she was building and how it was annoyingly behind schedule, she focused on her circle of expatriates. Some were folks we'd heard about or met in passing, like the lesbian couple, Maltese Patty and British Edevane. The girls regularly paraded their two enormous, short haired hounds on the *Paseo Vara de Rey*, the beasts' huge, tight balls shockingly visible. In between stories about her friends, Anna spoke of ex-Nazi commanders living off their pensions and frequenting a certain *alfresco* bar, and she elaborated on rumors of *Guardia Civil* horrors. It was said that American hippies, arrested by the *Guardia* for possession of pot, were hung by their thumbs for 24 hours before being kicked off the island. Quiet Ibiza was within the firm grasp of Franco's regime.

Despite the decades of *El Caudillo's* repression, the island had an established reputation of laissez-faire tolerance concerning foreigners. For as long as anyone could remember, Ibiza had provided a haven for outsiders landing on her shores—from philosophers to the beat generation, from the dissolute to the rich and famous. Just as Jews had been welcomed and protected from the Inquisition to Nazi persecution, so too had the perpetrators enjoying their *alfresco* bar. Stephen Armstrong, in his book *The White Island, Two Thousand Years of Pleasure in Ibiza*, relates the story of the Gestapo arriving on the island in 1942, demanding a list of resident Jews. Ibiza refused to comply. Armstrong makes the case that it would have been social and economic disaster to lose such a large population, as 30% of permanent island families had Jewish heritage.

Anna's scintillating array of characters, many of them bored and wounded under their bells and whistles, surrounded her with the constancy of amusing goings-on. But their most important function was as springboards to her past, a landscape she felt far more compelling than the present. When irritable, she endured her people, grabbing any opportunity to pass judgment on unwise choices and foolish behavior. While highly opinionated, she avoided verbal reflection that might reveal her own vulnerability. Anna considered herself tough and independent. Only once did she mention wanting a child. Something came up about the future and our desire to have kids, and Anna told us that when she was ready, when she had finally made the decision to have a child—in New York, with her second husband, Wachsmann—she couldn't get pregnant.

Anna seldom welcomed serious friendships, and insomuch as possible, feelings of compassion or sympathy were rarely indulged. She was continually surprised and a little offended by our close ties to the Palerm family—José, María and Antonia. For her, they were peasants, and not especially interesting. For them, she could never be more than *la Señora extranjera*, the foreign lady. Always polite, always perceptive, they understood and accepted she belonged to another world.

I learned to accept our friend in the ways I could. Her narratives carried us into other realms; she was a living museum of the past and so many things we respected and loved. Her galleries were always open to us: Europe before the Second World War, art, literature, the quality of night skies in Aix-en-Provence, survival in the time of the Nazis, and always, an appreciation of beauty and simplicity in all things. On the occasions when she came to dine and stay overnight, she kept us up for hours with her flamboyant storytelling. She was so magnetic, so fast, our nascent questions or doubts barely had a chance to gel. A voracious reader and shrewd observer of character, she was quick with wit. One morning after our chicory drink breakfast, as we walked her to the bus stop and a ride back to town, she declared I was still enough of a child, chronologically, to appear younger rather than older, upon awakening. On another occasion, learning that Alan was about to read

Chekhov's short stories for the first time—which of course she had—she declared it a pity that she did not have that pleasure to look forward to.

Besides youth, our contradictions may have attracted Anna. The innocence, tagging alongside an unwavering commitment to work. And running parallel to our happy independence and off-the-beaten-track lives, the traditional beliefs about love, marriage and fidelity, which Anna probably found shockingly outdated. We provided her with amusement and the opportunity to re-live her past.

In retrospect, I'm impressed by how well we all managed and accepted our lifestyle. Like us, Anna did not have a phone or electricity, and in the primitive *finca* she was renting when we met her, there was no bathroom. During those months her house was being built, she kept a pied-à-terre with some friends in town. Secretive about some things, she was straight forward when it came to her Social Security income paying for her small building project. I didn't understand the significance of Social Security for retired expatriates of limited means. On weekends, she went out to the *finca*. She assured us she easily managed the cactus patch—the Ibicenco outhouse. We could not have, and were grateful for our *casa's* amenities. As for the kitchen, we had the two burner gas cook top and ignored the large fireplace. Alan made a screened box and hung it from the kitchen ceiling to keep mice away from the cheese and *Tulipán,* (margarine). Everything else was stored in lidded pots or tins—bread, sugar, noodles, flour. When we craved milk, we mixed up *El Nido*—Nestles' whole milk powder—cocoa and water in a sealed glass jar. Lowering it into our cistern with a rope, we left it for several hours to get cold. In the decades since Ibiza, whenever we speak about our chocolate milkshakes cooling in the cistern, people are stunned.

After our café encounters with Anna over a coffee and pastry, we were always happy to catch our *Ruta San José* bus back to *Tienda Can Chocolate* and our *casa* at the foot of that red mountain.

---··•··---

'The Photographer, Her Lover and Her Dream', 1991,
Losers and Keepers in Argentina,
a book of fiction, published, 2001

"RENT A CHILD? HOW COULD we rent a child? What are you saying, Jess?" Victor Levin sounds irritable and threatened as he looks out across the hot summer fields. They are deep in the Argentine pampas near Rosario and the endless land stretching before him does not comfort his urban soul. The bus, *La Flecha de Santa Fé*, has stopped suddenly for yet another break. He should never have left New York, Victor realizes glumly. This is the third time the bus has stalled, choking and spluttering, the third time the smiling driver slides under the vehicle, assuring them that they mustn't worry, that they will get to Moisés Ville in time for the celebrations.

Half an hour has passed. The dubious passengers wait about in the heat. Some sit, some pace, some appear to enjoy the scenery. Victor glances at the crippled *Flecha*. He knows the driver isn't telling the whole story, and his sidekick, an overweight Indian girl, reveals even less. She wears a short blue skirt and white blouse with a *Flecha* Tours hostess pin that says Marisol. Marisol's still eyes and vapid face register nothing.

"I told you," Jess said, smiling, "through an agency. We rented a little boy through an agency."

Her voice eases his tension. "Like rent-a-car?" Victor asks, turning back to Jess. She's setting up her tripod, happily engaged, as usual. Her tall frame moves with grace and confidence in her loose cotton clothes, and the bags of cameras and lenses and film never seem to hinder. On the contrary, they hang from her like friendly appendages. There's a joyful generosity about Jess. Long ago, Victor decided it must have something to do with her height and that constant perspective, and with her belief that when human failings accumulate too greatly in any one person, he or she simply becomes "magical."

85

She's looking incredibly attractive in Argentina, he has to say that for the country. Her red hair has grown long and she's wearing it pulled back into a thick, curly braid. At that moment, there's a slight breeze, and the heat and brilliant light warm and soften her angular face. Her blue eyes are intense with concentration as she attaches the camera. He feels almost inspired, though they've lost ground during the time they've been apart—she here in Argentina, he in New York. Not that things were exactly terrific for the few months before her departure. He doesn't know why. Last week before he left New York, his sister, Masha, warned him. "You're going to have to give a little, if you intend on keeping Jess. Tell her, Victor, it's time you tell her about Robin."

But he can't. He can hardly bring himself to think about his daughter, about her death. After all these years, that pain is still his constant companion.

"I suppose it was like renting a car." Jess laughs. "The agency was in Mendoza. I don't know why Mendoza. We went in and asked to rent a child." Jess checks the focus. "You know where the idea comes from?"

Victor doesn't answer.

Jess looks up from the camera. Now what, she wonders? He's miserably unhappy, and he won't talk. Struggling to maintain her equilibrium, refusing to become unbalanced yet again by their relationship, Jess sets her attention and camera on the group of passengers directly behind Victor. They're laughing and complaining bitterly about the bus. Their name tags connect them to a Jewish Lions Club from Buenos Aires.

Earlier that day, while they'd all waited to board the buses in the dark hours of the Buenos Aires dawn, Jess listened to their annoying chatter. One of the Lions, he'd introduced himself as Judah and was clearly leader of the pack, explained the situation to some of the other passengers. "The members of my party are not descendants of your beloved and renowned village, Moisés Ville, the Jerusalem of South America!" He spoke in a loud, confident voice, wagging his impressive head of wavy white hair. "Nevertheless, we've decided on this excursion because it has all the makings of a good time!" He wore white shoes, a white belt, and baby blue pants. "We're all Jews!" Judah announced commandingly into that gray Buenos Aires stillness. "And we're going to help you celebrate Moisés Ville's centennial!" His wife, a short, plump woman with dyed black hair—high and puffy—clung to his arm. Her pasty face looked bewildered as she moved silently to his energetic body language. She wore many rings and her tiny feet were perched in spindly, transparent, plastic mules. "Moisés Ville, the cradle of Argentine Judaism!" Judah shouted out. Cheers and laughter followed among his companions while the other Moisés Ville passengers watched in silence.

Too much light, Jess realizes, adjusting the aperture. Hours ago, in that chilly dawn, she was embarrassed by the Lions, especially by Judah's aggressiveness. They were in sharp contrast to the other passengers, the ones for whom this pilgrimage would be a serious confirmation of their own lives, of all that existed before them, all that will after. Once again Jess focuses on Judah's wife—the uncertain face, the ringed fingers reaching tentatively for her hair.

Victor is still speechless. He reaches for the handkerchief in his pant pocket and wipes his face. He hates being so uncommunicative, but he cannot help himself. Jess dreams about renting a child, and she expects him to know where the idea came from? What does it matter? People are jabbering, he's hot and tired, his head throbs. Thoughts of Robin haven't helped. He feels drained. Of course it's always worse when he isn't in his lab. At least when he's working, his defenses are up. But when he's not involved in his research, a passivity settles over him and he withdraws into an inactive state—a form of retreat—a condition that makes self-defense virtually impossible.

An hour ago on the bus, he listened as Jess spoke enthusiastically about the final photographs she still needed for the book on Moisés Ville. She explained about illusive light, cast shadows and silhouettes. She told him about the unusually small bricks used in construction, about the century-old painted storefronts, now faded by time and circumstances. *Farmacia Juan Levisman, Panadería*

Portnoy. He listened, wondering how she could be so committed to a village that began and ended on a remote, godforsaken field? He listened, wondering how he could be jealous of an idea, a place he's never seen, an event that happened one hundred years ago? Last winter while she researched, Moisés Ville and the Baron Maurice de Hirsch were all she thought of—when she ate, when she slept, when she brushed her teeth. Victor grew tired of hearing about the Baron's philanthropy, his commitment to the cause, to his people.

"He got them out of Czarist Russia!" she called from the kitchen one evening as she prepared vegetables for their stir-fry dinner.

Victor pretended he didn't hear, sitting in the living room of their apartment, reading the newspaper. He knew she was standing over the stove still in her work clothes, herringbone blazer, leather boots, distractedly pouring oil into the wok.

"They were from the same cities in the Pale as your grandparents, as mine, and Hirsch resettled them as farmers on the virgin soil of the pampas. Their new homeland!"

It made him crazy that she never measured the oil, that she never wore an apron. She probably did it intentionally. He never helped in the kitchen. Masha was always warning him about that too. Jess' link to the famous Moisés Ville? Simply that one of her grandmothers passed through, staying in the colony for a year before emigrating to the United States. Nothing more. It seems a ridiculously thin thread connecting Jess to this incredibly aggravating country, Victor decides. He glances at the dead bus. He thinks of the freeways and the reckless driving, how they pass on the right side, at whim. Why does she want a connection? He thinks of the miserable economy and the near daily fluctuation of restaurant prices. Why does she always say "there, but for the grace of God, go I"? He wouldn't be surprised to learn that Argentineans don't pay their taxes. Jess has no stake in this country, yet her passion leaves him feeling miserably empty, angry because he can't understand.

An hour ago, the bus traveled on. Through the landscape of Rosario, through the landscape of Jess's obsessions. She watched as field after field of ochre wheat rolled up to the bus windows, meeting her voice in a gentle union of magic realism. Then, the crash landing into her dream. The crazy child-renting dream that synchronized with that peculiar noise coming from under the bus. Jess didn't notice until she saw the dramatic trail of black smoke, until she heard the driver quickly announce another short stop.

Victor's eyes are riveted to the bus.

"Victor?"

He turns. Jess is asking him something.

"The idea of renting a child, Victor?" Jess repeats. "Know where it comes from?"

The heat is overwhelming. He feels as though an eternity has passed in the moments since she asked. He shakes his head. "Can't imagine."

"Really?"

He realizes that Jess is going to attack again, with that energy and swiftness that is hers. She's going to attack their long-standing commitment to no marriage, no children. She's approaching forty. Despite her career—the freelancing, the numerous books of photographs, and now this grant to pursue her Moisés Ville project—none of it will matter. She wants a child. Wants, with the same intensity she wields her focused camera. In the end, women always do, Victor concludes somberly, as though he's lost a battle. He has his work at Columbia, his research and teaching. She has hers. They share lives. But none of this will matter. She wants a child. His sister warned him.

"Don't you remember, Victor, really?" Jess is amused by his distractibility. She loves that about him. Yet she knows it to be a sign that he isn't coping well, and she wishes she could help. But if he refuses to talk, how can she help? How many times has she thought this? Silence is nothing new with Victor, it's the game he plays best. She had high hopes for this visit, but they haven't reconnected smoothly. They haven't connected at all.

She watches as he stands with his hands in his pockets. His eyes turn from the fields to his feet kicking at pebbles, then up to her. She wonders in which cavern he has been detained. She knows his scientific mind works best in the compressed, intense spaces his imagination creates, one grotto leading to another. There, he gropes and struggles with the unheard of, the incomprehensible. Phenomenal ideas that grow out of those airless, lightless tunnels, like stalactites. She knows he spends his days in that lab methodically cutting up leeches and shrimp. He studies those veiny bits of greenish gray flesh—she's often thought they're the only real colors for him—charting their tiny nervous systems. Somehow, as she understands it, they are the closest animal life to the human brain. For Victor, these pampas and this talk of old Russian Jews must be like making a salad.

"Remember? In Buenos Aires," Jess continues, "we were told that it's not uncommon for professional beggars to rent small children from poor people. Business is better if they sit on a street corner with a baby in their arms, or if a small, hungry child stands at their side."

"I didn't remember," Victor says quietly. "That's unbelievable."

"I know. It's pretty shocking. Anyway, I'm sure that's where the idea of our renting a child came from."

A welcome breeze sweeps around them. Jess bends to blow dust off the lens.

"Babe," he looks at her, "why would we rent a child, if we've decided not to have any? It doesn't make sense."

He calls her Babe when he's nervous. "Vic, how can you say a dream doesn't make sense!" Does he catch the humor in her voice?

Jess watches as a group of fellow passengers make their way into the wheat field, heading for the only tree in sight, and in shade. The ombú's branches and thick foliage reach in all directions, creating a natural awning. Perhaps, Jess realizes, the time has come for her to deal with Victor's refusal to discuss children. She focuses her camera. Their children. A woman, slightly hunchbacked and wearing a blue dress, more midnight than royal, with a pattern of large rust chrysanthemums, hesitates in the field for a moment's rest. When she begins to move in the direction of the tree, Jess shoots quickly, easily. She finishes the roll.

The vociferous Lions hurry to the shade and seat themselves on a log under the far reaches of the branches. Other passengers find places to sit around the ombú's base, where the magnificent trunk divides into a bulky network of exaggerated, root-like protrusions. Jess wonders if nature intended those roots as companions for the branches, in the desolation of the pampas.

"I wonder what's wrong, and how long it will take him to figure it out?" Victor asks irritable.

Jess looks up.

Victor nods toward the driver who is still lying under the bus. Only his feet are visible. Two male passengers are squatting beside him. Marisol stands hugging her sides, staring down at the driver's feet. She looks bored, as though she's waiting in line at a government office.

Jess shrugs and returns to her camera. "You'll love Moisés Ville, Victor." She knows he's angry about the bus, and that he misses New York. She wishes he could enjoy the moment, wherever he is. "Do you want to hear the rest of my dream?" She asks, hoping to distract him.

"Sure," Victor says. "We went to an agency to rent a child. I can't wait to hear what happened next."

"Well, the agency said they didn't have a child at the moment, but that they could put together a package for us."

"A package?" Victor asks. "Like a travel agent's package? Hotel, excursions, two tickets to a show, all for the low price of—" Victor's laugh is dry, tired.

"I guess so." She knows the dream threatens him, but she perseveres. "They said they had the '*alma*', the soul, of a beautiful, unusual child, yet unborn, and they could put it into a vacant body."

"My God, Jess! Do you realize most people don't dream?" Victor takes out his handkerchief again and wipes the palms of his hands.

Jess ignores Victor's comment. "The only hitch was we had to have the child back to them by the end of the month, because the unborn baby would be ready for birth and would need its soul."

"But of course! We can't have a baby without a soul! Jess, I don't believe this!" He turns away, angrily. "Between your dream and the damn bus breaking down, all we need is a watch. It would melt by itself in this heat. Who needs Dali!"

"Look, Victor!" Jess points to some burros approaching the passengers under the ombú.

"Don't worry about the bus. This kind of thing happens all the time in Argentina." She unwraps another roll of film and loads the camera. She takes a series of shots directed toward the animals. "Can you imagine what those first colonists felt like when they laid eyes on the land? Moisés Ville is very much like this. Of course they had nothing, and there was nothing waiting for them, only flat, uncultivated fields."

"Like fools," Victor says. Jess has been trying to get him to relate to those colonists since he'd arrived in Argentina. He can't. He can hardly acknowledge any connection, except perhaps his having been born a Jew. Even that was an accidental fact of birth, irrelevant to his life.

"Victor, your grandparents went through Ellis Island, but they could have as easily ended up in Argentina, heading to one of these first colonies," Jess says, looking across the landscape.

"Not mine. Never. I do not come from a line of people who would have placed themselves in such ridiculous circumstances. Your grandmother had the right idea, leaving this place for New York." He watches her adjust the focus. "How much farther is it to the village? And remind me again why we're doing this?" Victor laughs anxiously. Now there are six men squatting beside the driver's feet.

"I told you," Jess says, breathing deeply and wiping her hands on her skirt before peering into the camera. Victor is being negative, and the heat is beginning to distress her. "I need to interview a few more people and there are still photos to take. I thought you might enjoy seeing the village, Victor. Besides," she looks up, trying not to sound hurt, "a centennial happens once every hundred years." Why is she apologizing? Jess wonders. "And it's nice to be away from the City, the pollution."

They both remain silent for a few moments.

"So, Babe, did we rent the child?" Victor asks quietly, sensing Jess's attempt to ease the strain.

"Yes, it was all arranged. We traveled for a month with him, from Jujuy down to the Patagonia. It was a wonderful time, and he was indeed as beautiful and unusual as one could hope for." Jess's voice becomes quiet and soft. "You became very attached to him, Victor."

"Dream on, my darling!"

"At the end of the month," Jess continues, calmly, "we returned him to the agency, as planned. Two days later, we were contacted and informed of the birth of the expected child, the one who was supposed to receive that soul. Remember?"

"How could I forget?"

"We were told we could visit him at the hospital."

"For God's sake, surely we didn't go, Jess!" Victor is disturbed.

"You wouldn't." Jess quickly swings her camera around and focuses on Victor, snapping, snapping. "The light's perfect, and the horizon behind you is beautiful," she explains. Snapping, snapping. What she doesn't explain is the sadness in his face.

"You know something? I don't know why I'm here," Victor suddenly complains, dejected. "Seriously, Jess, what am I doing in Argentina? I don't even speak the language. I should be in my lab in New York."

"For me. You came to visit, remember? I'm here for a few months, and you …"

"I'm sorry, Jess. I didn't mean it to sound that way. Of course. I came to see you." He attempts a smile. "I just can't relate to all this." He waves his hand out over the landscape. "It's all so disorganized, so unpredictable. Look at that damn bus! I don't do well without a sense of order."

"I know. What can I say?" Jess speaks quietly. "Everything you say about Argentina is true. I guess to be a survivor here, you have to roll with the punches, relax, expect nothing, and you'll probably find what you're looking for. It's such a beautiful country, Victor, and, I don't know, I guess I've become kind of attached."

"Attached? No!" The sarcasm has returned to Victor's voice. "Listen, Jess," he steps toward her, puts his hands on her shoulders. "I want you to hurry with this project and return to New York, where you belong. O.K.?" His eyes are nervous, his mouth anxious.

In the last few seconds, he's made a stab at two smiles. The first time all afternoon, Jess realizes. She knows all this Moisés Ville talk means nothing to him. For her, it's only the beginning. She still hasn't told him she's planning to extend her stay in Argentina, and that it will be another three months before she returns to New York.

A heavy silence settles between them. Victor turns to watch the driver pull himself out from under the bus. He stands talking to the other men about a short length of pipe he is examining. After a brief discussion, he walks off down the highway, the pipe dangling from his greasy hands.

"We're in for a bit of a wait," Victor says, nodding toward the figure moving away from the bus.

"Where's he going?" Jess asks, watching.

"Who knows. To get help, I hope. It could be hours."

Jess notices that most of the passengers remain very calm about the stalled bus and the disappearing driver. Perhaps it's the heat, or the late afternoon hour, but a trance-like mood settles over the lethargic group. A few of them stretch out along the grassy bank beside the bus, closing their eyes or pulling down their caps. Others remain at the tree. Some young people cluster around a transistor radio. Only the Lions Club group complains, unsuccessfully trying to stir up excitement among the other passengers.

At that moment, Marisol, the young hostess, approaches. She explains something in a monotone voice, waving one hand at bus, while inspecting the chewed nails of her other hand. Victor doesn't understand a word. She isn't big on eye contact, he decides, staring at the offensive pencil lines she has drawn in place of her plucked out brows. He can hardly concentrate on what she is saying. Jess engages her in conversation, pointing to her camera equipment. Marisol unlocks the storage compartment on the side the bus. Without smiling she points down the highway, mumbling something, then moves on to another group of passengers.

"She says there's a café where we can wait, about fifteen minutes down the highway. Some of the passengers are walking to it."

"What's wrong with the bus?" Victor asks.

Jess shrugs. "No one seems to know. She says the driver will pick up any passengers at the café, once it's fixed. Do you feel like a walk, Victor?" Jess puts away her camera and folds up her tripod. She packs them into the storage area and closes the door.

Jess and Victor start down the hot highway, the trail of passengers moving slowly ahead of them. "So, I suppose you went to the hospital to see the baby?" Victor turns to her.

"Of course." Jess smiles. "I arrived to find the mother and grandmother holding the infant in the light of a window. They had placed him on the ledge, proud of the dark Indian baby. I was taken aback by how wonderful he was, and I spoke admiringly of his beauty. When the infant heard my voice, he turned to me in recognition, crying and holding out his arms as though I was his mother."

"Jess, that's impossible! Newborns don't hold out their arms," Victor says seriously.

"I know, Victor, but he did. He wept, and he would not stop. It was not a baby's cry, rather that of an older child. I realized this was indeed our child—wiser through his travels—but trapped in the body of an infant, and I could do nothing for him. I felt horrible."

They walk in silence the rest of the way to the café. Victor knows the dream is some kind of turning point for Jess, but he isn't sure how, or about what. He feels depressed, alienated. He's sorry not to be more of a conversationalist. He's sorry he hasn't been able to explain about his daughter, Robin, and why, after her death, children can never again be part of his life.

As they approach the café, a small, sad place with a beaded curtain, Jess is stopped by a lone young girl about ten years old. She's dressed in old, faded clothes, but there is an attempted tidiness in her tucked-in blouse and the ribbons in her braids. A nagging cough accompanies her thin voice. She's selling something from a cigar box. The other passengers ignore the child, brushing rudely past her as they enter the modest establishment. Victor watches as Jess peers into the small box, asking the child about her wares. He notices that the girl has fine, white dust in the crevices of her skin—her toes, her fingers, even around her mouth. It's just dirt, Victor assures himself, the fine, white clay that she would have kicked up as she walked barefoot along a path. But there is something eerie about the whiteness, as though the child can't rid herself of a nagging premonition of her own death.

Jess speaks to the girl in gentle, quiet tones, smiling as she examines the articles in her box. A sudden ache of emotion strikes at Victor's stomach as he watches Jess's tall frame virtually melt with kindness toward the child. Somehow, this wonderful woman has the ability to make her own incredible presence seem less, so as not to overwhelm with her radiant health and good fortune at having been born in the Northern, rather than the Southern Hemisphere of neighboring continents. He sees Jess reach into her purse, withdraw some money, and hand it to the child. The girl smiles meekly as she wraps the items in a scrap of wrinkled paper. Oddly, it's at that moment that Victor knows something is terribly wrong.

They are sitting at a small round table inside the café. Jess realizes an hour has passed before they talk about it. It comes up rather casually, not the usual tense, compressed way that she knows fights and separations begin. They order more bottled water, and then she starts looking through her cigar box purchases. They are small, knitted things—a hot pad, a covering for a clay flowerpot, a long multicolored band, perhaps a belt. She examines them silently, upset. She throws her head back, her eyes closing for a few seconds. Finally she opens them and stares at the rotating ceiling fan.

"It's not going to work anymore, is it, Victor?" Jess says, still concentrating on the fan.

At first he pretends not to know what she means.

"Hmm?"

"Us. You and me. It's over, isn't it?"

"Jess?"

"You know want I mean. I want a child. I can't help myself. I think about it all the time, everything I do, everywhere I go." Jess's eyes close again.

"You're upset, Babe. It was probably that dusty girl." He tries to sound reassuring.

"No, it wasn't the dusty girl," Jess says, looking down at the knitted things spread over her lap. "I want my own baby, and you don't want one."

"Jess," Victor's voice is low. "Do we have to talk about this now?"

"Yes, now. Right now."

"Come on Jess, relax, have something to drink. Let's get you something cold." Victor turns quickly in his chair, signaling to get the waiter's attention. With his arm still raised, he looks back at her. "We're on our way to Moisés Ville, right, Babe?" He can hear the mild desperation in his silly, upbeat voice, but he continues anyway. "You have work to do, and I'll help you! Would you like me to pose? I could lean against one of the old synagogues …"

"Please, don't."

He says nothing.

"Victor, if you won't have a baby with me, I'm going to leave you."

Victor remains silent for a few minutes and then nods toward the bus hostess entering the café door.

"I think we may have other things to worry about at the moment."

Marisol stands near the door, looking slightly uncomfortable. She speaks quietly, without emotion. It's obvious she's talking about the bus, but Victor can't follow what she's saying.

"It's hopeless, they can't repair it," Jess says, her eyes on Marisol. "They've already contacted their Rosario office to send out another bus. Unfortunately it will be several hours."

Groans are heard around the café. Marisol's face shows no involvement as she stares at her fingernails and then at the far wall, as though waiting for her next cue. Her voice continues in its low drone. Silence falls over the café.

"For those passengers who do not wish to continue their journey, a bus will be passing through from Santa Fé in half an hour, destined for the capital." Jess continues translating, without looking at Victor. "Anyone who wishes can return immediately. Naturally tickets can be presented at the central office of *La Flecha de Santa Fé* for refunds."

"Refunds, my ass," Victor complains. "The way this country functions, I'd be surprised if the bus company admits this vehicle ever existed! As a matter of fact, I'll bet they'd even try to erase this route from the map!"

Jess has turned away from Marisol.

Victor knows she isn't listening to him. He watches as she pours more water into her glass, plays with her napkin, and finally looks at him.

"We're headed in different directions, aren't we, Victor?"

Victor shrugs.

"We are. I know it and you know it."

"What am I supposed to say?" Victor asks.

"Admit this isn't in my head."

Victor turns away from her. He watches the other passengers talking and complaining among themselves. They're probably trying to decide what to do—return to Buenos Aires, or take their chances with the new bus to Moisés Ville. These are the things that happen to him when he goes on vacation. He should simply never leave his lab.

"And all because of a baby," he finally says.

"Not all."

"I suppose you're going to talk about 'sharing', the way my sister does?"

"No, I'm not going to talk about anything, anymore."

Victor is overcome with frustration and anger. "So! Does this mean I'm to go back to Buenos Aires, pack my bag, and return to

New York? Am I correct, this relationship is over?! And what about you? Are you planning to come back to the apartment?"

"Of course. I'll be back in a couple of months and I can move stuff out. If it's in the way before I get back, I can arrange to have someone ..."

"No!" Victor turns from her, staring bitterly at the waiter who is wiping glasses. "I can't tell you how cheated I feel. Three years together, and where did they lead?"

"I know," Jess whispers. "I hoped they'd lead to a family."

"This is useless," Victor manages to say.

"Yes, it's been hopeless for a while, hasn't it?" Jess's voice is soft, gentle.

There are a few moments of silence, and finally Victor speaks quietly. "What will you do?" He sounds bewildered, lost.

Jess feels Victor is really asking her what he is to do. But she answers anyway.

"After I complete this project," Jess says, finishing off her drink, "I guess I'll probably look into renting a child." She tries to smile.

He doesn't respond.

"What about you?" Jess puts down her glass. "Victor?" she waits. "Don't you ever dream, Victor?" Her words are close, pressed with frustration and sadness. "Dream?"

Victor can't bring himself to tell her that for many years now, his dreams and his reality are one and the same.

The Saturnia arrives—
Spain, September, 1953-54

O<small>N THE OCEAN LINER</small>, S<small>ATURNIA</small>, we had a stateroom of our own for the voyage from New York to Barcelona. A year later, we were split up for the return trip—girls in one, boys in another. Several women shared our cabin including a large, morose girl from southern Italy. She was miserable and inclined to silence, so our conversation was limited. Evenings and mornings, she busied herself sniffing and powdering her blouses. My six-year-old sister, Jimena, was astonished. I pretended not to notice, and my mother glanced away, giving the Italian girl her privacy. My father and brothers bunked with several men. At night as we prepared for bed, Pa would knock on our door, checking to make sure all was in order. I'd heard my parents speaking about the *sinvergüenzas!*—those shameless men taking turns at the keyhole of the women's bathroom across the hall, their curiosity aroused by the group of nuns entering to bathe.

The sleeping compartments were stuffy with a lingering odor of seasick voyagers, come and gone. Regardless of the weather, we were happy to be on deck taking in the salty air and sea spray. During our initial voyage in early September, I was still obsessed with Roy Rogers and Dale Evans. Leo and I played cowboys at every chance—the ship's steel cable reels became our horses. We rode through red rock landscapes of cactus and sunsets while our parents walked the Saturnia's promenade and relaxed on canvas sling recliners, sipping their *maté*. My mother was never without her draw-string bag of supplies—*Yerba (*always *Cruz de Malta),* the gourd, *bombilla* (silver straw) and even a tiny kettle. It's unclear how she managed to get boiling water, but I can picture Pa going around to the kitchen, the little kettle dangling from his fingers.

The ocean liner's family entertainment included shuffleboard—unacceptable, my parents never played games with rules—and bobbing for apples, acceptable. Waiting at the barrel about to go under, an older girl at the stand beside me leaned over and whispered that a man had become a woman. I had no idea what she was talking about, but was pleased to capture an apple. Afterwards, munching on my fruit, I reported what I'd heard to my parents. No more dunking.

A day or so later, my father got me a lined notebook from the ship's tobacco and magazine stand and suggested I start keeping a journal. He probably figured that at the age of 10—almost a young lady—apple bobbing and Dale Evans should be left in the dust. So began my recording of where we went and what we saw. One Year Spent in Spain, the opus that convinced my mother I would become a writer—because Sergio Bagú said so, and because she needed to believe.

Many events remain vividly clear. The physical settings, who was present and exactly where I was in relation to the space and people around me. I've checked in with William about specific facts and dates. Some he confirms. Others are blurred by our conflicting recollections. I can say with confidence the wine turned vinegary from the Saturnia's rolling and pitching across the ocean, and much of the food tasted stale from storage, especially the oranges and bread. As for that comment about a man turning into a woman, it was a fact, a certainty I heard, not my imagination. Unaware of Christine Jorgensen or 'gender reassignment', probably not called that in 1953, I had no idea what the words meant, but they stayed with me.

Ten days after leaving the New York harbor, with brief stops in Halifax, Gibraltar and Portugal—my first diary entry is a description of Lisbon—the Saturnia finally docked in Barcelona.

Settling into the Hotel Bristol with our steamer trunk and suitcases, my siblings and I were grateful for our land legs and eager to be out and about in the mid-September weather. The museum visits began immediately. Catalan art on Montjuïc, the Gothic cathedral constructed over ruins of previous civilizations, the Mares Museum, the family home of Christopher Columbus, and more.

Stimulated and exhausted, outdoor café stops accompanied our visual and historical highs. At the end of tiring days, I spent evenings recording our adventures and pasting museum admissions stubs onto the cover of my diary. After two weeks of intensive sightseeing, when my dad was certain we were comfortably established in the Hotel Bristol, he boarded the train for France. In Paris, he would secure a car for the year.

With Pa gone, the routine eased and we spent quiet mornings in our hotel room. William read, Leo drew, and I had my diary. Jimena helped with the small pieces of nylon laundry Ma could manage in the hotel sink. On the balcony, our underwear fluttered from elastic cords and carousel clothes hangers brought from Iowa. Some days we had breakfast in the room—bread, cheese, and milk that Ma boiled on a hot plate. Skimming off the dirty foam, she made us swallow the warm milk with our disgusting cod liver oil, bribing us with talk of afternoon outings.

Under my mother's guidance, Barcelona was pleasant and leisurely. There were unhurried visits to the zoo, walks along the *Ramblas*, and the cool of early evenings as we strolled back to the hotel under ornate, iron streetlamps. On the day Ma took us to the Barcelona Maritime Museum—she wanted us to see models of La Pinta, La Niña and the Santa María—Pa was standing before an easel in a Paris print shop, somewhere around *Rue Jacob*.

Twelve years later, during one of those excursions from Ibiza to Paris, Alan and I wandered the same area trying to locate the same print dealer. I remember pausing at a quirky, neglected shop, intrigued that it belonged to Raymond Duncan—I rarely pass up historical or cultural trivia. Once a viable establishment that probably sold his famous, hand-made sandals, it was no longer enterable.

The deep window well looked abandoned. Leaning against the back wall were huge, faded photographs of Raymond's sister, Isadora, dancing around Greek columns, and at the front, a haphazard arrangement with bowls of grain and a small hand loom. Raymond, an old man of 92, was dying in the south of France. These had been his obsessions—classical Greece, hand-woven garments and a vegetarian diet—while the Great War raged and ended, and Jazz Age flappers rushed in.

The dormant tribute to fascinating lives in other times did not feel out of place in the lively Saint-Germain district. Longstanding art and antiquities dealers set the eclectic character of the neighborhood. The shops were old and rickety, but comfortably established with knowledgeable proprietors and a range of authentic collectables.

It's easy to imagine the encounter in that Paris print shop. My fixated father, the easel with Picasso's Minotauromachy, the waning afternoon light entering the multipaned windows.

In 1935 while Picasso worked on the print, Mauricio was 21. I don't know when he first saw it, or if he knew it only in reproduction. In 1943 when his Guggenheim Fellowship took him to New York, he regularly studied the print collection at the Metropolitan Museum. If the original existed in the Met's collection, or at the Museum of Modern Art, or the New York City Public Library, the likelihood is he would have seen it. Regardless, there he was in that Parisian shop, the Minotauromachy calling to him with all its splendor.

But it was not to be. His family waited in a Barcelona hotel and the travelers cheques in his nylon money belt had another purpose. Leaving the shop, he refocused on what brought him to Paris.

Before departing from the States, there had been letters back and forth with the Pacific Motor Sales office in Chicago concerning car rentals through the European Pamosa plan. Finding his way to Pacific Motor Sales, 65 Avenue d'Iéna, arrangements were completed for an English Ford Consul. The American Express travelers cheques met their destiny.

The next day, managing the complexities of Parisian traffic—for years he would talk of circling the *Arc de Triomphe* multiple times not knowing which avenue to take—and without the benefit of GPS, my father left Paris and the print behind, driving back to Spain through the Pyrenees.

Returning to us at the Hotel Bristol, he spoke so reverently about Paris, it was as though he'd fallen in love. We listened as he suggested that when one of his bad moods hit, we ought to remind him of the city's magnificence and elegance. Then he spoke about the Picasso. I was well acquainted with the print; a reproduction used to hang on his studio door when I was a kid. The image was so familiar, so close to Pa's own prints from 1946 to 48, especially the series, For an Eye an Eye and El Pájaro, I assumed the Minotauromachy was his. Picasso's technical and aesthetic genius would continue its trajectory of influence well into the future.

Just as my parents breathed a sigh of relief (the Ford meant no more public transportation, no more dirty train stations), a cloud of illness emerged on the horizon. In the month before leaving Iowa for Spain—strep throat. The four of us came down with serious cases. Despite multiple doses of sulfa, William's was not eradicated. During our museum breaks in Barcelona, it was hard to ignore his fatigue. Seeing his head buried in folded arms at café tables, Ma worried, Pa became nervous and irritable. It was the same when any malaise did the rounds. His stormy anger passed over our heads, charging into fate. Throughout our stay, his apprehension over illness would cause Spanish tin forks to buckle in his fists, clattering dishes, spilled wine, and crumbled bread. At the end of those tense meals, his place at the table was such a mess, a pack of restless rodents might have passed through.

Cataluña, 1953

O N GOOD DAYS, WHEN EVERYONE was feeling up to outings, we carried on with the museums and sites. Our explorations included the prehistoric caves at Tirig, down the coast from Barcelona near Castellón de la Plana. Though called caves, most of the rock paintings of the Spanish Levantine are in shelters, *abrigos*. I'm not sure how my father connected with Juan Bautista Porcar Ripollés, painter and archeologist. Known for his dedication to cave art, Porcar (as we referred to him) was obsessed with a protective responsibility for the Paleolithic caverns. We were fortunate to have him lead our private excursion. Though I considered him an old man, he was in fact 65 and remarkably agile. After an hour's drive from Castellón, we had a three-mile walk through fields and vineyards surrounded by majestic highlands. It was a landscape of solitude and peace, but for my younger siblings, attacks of diarrhea followed the delicious clusters of grapes. As we approached the location, the mountainous terrain became treacherous. The narrow ledge leading to the cave was alarming and the kids were pale and lethargic with upset stomachs and exhaustion. Ma held on to Leonardo and Pa lifted Jimena to his shoulders—a sight that would become familiar that year.

Our nimble guide arrived before us. We found him crouching at the wall, gently splashing water on the rock. Leaning back with satisfaction, he watched as delicate drawings emerged—reddish deer and hunters, wet, glistening with awakened energy. I remember standing at that recessed wall, listening to the adults speak, excited by the day's adventure.

I was too immature to comprehend the significance of that stone canvas, but not too young to grasp the passion in Porcar's voice. He became emotional, almost frustrated as he spoke about the site, telling us we were witnesses to a dwindling flame. It was only a question of time before the vandalism would resume, the chipping of rock, the hunt for souvenirs. Eventually he would die, and yes, there would be other guides, but not like him. He'd been protecting the site since its discovery in 1917. The ones who followed would not know how to guard, not like him, and the caves would be ruined. The flame would be out.

Recently, I heard a 'Porcar' anecdote from my brothers. Once again, both William and Leo had their separate versions—variations on a story I was unaware of. Approximately 12 years after we visited the cave, Pa received a telegram from Porcar, requesting urgent assistance for another site in need of an enclosure to protect it from ongoing vandalism. The plea for help came during the summer when Pa was in Maine, visiting with his friend, Austin Lamont, activist and art patron. Austin volunteered financial support for the project. In the end, the local Castellón community declined foreign assistance and raised the necessary funds. I can visualize those inhabitants of the Spanish Levante, men and women alike, trekking up a mountain with *boinas, (berets) botas* (wine bags) and walking sticks, proudly declaring the site theirs to look after.

Mission accomplished. How wise Porcar was reaching out to my father—a man who'd led his wife and four children through fields, vineyards and up cliffs, just so they might stand at a birthplace of art.

In 1994, the Valltorta Museum was created to promote the protection of rock art in the region of Valencia. Porcar died 20 years before. The 'open-air' museum of three caves includes the *Cova dels Cavalls*, cave of the horses, the one we were taken to. Reading about it, I was relieved to learn of the addition of railings along the mountain ledge.

That night in the Castellón hotel, boiled, white rice was piled high on our plates. It would become our Spanish diarrhea cure.

At the end of September, after more than a month of sight-seeing, my parents decided it was time to move on, time for the children to attend school. We collected our belongings, packed into the Ford and left for Madrid. I assume our steamer trunk was shipped ahead, possibly to the American Express office. My mother was thrilled—we were going to Castilla, the land of her ancestors.

Madrid, 1953

WE ARRIVED IN MADRID OCTOBER 9th. *Hotel Zaragoza*, 22 Calle del Principe, became home while my parents searched for a more permanent accommodation. The owner of the hotel, a tall, angry woman in her late fifties, ran the place with a tight fist and a dry smile. She looked like an eagle. In all the decades since, I haven't been able to pull up her name, but in my mind, she's become *Señora* Aguilar. We rarely saw her husband, *Señor* Aguilar, but there was a small grandson in residence and a pretty niece in her twenties who managed the switchboard. Someone answered to the name of *Jesús*, either the grandson or the *mozo*, a scrawny errand boy with a toothy grin. As a 10-year-old Iowa girl, I was blown away by the name, *Jesús*.

Despite *Señora* Aguilar, the *Zaragoza* was comfortable and pleasant. We settled into an arrangement of adjoining rooms. Our parents' was the largest, with floor length windows and shallow cast iron balconies overlooking Plaza Santa Ana. The sunshine was inviting, especially as cool, fall days approached. Every morning one of the chambermaids went down to the street vendor and brought up warm churros strung on green water reeds. *Café con leche* and hot chocolate thickened with cornstarch, bananas, and occasionally hard-boiled eggs. In the late afternoons, Ma would take us down to the plaza while we waited for the dinner hour. In my mind, the Santa Ana was a small, intimate square, contrary to current photos of its vast size and impressive, surrounding architecture. Nursemaids and small children, the confectionary kiosk with those white, marble size anise candies, the smell of roasting chestnuts and the one-man-band and his mangy monkey. In the evenings, joining the other guests in the lounge, we played chess or tried to behave and focus on the adult conversations around us.

One night, the gypsies arrived—their clothes, instruments and bundles shocking the monotone lobby into brilliant Technicolor. I immediately befriended the troupe and they were soon draping me in their costumes and jewelry, teaching me their songs. Hurrying off to their rooms at any opportunity, I became so involved listening to their chatter and music, my parents had to haul me back, telling me to mind my business and stick to our rooms. I was miserable. The main guitar player, the attractive man with dark eyes and slicked, black hair, had asked me to run away with them.

I turned my attention to the switchboard. With the help of *Señora* Aguilar's niece, it was not difficult to master. On occasions when the young lady was absent from her post, I managed to make phone connections for guests staying at the *Zaragoza*. My innocent but persistent 'lack of boundaries' became a recurring annoyance for my parents—an ongoing theme of my youth, and beyond.

No more switchboard. My parents suggested I concentrate on my diary, unaware of the awaiting catastrophe. Aguilar was horrified when she saw me at the small desk in the lounge, writing with my left hand. Without hesitation, she commanded me to use the correct hand. Pointing to the painting of the Virgin hanging above the desk, she announced that if I continued my sinister ways, the holy Virgin would eat my eyes out. I found it hard to believe of the pretty woman with the halo and blue robe. Again, my exasperated parents had to intercede, insisting on the privacy of our rooms.

Shortly after the gypsies left, an apartment became available at 77 Francisco Silvela, a sedate building in an upscale neighborhood. We were happy to leave the *Zaragoza*; we'd been there over a month. It may have taken that long because of my father's bottom line to the realtor, which I heard him repeat for my mother's benefit.

"I didn't bring my children to Spain on a Guggenheim to make them live in a lousy apartment. They will see enough misery. Nothing old or dirty."

Clean it was, well-appointed, somber, and according to Pa, lacking in taste. Traditional rose chintz slipcovers and curtains dominated the small parlor dining room. The heavy furniture was oppressive. The bedrooms, remarkably dreary. I was drawn to the small laundry off the kitchen with its tiled walls, counters and a stone washboard built into the stone sink. During our stay, while assisting Faustina, I learned about washing clothes. Spain had few machines, and certainly no washers, dryers or dishwashers. 'Faustina', like the Roman empress, William pointed out. But unlike the empress, who surely didn't wash her own gowns, our Faustina laundered, cleaned and helped with the marketing and cooking. She was with us several days a week and we came to depend on her practical, positive manner.

The only subject that rocked her steady good cheer was the war with its *tragedias y atrocidades*. In 1953, the Spanish Civil War had been over for more than a decade but the country's plight continued with its wounded economy and the war's legacy of heartbreak. Franco was all-powerful; repression and gloom were rooted in the nation's temperament. Hardship and hunger still accompanied families fractured by political alignments—the Loyalists, the Fascists—sons against fathers, brothers against brothers. All we knew about Faustina was that her *novio*, boyfriend, had been killed in the war and that she lived with her sister's family. In the evenings, she insisted on staying until she'd served us dinner and cleaned up. Every night before she left our apartment, Ma asked me to wrap up a couple potatoes, eggs and an onion, so our tired Faustina could make herself an omelet when she got home. I loved making those little newspaper parcels. It wasn't until we began our departure preparations that Faustina confessed. Her little nephews would miss their eggs.

The Prussian blue, velvet drapes adorning the entrance foyer were a hiding place for my sister's nimble little body, her tiny feet tucking neatly under the gold fringe. My fascination was the laundry, those blue drapes were Jimena's. Disappearing into their folds, she'd twirl the gold rope ties and watch the tassels spin, listening to the chatter of our voices and the sound of rain splashing on the terrace. An intense smell of dry-cleaning chemicals emanated from that yardage, and despite the foyer doors that opened directly onto the terrace, it was impossible to ventilate the small space.

Aside from that annoying odor and concerns that my younger siblings might cause damage—Jimena was constantly jumping on the upholstered settee—Ma seemed happy with our new place. I think she may have liked it for exactly the reasons Pa didn't. Slip covers on stuffed furniture, drapes, the china cabinet and side tables of carved, dark wood. They may have reminded her of our arrival in Iowa City and the months we lived at the University of Iowa's presidential mansion. Because of the post-war housing shortage, Dr. and Mrs. Virgil Hancher had graciously welcomed us to their residence. Or possibly, the apartment's furnishings took her back to her parental home and what she was accustomed to. The kind of furnishings Mauricio was never interested in.

He would have been satisfied with the simplest wooden table and bed. When it was necessary to cover glass, bamboo blinds were his fallback, his concession to conformity. No fabric on windows, no fabric on furniture, leather only. One full length mirror, because my mother insisted, but only one. Mirrors encouraged narcissism. No candles because they reeked of religion and death. My father had lots of *no's* during my childhood.

In Madrid, I thought him very handsome—tall and lean, his hair jet black. He moved with energy and communicated rapidly, his voice enthusiastic, his eyes eager. When he was in good spirits, joking and laughing, his trademark mustache brightening his youthful face, we kids were happy. We wanted to please him. He was the center of our universe. When a dark mood pulled at him, we all fell.

He loved us, but his work was his center. Knowing he'd have a one-man show in Spain, he brought portfolios of prints from Iowa. They were stored in the unheated end bedroom of the apartment, along with stacks of paper and copper plates, burins, inks and tubes of oil paint. He never used the space, but supplies waited on the table. If I was sent there on an errand, I lingered, feeling the crayon pastels, the pads of thick drawing paper, the chill. I sniffed at the bottle of turpentine and unscrewed a tube of crimson paint to test the color on a fingernail.

Shortly after we moved into our apartment, William was admitted to a medical clinic for the treatment of rheumatic fever. It escapes me how long he was there, but when he finally returned home, his recovery involved daily penicillin injections my father learned to administer. His improvement was slow and he was understandably cautious, avoiding fatigue and learning to conserve his energy. Habits that would stay with him. As soon as he felt well enough to travel, we began taking day trips to sites near Madrid, including the royal palace at Aranjuez and the Casa del Campo Park. The Campo Park was a favorite outing for picnicking and wading in the Manzanares River. The longer journeys to Toledo, Segovia, Avila and Cardiel de los Montes, our maternal grandmother's village, home of the Medinas, took more preparation and overnight stays.

When our Argentine family joined us in Madrid, excursions were carefully planned so everyone had a chance to travel, and our little Ford was a veritable wonder of transportation. I was sorry not to be on the trip to Cardiel del los Montes, but I made up for it when Alan and I visited the village. Parking our rented car in the center square, I inquired of some elderly men sitting on a bench if they knew of any Medinas in the village. '*Pues caramba, yo soy Medina!*' Word spread like the wind and within a short time, I was surrounded by Medinas and hearing stories of the young Pilar, and the *genio,* Luis Barragán, who won her heart and wooed her away to the Argentine.

Tales of Cardiel, El Burgo de Osma and Berlanga de Duero in Soria—land of the Barragáns—flourished. The combining of stories and facts in my own fiction, as I re-invented what I'd heard and knew, became my custom. Not unusual for a writer. It didn't take long for the line between reality and fiction to blur, on paper and in my head. Also, I suspect, not unusual for a writer.

Excerpts

'The History' and 'Reyna's Journal'

from *ONE APRIL AFTERNOON*

in the time of Silberman and Gould

unpublished novel, 2010

"Reynamisia Toledano Ribera, you are the keeper," Don Jerónimo Toledano announced in his deep, melodic voice.

Standing in a rectangle of sunlight on the wooden floor—one long window had its shutter open and the pane pulled up—seven-year-old Reyna glanced timidly at her beloved great uncle, the mayor of *La Fuerza*.

Despite his commanding presence, a colossal figure with a majestic head of untamed, curly white hair and a drifting, right eye, Jerónimo was a shy, unassuming man. Uncomfortable situations often left him tongue-tied, his pulse throbbing under his jaw, his weak eye darting with nervousness. He never wanted to be mayor, a title thrust upon him because of his physical stature and the historic significance of the Toledano name. Nevertheless, he persevered in his civic obligations. Only with family did he forget his reticence, only with birds and children did he choose to sing flamenco and recite poetry—sometimes his own.

So when Reyna heard her great maternal uncle's 'Reynamisia', ringing with the certainty of a silver waterfall or a burst of stars in the black night, she could hardly contain her excitement, for she'd always been Reyna, simply Reyna. He took her name to places she'd never known. If voices had color and texture, Don Jerónimo's would be caramel satin, like his beloved cognac.

The year was 1925, and the place, the mayoral office in the Town Hall of La Fuerza Toledano, a small town in La Mancha, Spain. Don Jerónimo Toledano stood quite still beside his antique desk, left hand behind his back, right hand extended with the huge,

113

iron key, particles of dust drifting about him in the light. He well understood the need for patience. Waiting, he glanced out the open window. A perfect sky, a beautiful afternoon—perhaps later, he could walk along the river. Don Jerónimo smiled. He felt a tender attachment to this endearing little girl with her pale face and black ringlets, the tiny white pinafore.

Was she to take the key? Reyna blushed, eyes averted to the old runner of maroon velvet draped on the desktop. Her fingers traced the embroidered inscription and tiny, gold lions. 'For God and …' The worn letters were hard to make out. 'For God …' a gasp caught in her throat '… and …' her heart began to thump.

Could it be? Day after day, week after week, she'd stood in that very position, her hand moving slowly across those letters. Narrowing her eyes, she looked again, again touching the embroidery. When had these letters become words? WORDS! Eagerness rushed her. WORDS! In disbelief, she glanced quickly around the room. Nothing had changed. Her friend, Maribel, was still scratching her elbow, the other children lingered expectantly, Don Jerónimo waited.

How long had she waited for this moment? How long had she watched adults squinting in the sun as they stopped to read bullfight posters, or swaying with the movement of subway cars, their faces buried in newspapers, or her brother, Juan, studying his schoolbooks? Through days and years she'd waited, through the landscapes of her baby life. Her Grandma in the kitchen, her Ma resting on the patio, and Juan working solemnly at his easel while she skipped rope with her chanting cousins. When the shipments arrived in her father's grocery, the aroma of coffee beans and dried cod drifted about the pottery jars and burlap sacks, all stamped with letters and numbers. Now, when he wrapped her in an apron and lifted her onto the counter, kissing her tenderly, smiling and sticking a pencil behind her ear—he was always so eager when the shipments came—now she could help him with the inspection. Through days and years she'd waited for this moment, waited to read those letters and numbers.

Reyna wanted to conquer her baby shyness and turn happy cartwheels around Don Jerónimo Toledano. She wanted to climb onto the windowsills and proclaim to the world, 'I Read!' But no, she would not. The sight of Juan sulking in the corridor, the realization that his reading assistance would soon become unnecessary, was too much. Before long, Reyna would no longer ask for help and she knew what this would do to him—the silence and far away gaze, the furrowed brow, how he would make this his new trouble, drawing it close like a great cape. Reyna fought back tears as she stared at the old velvet with its brave tassels, once golden, now rusty and still. The silver inkpots closed in conclusion. The large ledger opened to a page covered in numbers and letters too small and exhausted to carry their weight. There was a great deal to cry about, but everything was different now. Wiping her eyes, she bravely pulled herself together. Was she to lift her hand, small and white, the velvet so warm, lift her hand and reach for that key? Would she be able to hold such a heavy piece of iron? Yes, Reyna decided, looking up.

The other children stood a few respectful steps behind Reynamisia Toledano Ribera. They knew Juan and his sister were somehow descended of royal lions and they'd heard the mayor bestow her with the title of 'keeper'. They waited quietly in the somber room while Juan remained in the vestibule, refusing to attend this honor bestowed on his little sister. Curiosity nudged him in the direction of the doorway. Watching, listening, he fought back tears as he thought of Velázquez' Surrender of Breda, the large iron key handed from one soldier to another, compassion softening the victor's face.

Glancing up and away to hide his emotion, young Juan Toledano Ribera focused on the wooden shield of *La Fuerza* hanging on the wall above Don Jerónimo's desk. Divided into quarters, each had a different image: the mountain, the turreted castle, the olive grove, the river. White doves and olive branches worked the gold-leaf border. Beside this symbol of *La Fuerza*, the coat of arms of the esteemed Toledanos, another sign of respected, recorded history—two red lions, crowned and rampant, paws raised over a dead knight in armor, sword and shield at his side. The parchment was cracked and water-stained. The roof, Juan realized, had probably leaked for decades. He desperately wanted to believe that none of this was important—not the escutcheon or those red lions, not the key or their great uncle's statement that his younger sister, Reyna, was the keeper.

[EXCERPT FROM REYNA'S JOURNALS]

All told, we were six. Don Jerónimo would not have liked more; six was enough. The same six children climbed the mountain. It was a ritual. We climbed and climbed, grabbing onto scrubby bushes and branches on our way up. There was always a breeze at the top, some days, a wind. Our hair whipped in our faces as we looked down at the orderly olive groves hugging the mountainside and *La Fuerza* nestled comfortably in the bend of the river. The other children waited patiently as I lifted the key with both hands and carefully pushed it into the great, steel lock of the castle's door. It took all my strength to turn it, and finally, all six of us had to push on the huge doors. That was when my brother, Juan, forgot his jealousy and became the leader of our small group, taking charge of the heave-ho command. He was strong and handsome with his dark hair and brooding face. How I admired and adored him! We shoved and pushed and the doors creaked and groaned, finally giving way. We loved that magical moment when the doors finally yielded, opening to the sky! The castle no longer had a roof.

When my family arrived in *La Fuerza*, Don Jerónimo himself took us up the first time. Wearing his billowing pants, he was the sail of our ship as he led the way up the mountain. He maneuvered the incline with his walking stick and the picnic lunch my great aunts had packed. I was a fussy eater so I loved picnics. Outdoors no one noticed what I wasn't eating, especially that day. We all went, Juan and I, our parents. Once inside the broken walls, Don Jerónimo found us places to sit before he proceeded to point out the architectural remains with his walking stick. My mother was feeling very well that day and her eyes flashed with excitement. She remembered everything about the castle. It had been her playground. Her outfit was the Panama hat and a loose, flowing outfit in light pinks and green, her favorite colors that year.

Though my father was always respectfully attentive when *Don* Jerónimo spoke, I noticed a rare seriousness in his face as he looked out over the landscape surrounding the castle. Was he weighing the proposal to remain in *La Fuerza*? I'd heard my parents discussing *Don* Jerónimo's offer to have father take over the management of Vinos Toledano. Or was he yielding to the pull of Buenos Aires, worrying about his next business venture, and whether he would be able to raise the necessary funds? Whatever his preoccupying thoughts, he banished them and turned back to his family, pleased to see his wife, so radiant in the presence of her old uncle. It was a good day for her, though the rheumatic attacks had become more frequent and for longer periods, and lately, she seemed to spend most of her time in pain. I'd heard my father say that soon we would have to travel north, to Soria.

It was a beautiful day at the top of the mountain, not too hot, not too windy. We listened as Don Jerónimo spoke about the original rounded tower, still standing. The 'keep', he explained, was very old, possibly constructed by the early Iberians. Conceived as the original brain and heart of the castle, it was the first structure to go up in defense of its designated territory, and the last to fall to invaders—and invaders there were plenty.

'Romans!' Don Jerónimo shouted out as he pointed his stick to some crumbling foundations of the north wall. 'A sure sign of that unparalleled civilization, perhaps even Hadrian himself, for *La Fuerza* of the *Mancha* was in the line of his path.' Once Roman, now home to wild herbs and baby's breath.

'Moors!' He swung around to the fragment of the eastern wall. Twirling his stick above his head, he brought it down, gracefully pointing to the only remaining arches in the castle, intact double horseshoes, Moorish. His face, damp from the exertion, beamed with excitement, his white hair a frenzied halo. I can still see his happiness. Don Jerónimo, a man in white, standing in the mint and stones in his espadrilles and those crazy pants he'd made from his mother's sheets.

'Then in 1085,' Don Jerónimo continued, 'Rodrigo Toledano came into this castle's story. Rodrigo was a young nobleman and his family had a magnificent crest.' At that moment, Don Jerónimo stopped talking and turned to my mother who was sitting on a low, moss-covered wall with my father. She looked so healthy with a flush in her cheeks. It had rained the day before and I found the colors intense and distinct from one another, the moss and gray stone, the turquoise sky, my mother's dark eyes. Don Jerónimo bowed deeply and dramatically to Isabella, as though she was a queen. When he straightened up, he continued the story about Rodrigo and his family's crest, the two crowned red lions facing each other. 'Rodrigo fought bravely alongside El Cid as one of his captains and he helped drive the infidels out of Toledo. As a reward for his bravery and loyalty, the King of Spain, Alfonso VI, gave Rodrigo Toledano the castle of *La Fuerza* of the *Mancha*. That first Toledano became a feudal lord and this castle remained in our family for several centuries.' Again Don Jerónimo smiled, bowing to Isabella. 'During Rodrigo's watch, improvements were made and the castle became a home, not just a fortress.' The walking stick pointed to the remains of a tiled, interior wall. 'He put in staircases and latrines; he had a family, children and grandchildren. He worked the land and planted the olive groves. In time, the king demanded that the nobility abandon their castles and move closer to the court. Rodrigo refused, remaining at his castle.' Don Jerónimo explained that Rodrigo kept a diary, but written records ended after his death. Don Rodrigo died in battle.

Others came and went—more changes and additions, more battles, more invasions. Times changed, and wars and weapons. The French came, cannons and cannon balls. 'They were terrible, the French,' Don Jerónimo said, 'such devastation, and all for sport. In Egypt, French soldiers shot the face off the sphinx! They used her for target practice. Can you believe that? God knows what all they did here in Spain! They're such a destructive people, the French!'

What became of the squat turrets and partial arches was an exquisite state of crumbling abandonment. Poachers and vandals came to loot doors and furniture for their own farms, stones and gates for their roads and fences. Highwaymen and ruffians passed through, and finally it became home to the destitute, who had no other place to go. After the poor, nature came to dwell; trees and bushes, small animals and mint, complete wild gardens took up residence within the castle. Its final abandonment had to have come when the roof finally fell in and the great wooden doors opened to the sky. Then we, the children, came.

Ibiza, May 1965

UPON THE COMPLETION OF THE studio's north window, we settled into a comfortable rhythm of work and daily activities. Without the conveniences of modern living, housekeeping was a simple routine rather than a challenge. We prepared uncomplicated meals relying on legumes, eggs, canned tuna, almonds and fresh vegetables. María, who was becoming more relaxed with us, insisted we try her goat's milk cheese. Ibiza's arid climate contributed to an overpowering flavor I found unbearable, though it didn't bother Alan. Lack of rain was a regular problem on Ibiza. My letters repeatedly mention stretches of near drought conditions. In August of '65, I wrote that it hadn't rained since the winter before and farmers were worried about their crops and cisterns.

Next door, *Tienda Can Chocolate* stocked ordinary staples including wine and olive oil, dried beans, noodles and chicory, the ground root that passed for coffee in the country *tiendas*. Every other day, huge round loaves of unsalted country bread were delivered to the small shops along *la Carretera de San José*. We always asked for half a loaf, but it caused María Chocolate no end of anxiety. Scuffing about the shop's dim interior in old *alpargatas*, her dirty skirt swept the floor as she fretted about who would buy the other half. Flies rode her forehead and an annoyed sucking sound revealed three remaining teeth.

You can imagine my shock when we learned from José that María Chocolate was married to a much younger man. Dark and good-looking—if your taste runs to cowboys from Murcia—Ramón was employed in Ibiza's hotel industry. Occasionally we saw him coming or going from the *tienda*, early in the morning or late at night. Always dressed in tight jeans and a denim jacket, he wore a cowboy hat and rode a large motorcycle. When they were married, María Chocolate, was 45 and Ramón 20. The wedding took place in their ancient parish church of Sant Jordi, with its sun-drenched white walls, tiny windows and crenellated roof. I tried to imagine the highway journey in Juan's horse and cart, the white veil blowing in the breeze, Ramón riding beside on his cycle.

In letters home to Iowa, I quoted Alan's comment that María Chocolate could have escaped from one of Goya's *Caprichos*.

Juan, never had a problem with our request for half a loaf of bread, and we were grateful when he was the one appearing through the dusky curtain as the doorbell jingled behind us. Always polite and pleasant, Juan was pleased to answer our questions about the island's history and he was particularly knowledgeable about the wild plants and herbs we encountered on our walks.

We washed dishes in a plastic tub under the bougainvillea at the end of the veranda, and twice a week, I laundered our nylons. José and María quickly recommended their widowed neighbor and her daughter, Rita. The widow and Rita hand washed our sheets, towels and Alan's painting pants.

The family was so impoverished, there were years they could not afford a piglet to fatten for butchering. We never learned the widow's name, she was simply *la lavandera*, and Rita, *la hija de la lavandera*, the wash lady and the wash lady's daughter. *La abuelita*, the toothless grandma, lived with them. A tiny black cocoon, she spent her days on the doorstep cackling happily to herself as she spun sheep's wool with a stick.

Later, when we were on more familiar terms, José told us about *la lavandera*. The family had lived there since he could remember, and though called a widow, she had never married. She'd given birth to three daughters 10 years apart, and each by different men. I found her story fascinating. She seemed so shy and modest, wearing the long skirts and black head scarf under a straw hat. Whenever we delivered our laundry, Rita was friendly and upbeat, but their hardscrabble existence was painfully apparent.

Like many country women of Ibiza, *la lavandera* spent her free moments producing the island's traditional, pulled thread creations. Tablecloths and other large items required an embroidery hoop, but the small handkerchiefs could be worked while tending goats in the fields. The squares of pastel cotton were wrapped in aprons to keep clean. It was not hard work, Antonia laughingly assured me, deferring to her brother to explain how the piecework, sold to tourist shops in town, brought in the desired extra pesetas.

Besides her impoverished circumstances, *la lavandera* had a gastric ailment. Whether it was due to an ulcer or what we now call stress—a history of three children and no husband, not to mention continual hardship and an old mother to support—nausea sent *la lavandera* to vomit in the cactus patch several times a day. Her handiwork was tainted with a bilious odor. Rita, an industrious, devoted daughter, had trouble making sales to the Ibiza shopkeepers. I felt sorry for them and bought a heap of the carefully done, malodorous squares. Wrapping them in *frígola*, I hoped to freshen them, but the aromatic herb did not help. Years later, realizing they could never be gifted and that my memories of Ibiza would keep without them, I finally threw them out.

I tried conjuring up scenarios for *la lavandera* as a young woman and the three men who paid her those visits, 10 years apart. We met the oldest daughter who occasionally came to visit her family. Short and heavyset with black hair, she did not resemble Rita. I wondered about the third daughter. And what about *la abuelita*? Did she continue spinning through it all? María Chocolate must have been apoplectic that such indiscretions were taking place on the mountain behind her. Conceivably her brother, Juan, and her husband, Ramón, were able to calm her. Having lived with his sister all his life, Juan must have been accustomed to histrionics. I was comforted knowing the Palerms took the situation in stride, acknowledging that sometimes, such things happen.

I discreetly hung our nylon underwear on a line strung between the orange trees on the other side of the house, confident they were out of view, away from the inquisitive eyes of *Tienda*

Can Chocolate. But María Chocolate was all-knowing. Whenever I went in to make purchases, she let me know what we'd been doing during the day, and the day before. It seems she was not equipped with night vision. She knew when I washed clothes on the veranda, when we hurried down the highway to catch the bus, when we went up the mountain—though why we had to go up there so often she couldn't imagine. Flustered, I considered telling her it was none of her business. Instead, like the man who stood at the train station ticket booth staring at the buxom attendant and asking for two 'pickets to Tittsburgh', I asked for half a pound of noodles and two tins of tuna.

Summer arrived on the island. We learned to close up the house and stay in when the sun was at its strongest. Early evening was for climbing the mountain to buy eggs and visit with our new friends. We picked up Ibicenco vocabulary and the Palerms' Spanish improved, though María and Antonia would never speak the language with ease. In my weekly correspondence home to my family, I detailed our daily lives, our interactions with the Palerms, our house and the surrounding landscape. I even began referring to the mountain as 'ours'. We were wildly happy and I always signed off with the hope that my parents would come to visit.

Madrid, autumn, 1953

ESTABLISHED IN OUR MADRID APARTMENT, Leo and I were enrolled in school, *El Colegio Británico*. At six, Jimena was considered too young, and for William, the American High School was a possibility. It never happened. Possibly, lingering fatigue from the rheumatic fever kept him from attending. He ended up 'home schooling' himself with the Iowa textbooks that accompanied us to Spain. William was always an independent learner, a self-starter.

I was excited about my classes and friends, and I loved my British teacher, Mr. Phillips, who looked like David Niven. All the courses were conducted in English except for math and religion, both taught in Spanish. After the first week I was excused from math—a lost cause, even in English—and my parents were adamant about my not attending religious instruction. While those classes were in session, I was permitted to go up to the school's attic where I kept busy with schoolwork or rummaged through stored theatrical props. The high windows provided a fine view down to the gravel playground with its empty planters and stone garden benches—the thin dusting of snow turning everything light gray like the Madrid sky.

The priest taught religion and the headmistress taught math. Mr. Phillips, free of teaching responsibilities, began joining me in the attic. He read to me, performed his repertoire of magician's tricks, and told me stories about his WWII service a decade before. When war memories rushed in, Mr. Phillips grew pensive, but he always came back, refreshed, ready for the next task. His most lasting contribution to my education was having me read to him from my diary. I was happy to comply. I doubt he was interested in my family's Spanish adventures. More likely my 10-year-old diligence intrigued him, especially because I couldn't read very well.

I never questioned the act of writing. Recording my adventures was instinctive and unrelated to my reading difficulties. My parents were not alarmed, to the best of my knowledge. If concerns had penetrated the foundations of those formidable towers of defense, they probably ended up transformed into positive reasons for not worrying or coercing. Waiting for maturation to correct the reading problem, my artist father maintained his hands-off respect for independence and the creative personality—more or less the idea, in more or less his language. It was a child-rearing principle he fiercely adhered to, especially when his children faced learning challenges. And any teacher who dared question his parenting could go to hell. My mother, always gentle and protective of us, was rarely confrontational.

Despite my reading deficiency, I managed well enough for *El Colegio Británico's* schoolwork, and the memorizing and reciting of English poetry was a joy I excelled at. It wasn't until I returned to Iowa that my sixth grade teacher determined I was behind grade level. Fortunately, he took on the challenge to help me catch up. By seventh grade, I was reading *The Good Earth* and *Moby Dick*.

It's occurred to me that the perceptive Mr. Phillips may have been onto a strategy of reading lessons to undertake while the rest of the school was busy with math and religion. Lamentably, I left school before the opportunity arose, but not before other students began joining us in the attic. They too had secured parental permission to skip religion class. We soon had a club, until the headmistress and the priest put an end to the rebellion. I have lovely memories of those attic adventures with a kind and affable teacher.

School in the morning, home for the mid-day meal, and afterwards, homework. Leo never appeared to do any. Instead, he drew. Brick by brick castles covering huge sheets of paper. After lunch, still in his school uniform—shirt and shorts in disarray, little tie askew—he struggled to tape more paper onto his drawings. His school bag of *deberes*, lessons, dropped under the table. I, on the other hand, assiduously completed assignments before taking up chess with William, making doll clothes, or helping Faustina with the laundry. Mid-week expeditions to a new museum were adventures we all looked forward to.

In the same way I perceived Pa's pleasure with my ease navigating the year's happenings, I sensed that Ma never worried about me. She was often preoccupied with illness in the family. As the winter progressed and more difficulties presented—from her father's heart attacks and eventual passing to problems between my father and Uncle Luis—my mother's tranquility seemed increasingly fugitive, her attitude, more frustrated than happy.

One rainy afternoon Pa rushed into the apartment carrying a parcel wrapped in newspaper. On the way home from the museum, he'd hit the flea market. His habit of stopping by *El Rastro* nourished his curiosity and calmed his mood. We were never surprised by the odd shaped bundles, large and small, the 'finds'. Dropping to a chair in the foyer, his hair wet from the drizzle, he began removing the wrapping and told me to get Ma.

"What do you think?!" He asked excitedly, rubbing his inky-newsprint-fingers over the antique, ceramic plate.

Under the *schmutz* of dirt and grease, a crown floated over two ochre lions, rampant and facing each other, paws gripping a shield depicting a blue swan over waves. As an adult, I realized the background was a primitive rendition of fleur-de-lis, but that learned information was irrelevant to my initial response. On that rainy day, I saw a sprinkling of blue wildflowers behind those lions. We listened to Pa's description of a coat of arms, how it was the proud symbol of an old family, like the Barragáns, or Fernández or Medinas, all my mother's people.

"Magnificent, isn't it!" He held it up at arm's length, his hair still dripping, his face glistening with excitement.

Ma was not impressed. She saw the spots of tar, the chipped rim. Spur marks remained from the three-legged stilt, an indication of ordinary ware stacked for a routine firing. The production of multiples conceivably meant the ceramic was a town's symbol, rather than a family's—but none of that mattered. I liked how Pa gathered up the Barragáns, Fernández and Medinas, lifting them high above our heads as he spoke, as he admired his piece. I don't believe my mother was any more aware of stilts or the production of multiples than I was, but that too was immaterial. Her understanding was absolute: the ceramic was an unassuming piece of history.

"It needs cleaning," she said firmly, her mouth a thin, taut line. We all knew how she detested the *Rastro*. Never considering those flea market excursions fun, she became frantic if we touched anything, convinced our curious hands would absorb and disseminate ancient germs.

Disappointed, my father asked me to take his treasure back to the storage room and he promised my mother he would attack it with turpentine.

Ma was correct that it was humble and unrefined. Regardless, I was riveted—the chunky feel, the red clay peeking out from under a creamy engobe and transparent glaze. The simple crown had a stenciled quality, but the primitive lions were irregular, like the blue outlining and shield. No self-importance. A conception and completion free of traditional heraldic markings: gold swirls and curls, borders and edging, royal reds and blues.

Was that my introduction to clay? At 10, I understood nothing of heraldry, nothing of stencils, engobes and lead glazes. But I knew that ceramic spoke to me, like our Christ from Burgos.

Now we're both older, both needy as we mend the cracks of time. My bottle of glue, the plate's memory of things I've forgotten or never knew. A link embedded in that earthenware stretches back to a key year of my youth, and forward to the future and my passion for clay—harbinger of the pottery studio I would set up in Ontario.

Teeswater, Ontario 1970

O N A BRISK AUTUMN DAY in 1970, an ancient dough mixer was transported from a small town's defunct bakery to our Teeswater barn. After the wiring upgrade, an oiling and cleaning, we were ready for production: clay, instead of bread. Rachel, seven months old and glued to my right hip, accompanied as I prepared for a mixing. Recipes had to be double checked, the water hose set up from the house basement to the barn, dry materials inspected—the 100 pound bags of kaolin, Buckingham feldspar, flint, and so on. Finally, lidded plastic barrels were positioned to receive and store the clay body. Our daughter, Rachel Simcha, was born March 21st, 10 months after we left Regina.

In all my talk of infertility and the harshness of Saskatchewan winters, I should have mentioned I fell in love with clay, a certainty that made those freezing prairies tolerable. Shortly after we arrived in Regina, Alan encouraged me to sign up for a couple night classes. I might enjoy pottery, he said; after all, it ran in my family. Both William and Tomas were accomplished potters as students. I'd never touched clay, yet the chances for a familial link, a positive involvement, were looking good. I was a writer, dedicated to my fiction, so it was not about abandonment, but the potter's wheel offered a new adventure. Instant gratification and the union of visual curiosity and manual dexterity, something my typewriter could not do.

Carried into a new world, the art department's pottery studios became my pleasure: tubs of slops and vats of glaze, porcelain's white elasticity, the smell of bisque firings as pots released their last, earthly moisture. Learning and experimentation were in progress. Marilyn Levine, a chemist turned ceramist, quietly lectured on the composition of clay bodies and glaze recipes. Jack Sures, head of the department, taught kiln styles and firing techniques. They were both available to help with the wheel, but after initial demonstrations, we were expected to proceed on our own until we got it. I was surrounded by the excitement of perseverance and discovery.

During those semesters, I watched as Marilyn abandoned her heavy, finger-ribbed stoneware—dinner sets in speckled, muted colors—and began testing the use of fiberglass in clay. Developing a new recipe that lent itself to the rolling pin, she was soon shaping realistic, well-worn boots, bags and vests. The fiberglass burned out in the firing resulting in lightweight trompe-l'oeil clay garments. Swiftly endorsed in cutting-edge California, the innovative technique led to unprecedented success for Marilyn. The shy scientist/ potter found herself at the forefront of the American funk art movement. Eventually, Marilyn left Saskatchewan, enticed away by the golden state.

That first winter in Regina, Alan and I got into the habit of grabbing a couch nap after dinner, then walking to the art school for a few hours of work. Having gained access to the pottery studios through extension classes, thus not a 'real' art student pursuing a degree, I could ignore departmental politics. The studios weren't as busy after hours, so evenings were opportune for endless throwing and centering—a new language I found both exhilarating and exhausting.

If no one was waiting for a wheel and my wedge of clay could be left for a few moments, I'd grab a quick coffee in the cafeteria. I used to run into Tom Mansard, a pianist who taught in the music department. We knew each other only from those breaks at the vending machines. On one occasion, he suggested introducing me to a handsome artist he'd met over lunch hour. Tom was certain we would make beautiful babies. Just as time helped dispel his embarrassment that he didn't know, time would also prove him correct about the babies. I've always considered that incident a stroke of magic.

My affinity to clay followed me from Saskatchewan across the country to Ontario, where the basement of our Teeswater farmhouse became the pottery. In cold weather, the stone walls took on the furnace's warmth; on hot days, their thickness kept the space cool. The wheel and wedging table were centered under fluorescent fixtures and the area beneath the staircase was ideal for a plastic-walled damp box. Alan built large shelves for tools and glaze supplies. Calipers hung from beams along with our musical neighbor's discarded guitar strings—indispensable for cutting clay. Barrels of dry ingredients lined the basement walls and rows of thrown pots awaited their first firing. I would soon have to build a kiln.

Alan painted in his barn studio, I wrote and researched kiln designs, and Rachel went off to a babysitter three half days a week. We regularly kept her up late into the evening. In the mornings, she'd go back to sleep after her bottle and I could get in a couple hours. Our parenting might be considered questionable, but Rachel was easy-going and content, and I, determined.

Our bright farmhouse with its happy southern windows and sanded pine floors was a labor of love. We'd completed the serious renovations the previous summer with our friends from Saskatchewan, but there was always more to do—bookshelves and closets to build, windowsills and baseboards to strip and varnish. Between home maintenance and our own work, weekdays were full. Saturday farm auctions became our entertainment.

Lured by the range of local craftsmanship, Alan was soon returning home with 'finds' of primitive pine furniture and earthenware crockery, vintage pieces considered undesirable because of their minimalism and lack of pretension. Lead-glazed black and redware pitchers, jugs and crocks began arriving in different sizes—graceful, ballasted shapes, echoing their makers and makers' wives, all thrown by the same, steady hands.

In the late 1800's, Bruce County, our corner of Southern Ontario, had nine potteries owned and operated by farmer potters. Unable to work their fields during winter months, those industrious men utilized their lands' clay pits and hardwood bush to throw pots and fire kilns. They generally employed at least one assistant to help with the digging and processing of clay, throwing, glazing and kiln firings that could take several days. The pots sold locally to general stores and neighbors—vessels for butter, molasses, fruit preserves, anything requiring storing.

With the help of a local antique 'picker' from Mildmay, a small town not far from our farm, we soon learned that the pieces Alan had begun gathering were attributed to Ignatius Bitschy, a German immigrant to the area. In 1870 he established a pottery on the outskirts of the village. A productive enterprise, Ignatius and his assistant threw 100 to 150 crocks a day, the larger ones selling for 10 cents each. It's easy to imagine a neighbor approaching with horse and wagon and perhaps eggs in exchange, as his wife requested a new jug for the spring production of maple syrup.

Bitschy was typical of Bruce County farmer potters. They raised families, farmed, labored at their trade and passed. When we moved to the area, Ignatius Bitschy was rooted in the folklore of Mildmay. There is still an Ignatz Street at the south end of town, just off Highway 9. After his passing, Bitschy's earthenware legacy silently slipped into history. In fact, at least one expert would later claim that no known pieces could be traced to the Bitschy workshop. He was mistaken, according to the residents of Mildmay. Though not signed, his pots were easily identified—striking for their rich color, signature neck ribs, shoulder and waist rings.

According to a 1989 publication of the Mildmay-Carrick Historical Society, the town's residents could identify the location of his home, pottery, and clay pit, as well as the exact spot on the road to Clifford—the source of high lead clay Bitschy used for glazes. Some recalled that 'a great fire of hemlock was kindled' in the brick kiln. Bitschy, like any potter, well knew that a firing mishap could result in a disaster of near biblical proportions—the molten mess and charred remains of long, hard work.

For years Bitschy's crocks and jugs dozed in farmhouse cellars, accompanied by baskets of empty sealers and abandoned storm windows. But old folks pass, properties are sold and yard auctions follow.

As the contents of a house and basement are emptied onto dewy grass, the accessories of decades tell a home's story. Large or small, comfortable or poor, the desire for aesthetic nourishment is palpable: lace curtains and tinted family portraits, treasured furniture, picture calendars still hanging on flowered, wallpapered walls. English decorative china dictated the taste of kitchen and tableware, a tradition that lingers on.

In the early 1970's, the Bruce County auction attendee with eyes on a Spode platter or Royal Doulton figurine, may not have noticed the quiet artist moving slowly from table to table of household effects. Pausing to wipe his glasses, he smiles at the stoic farmwife as she bravely lays out yellowing linen and her grandmother's dishes—things of no interest to her children. Stopping to chat amiably with an acquaintance or two, the artist's manner is polite and low-keyed—a contrast to the professional 'pickers' who arrive early to peck and poke around. Ostentatiously incognito, with straw hats and dark, Amish-type jackets, they resemble a flock of crows on a spring field. Silently rummaging through crated possessions, they manage to reduce honorable lives and dignified homes to stacks of 'collectibles', at best, piles of 'junk', at worst.

EXCERPTS
'Auction', 1985
from a story collection in progress,
This I Can Tell You

AUGUSTA WATCHES THE MOVERS THROUGH the screen door. They seem decidedly incompetent with their dangling arms and stupid, leering grins. She refuses to worry. Sidney Armstrong, of ARMSTRONG ESTATE SALES has been hired to handle her auction, and if he's sent out those boys to move her furniture, so be it. There won't be a moment's peace between the movers shouting from one room to another, and her niece, Rose, fussing over the possibility of rain or some other nonsense. Augusta doesn't care if the linens get wet, besides, it doesn't feel like rain to her. She looks out across the back garden—a lovely day, and by four, possibly five, it'll all be over. Those bits and pieces, the accessories of life, will no longer be hers. What happens tomorrow? The Senior Home is an outrage. She'll be better off at Rose's.

Senility has chosen a bad time to finish its job on Admiral, Augusta muses, picking up a piece of toast from the saucer. The poor dog refused to leave her bed this morning. Never mind, he's still a comfort, and it's good to know old age is just as hard on him. The difference is that no one cares if a dog talks to himself. Augusta bites into her toast. It's a low, groaning monolog—been going on for years. They've only recently found out about her. That's why the haste to get her into the home where she'll be with all the other old people who talk to themselves. Do they really believe the 'talking' problem will end? Augusta wonders, raising the cup to her mouth. Rose has been up in the bedroom for ages. What is she doing? Still prodding Admiral off the bed?

Pushing open the door, Augusta carefully steps onto the wooden deck then down to the grass. She had the lad mow yesterday. It looks fresh and tidy. Carrying the cup in her right hand

and the cane on her arm, she circles the house to the front lawn. Augusta catches her reflection in the oval dressing mirror placed against one of the maples in the curve of the drive. At 80, she's still striking, tall and straight, with a shock of white hair showing under her hat. From behind, do her shoulders betray her age? She remembers when the sloping shoulders happened to her own mother. Augusta adjusts her hat. Striking, yes, but she was never especially pretty or naturally graceful. Her sister-in-law, Mary, now that was exquisiteness, even if she was mad enough for the entire village and the whole of time. 'Mad Mary', they called her. 'Mad Mary', walking around her garden by the light of a full moon, not a stitch on. Lyle had to put up that fence to keep curious eyes out and his Mary in during her somnambular strolls. The doctors were never certain what to make of it. And Quinn? 'A disturbance of the mind,' that's what her Quinn always said. A good pharmacist, like his father before him, Quinn understood about these things, about how sometimes medications aren't worth a fig. How did Rose come out so practical? Augusta suddenly wonders. Perhaps it was all those nights of her youth when she'd have to take a bathrobe down to her mother and lead her back to bed. Rose didn't get her mother's beauty, for sure, but she didn't get the madness either.

None of that matters now, looks or madness. It doesn't matter that Augusta came from a good family, was surrounded by fine things, and knew how to behave. It doesn't matter that she and Quinn were once called *Mr. & Mrs. Bridgeport*. Time and neglect take their toll. On autumn days when she bundles up in her once handsome, tweed outfits and takes her reluctant Admiral for a walk, it doesn't bother her that cuffs are threadbare, or that she no longer cares enough to summon her seamstress, Darlow, for repairs.

"Mrs. Ferguson, where do you want your rocker?"

One of Sid Armstrong's boys carries the wooden rocker toward her across the lawn, his black hair still damp and combed.

"You can sit in it to watch the proceedings."

Augusta signals him back. The fool, does he think she's going to sit out on the lawn with no protection from the sun? "Under the big maple beside the veranda," she snaps impatiently.

He smiles and nods in agreement, turning back.

She's surrounded by fools. The cup shakes in Augusta's hand. What's so terrible about an old woman living alone? If Edward were alive, he would never have allowed this to happen to his mother. The house would never have been put on the market. Whoever heard of an electrician buying a big house? Don't those people live above their shops? They'll probably pull up all the flowers beds. That's what people do now when they're too young to be bothered or too old to see and bend. It's better that way. There's nothing worse than an untended perennial bed. The house would have gone to Edward, and naturally, he would have insisted she live with him and his family.

Augusta fixes the cushion on her rocker and sits down. Placing her cup carefully on the grass, she pulls a handkerchief out of her pocket. She's lived alone this long, what would a little longer matter? She removes her hat and leans back against the rocker, dabbing at her face with the linen. That young doctor carries on about her heart. What does he know? And Polly, who's supposed to clean, would rather prattle, day in and day out. 'One of these nights, Mrs. Augusta will fall down the stairs.' The kind of 'licking and promising' that Polly does, even Admiral could do, with a dust rag tied to his snout.

What ever happened to their Scottie Nell? Now there was a girl who knew how to do things properly, even if she was overly fond of her drink. Augusta never paid attention to her spiritual side— her talk of heaven and so on and so forth. Nell returned to Scotland for her father's funeral and never came back. Augusta got Quinn to call, all the way to Scotland, but the girl said she was home to stay. And Rose, coming around with those articles she prints at the library, news clips concerning old women who've been bludgeoned to death in their sleep. It's always faraway places—Halifax, Vancouver, the Sault—never within a hundred miles of Bridgeport.

[EXCERPT]

Quinn would have appreciated the perfection of her Centennial rose, Augusta muses. He enjoyed reading the paper beside the birdbath, but she could never get him to give up the horrid canvas swing chair that belonged to his mother's lawn set, a relic from the twenties. It looked so out of place with the nice wicker she ordered through a catalog. Quinn passed away too young. She's been lonely without him and Edward. He would have gone on to greatness, her Edward. Now she has only her daughter, Melinda, and her niece, Rose. The peonies should be dug up and separated. That young lad who does the lawn and gardens isn't as conscientious as old Elijah. Poor Elijah. Didn't his son put him away in that nursing home down near London? It's a shame to let peonies go for so long. Augusta recalls how thick the daffodils were in spring, but the blooms are getting smaller. They too must be separated. Quinn was too young. She'd been nagging him to call the heart specialist in London, but he kept putting it off.

Perennial beds take work and the young folks who want the place probably don't even care about flowers. Rose mentioned the fellow would be commuting to Maitland Bay Power on the lake. For two generations the house has belonged to Bridgeport's pharmacist. Everything is different now, why there isn't even a pharmacy in town. That young doctor from Ferrisburg who's been looking after her—the Catholic boy, turns out he's not so bad after all—it seems he's leaving. Now that she's getting used to him, he's up and leaving.

What is she going to do with herself in that miserable place? Play cards in the dining room and attend the bingo nights in the Town Hall? Why does she have to associate with those people now if she never has before? A month ago, Rose took her over for a visit and Augusta found the whole thing appalling, especially all those old people who'd be living so close to her. Imagine not being allowed to bring over her own bed. Rose has offered to take her in, but how could she live with such a fusser? As for Melinda … Augusta glances over the front lawn. All the furniture is out now. Didn't Rose say Melinda was coming?

The cool morning air has vanished and Augusta is already feeling the heat. The beds and dressers are set up along the edge of the yard. It's a shock seeing them outside. They seem so exposed and vulnerable. The house always felt comfortably full, but now that everything is out, the pieces of furniture seem displaced, no longer part of her life.

Her husband and son are gone. She's left with a troubled daughter and a spinster niece. Rose is a good girl and maybe she couldn't help spraining her ankle. Augusta shouldn't have gotten angry. There are no more Fergusons. Here she is, sitting in her nursing rocker, surrounded by the ghosts of memories. All those pieces of furniture with empty drawers and shelves, apparently, they've become 'antiques'.

"It would be an honor and privilege to handle the Ferguson auction," Sidney Armstrong said in a serious voice when Rose first had him come to discuss the sale. Polly showed him to the parlor and offered him lemonade, but he said he'd prefer a glass of cool water. He drank half the glass down and then took a swig and swished it around his mouth as though he would spit it back. He finally swallowed. Augusta was appalled.

Why must she deal with him? His hand is moist, and middle age is making him flabby. Augusta noticed his dark suit when he came to the house, surely left over from his undertaking days. For generations the Armstrong name had been associated with the funeral business, until Sidney decided he could do better handling widow's estates and retaining twenty-five percent. No doubt his wife makes him wear it, telling him no one will listen to him if he isn't dressed in a suit. She's right. Augusta knows he's only trying to be friendly, but she can't stand the sight of him.

One of the workers places Edward's black rocking horse beside the cherry desk—lonely little thing, all those years in the attic, rocking away. Why have they put the china cupboard and buffet so far from the table? Surely they aren't splitting up her dining room suite …!

Teeswater, Ontario, The Kiln, 1970

ALAN SYSTEMATICALLY ACQUIRED EVERY BITSCHY pot he found surfacing from those farm basements. Our collection grew by leaps and bounds and in 1991, we gifted the majority to the Bruce County Museum and Cultural Centre in Southampton, Ontario—an assemblage that surely laid waste the theory that no known pieces could be attributed to the Bitschy pottery. A question lingers. Among the makers and egg-trading-takers of those earthenware crocks and pitchers, did elegance of form and simplicity of surface attract visual curiosity—then as now—or was it only about frugality and utilitarian restraint?

When Rachel celebrated her first birthday in March of '71, she was surrounded by our two cats and lots of pots. They'd spilled over from kitchen shelves onto the dining room windowsills and floor, the crocks a fine size for our blooming geraniums. We were excited about spring. Plans were in place for the Ontario Department of Lands and Forest to plant 16 of our 100 acres of non-farmable, rolling land with pine and walnut trees. And in March, plans were in place for a catenary arch kiln.

With the assistance of books and recollections of the University of Saskatchewan's kilns, my project was underway. Advice and instructions arrived from Jack Sures in Regina, from my brother, William, in Pennsylvania. Detailed ink diagrams on small, graphed notebook paper, Jack's. Notes on numerous yellow foolscap pages, William's. They've recently surfaced along with my notated clay and glaze recipes in a logbook of firings.

Jack sent greetings for toddler Rachel—now a mother of a teenage daughter. William included plans for the propane gas burners he would build for my kiln. Two artists, university professors. Their vast knowledge and matter-of-fact characters made them natural teachers.

All options must be considered, they insisted. Updraft, downdraft, two burner ports or four, this possibility or that. I had little knowledge and no practical kiln building experience. Experimentation. Trial by error. There would be setbacks, of course. If things didn't turn out, the kiln could always be reconstructed, William said, reminding me that the catenary arch required no mortar. Undeterred by their certainty and my lack, I persevered.

Jack had been a good teacher, a harsh critic, especially in the presence of skill and a distinct voice, his stinging deprecation hard to forget. William, always brotherly, but firm. Both of them signed their graphed and yellow paper epistles with 'love'—so strange, when dealing with insulated firebricks, flues and baffle walls. I suppose the 'love' carried invisible hurrahs. With Alan's help and encouragement, I built my kiln, just beyond the house and yard, where the cut grass ended and the empty field began.

In the spring, we hired a mother's helper who came on weekdays so work could continue in the studio and pottery. Our Bitschy pots inspired me and I was eager to try the local red clay. We read and researched, and Alan was interviewed by a local radio station about our hunt for early potteries and clay pits. He gave out our contact information and we received multiple letters with maps, diagrams and invitations to drop by. In addition, we interviewed the widow of Teeswater's long-standing former doctor. Our thinking was that such an alert, elderly resident might surely have valuable recollections. A tall, elegant lady in her mid-eighties, the doctor's wife had come to Teeswater as a young bride of 18. She told us she was unable to help us because 'she wasn't from Teeswater'—65 years later, and still an 'outsider'.

Eventually we learned the locations of some of the old potteries, but the original clay pits were long gone. When our good friend and neighbor, Wilma, told me that she and her brothers used to make coil pots from clay they dug up on their home farm, we were off and running. Her husband, Ken, provided the truck, empty fertilizer bags and sisal ties. Wilma's older brother was still on the home farm. Though dubious about the whole project, in the end he acquiesced. If a couple of fools wanted to dig up mud, that was fine with him. The red clay had a moist, crumbly quality, and very little preparation was necessary. Dumping a fertilizer bag onto a large piece of heavy plastic, I removed the stray roots, sprinkled on water, wedged it up, and it was ready for the wheel. Any remaining vegetation burned out in the firing leaving tiny brown spots on its deep, red surface. Wilma was elated with the finished pots she could distribute to her brothers—clay from their home farm—and I enjoyed a sense of continuity with those early Bruce County farmer/potters.

Of all the things we learned in Teeswater, probably the most important was the lesson of good neighbors. Our first Teeswater winter when I was pregnant with Rachel, we had multiple blinding snowstorms that knocked out phone lines and power, sometimes for days on end. In the final stages of completing my BA in correspondence, I occasionally accompanied Alan to Guelph where he was teaching drawing at the University. I studied in the library while he taught. Other days I remained at home. In my last few weeks, Wilma was concerned I might go into labor alone and during a storm. She told me if I needed help and could not reach anyone because the phone lines were down, I should put one of our kitchen chairs out on the front veranda. The black chair in white snow would be visible from her attic window, and she'd go up to check every 20 minutes until Alan got home. We still have some of those old spindle back chairs. I never see them without feeling my neighbor's presence.

Our second child, Anna Chaia, arrived exactly two years and three days after her sister. Two beautiful little girls. The kids and home, a large vegetable garden, the pottery—by then dubbed Culross Crockery—I was completely absorbed. Writing was out.

I threw pots, experimented with glazes, mixed enormous batches of clay in my old dough mixer, perfected a porcelain recipe, and patiently waited during many experimental firings. I relied on our weekday babysitters.

Weekends were reserved for a change of pace and activities I could do with a toddler and baby. No pottery. With Alan often gone to auctions, the girls and I baked cookies and bread, did laundry, listened to kids' records and read stories. At the end of those Saturday afternoons we sat on the veranda waiting for Alan's return. Watching as our car crept down the lane, loaded to the gills, I was never surprised by the dry sinks, rockers and the bottom half of a flatback strapped to the roof. Our farmhouse was soon filled with Amish quilts, Mennonite furniture, wrought iron kitchen utensils and salt glazed five gallon crocks. Our lives were full and happy.

In that brief period, Culross Crockery pots sold at fairs and craft shops in the area, and I taught a few extension courses for Georgian College based in Owen Sound. The classes were held at the Kincardine high school, a half hour drive from our farm. In August of 1975, lugging my wheel and bags of clay in the trunk of the car, I taught my last class for Georgian College, eight months pregnant with our third. Daniel Aaron was born September 1.

After a decade of living in Teeswater and a short stretch in San Antonio, where Alan taught printmaking at the University of Texas, we moved to Iowa City so our kids could be near grandparents. By then, Teeswater had become a summer residence, and it was during vacation months that Alan and I started offering kid's classes in pottery and drawing.

Eager children, happy parents. On the last day of those sessions, the families were invited to see what had been going on. They arrived prepared to video tape, well before the convenience of cell phones. The bulky cameras and equipment were out of sync with the timeless ease of the studio and the children's candid work, especially the wall of drawings done with sticks and pots of ink.

"We're off to find a drawing stick!" The first lesson on the first day of class, as curious kids followed their teacher into our woods.

"How thick should it be, Mr. Weinstein?" Crouching, small hands moved leaves and pinecones. "Is this one good?" Straightening up, pushing hair out of hopeful faces, excited children called out. "Can you sharpen mine, Mr. Weinstein?"

Some tall, some short, they maneuvered the wooded paths in their oversize painting shirts—Alan's old tees—a flock of multicolored, long-leg flamingos.

Overwhelmed by the exercise, the parents were shocked that art could be created with the simplest of tools. Even the most chatty and self-confident fell silent, their high-tech cameras abruptly obsolete.

We had fun teaching, but it was exhausting, too much energy pinched from our own work. I've moved on since then, long ago leaving pottery behind. I had to focus—our growing family, my writing. We make our choices.

Nonetheless, that time remains significant and those 24-hour firings have stayed with me. Peering into peepholes to check the kiln's progress, I retreated patiently to the hammock while my house and family slept under night skies. It was usually dawn before cones 9 and 10 finally softened into those lovely curves, like exhausted dancers in white.

There were good firings and bad, frustrations, excitements, and the peace that always came from having clay in my hands. I worked new shapes until they felt right. But once there, doing the same thing repeatedly was tiresome, boring. I could never have been a production potter. What I loved about clay was the experimenting, the moving on.

Two summers ago, my artist nephew came to visit us in Teeswater. A printmaker by training, he was intrigued by the remnants of the pottery studio. Unglazed pots, wheels, the electric kiln wrapped in plastic, the remains of the catenary arch kiln, the barrel of 25-year-old porcelain. (Every summer I give it a sustaining drink of water.) His excitement and desire sparked an old flame. If he came to play with clay, he asked, would I?

After so long? Maybe.

When our kids were little, I tried to interest them in pottery, setting them up at the picnic table under the apple tree to form coil pots and slab structures, but they fought over the old rolling pin. They all tried the wheel, but none of them were drawn to clay. I may still be waiting for someone to entice me. My nephew came close.

By the time Alan and I were dating, my mother had grown fond of our rampant lions from the *Rastro*. At 404 South Summit, she kept the plate on the dining table with an arrangement of bananas. There was something comforting about the yellow skins on the thick, creamy ceramic. As for the lions, Alan suggested they might be a symbol of royalty, like the lions of Judah and the House of David.

'The Swimmer from Vanishing Point', 1989
No Peace at Versailles, and other stories,
published, 1990

WHEN MY YOUNGER SISTER, JACQUELINE, asked if this year I would please take a cottage with her at Vanishing Point, our old childhood vacation spot, I surprised both of us by saying I'd think about it. I've never really done the beach, at least not as an adult. I'm not especially fond of the sun, not to mention all my other priorities, but I've never been 45 either.

I'm Dora Maar, by the way. Need I tell you that our father, Pierre Bollet, who owned and operated a men's clothing store in London, Ontario, loved Picasso? He named the first three of us Dora Maar, Olga and Jacqueline. I inherited mother's restless, discontented soul and Scottish genes—her height and red hair, fair skin and strong jaw. A far cry from my calm father and Picasso's Dora Maar. When our mother, well pregnant for the fourth time, informed our short, adoring Québécois father that this was it, no more, he prayed for another girl. His prayer was answered and he named the tiny, red, wrinkled infant, Marie Thérèse Françoise Fernande. Of course she was always Frannie to us. Free-spirited and pig-tailed, with a hint of pigeon toes and one lazy eye, a tom-boy, blessed with the names of three of Picasso's beautiful women. Naturally our names caused some discomfort in Anglo-Saxon, London, Ontario, where Bollet became Bowlit. And in the Catholic parochial system that fate had thrust us upon, Picasso was neither viewed with awe, nor humor. Nevertheless, we carried the names with pride and dignity, in deference to our father, despite the fact that they were legacies of misery, madness and suicide.

My husband, Nate, hardworking and conscientious, thinks the beach is a wonderful idea, although his instinct is to avoid the sun even more than I do. For him, August promises solid work, commuting back and forth from his Toronto architectural office to the firm's housing project for the elderly in Oshawa. But I deserve a break, he insists. Perhaps a little too eagerly? Nate, like all of us, I suppose, is struggling with some form of mid-life crisis. Having recently become obsessed with his own mortality and lack of hedonistic pursuits, he has forced the Yuppies' R. & R. into his vocabulary. He's concluded that perhaps we should 'lighten up', to quote our Army Surplus attired daughters. He's quite right about a break. I've just finished editing another high school French book. He understands that in the last couple of years, things have seemed particularly bleak and pointless when I finish those textbooks; he understands the despondency, the restlessness. It wasn't always true of course. I used to enjoy my editing, especially when the girls were younger. My publisher used to say I was indispensable. Nate says our last child, our five-year-old Ben—who waits patiently for his parents to have time—will love the beach.

We pack Jacqueline's station wagon on the 5th of August. Ben and Joshua—Jackie's five-year-old—as well as Joshua's two dachshund dogs, are beside themselves with excitement. They're already unpacking the bag of He-Man toys.

"Yesterday I went to Chinatown."

I throw the last bag of clothes into the back of the car and glance up at Nate. "Chinatown?" He's standing beside the car holding a package.

"I'm worried about the sun. You're not used to it." He unwraps a large, paper umbrella, covered with dragons and incredible blossoms.

"I wanted to get one of those spectacular bamboo helmets the rice pickers use, but I didn't think you'd wear it. I couldn't resist this!"

Despite his mother's early Alzheimer's, the relentless work to establish his firm, the tribulations of our twin daughters' rebellions, despite it all, bamboo and paper can still excite him, mid-life crisis or not.

"The guy said it'll keep off almost anything—sun, rain, snow!"

And thus, the moment of cold feet. The moment the whole idea strikes me as sheer stupidity. What business do I have going off to the beach? Never mind exhaustion and a five-year-old son. There is other work to start. Why am leaving my husband for three weeks? Isn't that what *The Seven Year Itch* was about? That goofy husband getting rid of his wife and kids so he could play with Marilyn Monroe? Of course Nate isn't exactly goofy, I remind myself.

"Don't you like it?" he asks, opening and closing the umbrella. "I thought it'd be good for the sun."

"I love it, Nate." I run my hand over the fan folded paper. We kiss good-bye and he leans in through the car window, placing the umbrella into the back beside the bag of beach toys.

Perhaps not goofy, but why is he so eager to get me off? I hate being forty-five. There are days when everything seems gray, saggy or suspicious. The house in Rosedale, the clothes in the closets, and on occasion, my mind. Nate's face isn't gray or saggy. He's smiling, his arms resting on the window frame. He strokes my hair, mumbling something about relaxing, enjoying the water, that he'll miss me. His eyes are clear and upbeat—always receptive, always giving, despite the hurdles life throws him. Yet I can't help thinking gray. At one end of the scale, senile parents, and at the other, teenage children engulfing us, like algae in water, spreading, cutting off the air supply. When we free ourselves long enough to come up for a gasp, we find that it's precisely our patience that has worn down our crisp edges and is turning us to moss. I'm not really worried about the *Seven Year Itch* stuff. We have a good marriage. I know we've been lucky really, compared to some of our friends. Lucky with the kids, our work, that we're still lovers. Does Nate think in saggy, gray patches? I suspect not. We kiss good-bye again. He's right, it's time for the beach. Nate reaches into the backseat cuffing Ben playfully, promising to come up for a weekend, at least.

After an hour of traffic, we meander through beautiful, leisurely farm country. Jackie insists on driving. I feel comfortably drowsy, and the boys and dogs are good. The radio is on—the sound of the local station hasn't changed. The swap shop still advertises old cellar windows and bushel baskets of sealers. The announcer still reads out recipes before the local news. '... beaches are open again for swimming after an accidental sewage spill further north ... peaches from the Niagara fruit belt are expected on the market by next week. Crystal Dunn, from Seaforth, is still missing.' I lean my head against the back of the seat, wondering, briefly, who Crystal Dunn is.

Minutes later I'm pleasantly surprised to recognize landmarks in the landscape—the blue barn at the turn off to the lake route, a yellow brick farmhouse with a turret, another with a remarkable, gingerbread veranda. Jackie made all the arrangements for the cottage. As she drives, she recalls our grandmother's place and the long afternoons at the water, the spectacular sunsets. We reminisce about our father, how he'd remain in the city all week tending the store. It gave him great satisfaction knowing that his wife and daughters were at Vanishing Point, enjoying the sun and water, having a vacation. On Saturday nights, he'd close up and drive out to the beach for Sunday with his girls. I can still see our parents at the water. Mother had presence; her stature and flaming red hair, her confidence and carriage. She wore two piece, striped bathing suits and always looked beautiful. Her own mother had wanted her to go on the stage. She never did; she raised her girls instead, and rested. At the beach, on the lounger, she surrounded herself with umbrellas and straw hats, cold drinks, fruit, magazines and cigarettes. Whenever I get within sight of a lake, I smell her cocoa butter tanning lotion, her cigarettes. Breathless from running, we brought her iridescent sea shells and bits of quartz. She held them in her long fingers with the red nails, studying them intensely, as precious objects. Were there answers in those muted colors and bits of dancing light? Was her restlessness stilled? Father in the chair beside her, reading, his short, barrel build upright—he always brought mother certain comfort, peace. The water was clear and the sand white, and at night, large street lamps like the ones from the Paris métros, lit the boardwalk the length of the beach. Our father had taken us all to Paris once—for Picasso of course—that's how we knew about the métros. Our parents are both dead now.

Jackie has turned off the highway and onto a blacktop side road.

"Have you been to Vanishing Point recently?" I ask.

Jacqueline shakes her head. "I've taken Joshua to Georgian Bay for the last few summers."

I nod. "Maybe the water—"

"Mom! Mom!"

I hear Ben scrambling forward in the back of the wagon.

"Just a minute Ben, let me finish." I pat his hand. "Maybe the water's polluted and the sand is dirty."

"Joshua has to pee! Joshua has to pee!" Ben's voice is behind my ear, he's tapping my arm with Skelator.

"Oh boy. Are you sure?" I ask, turning around.

Joshua nods urgently, pressing down on his jeans.

Jacqueline glances into the rear view mirror to catch sight of her son. "He's sure," she agrees, pulling off to the side of the road. "O.K. kid, let's go, out the back." She jumps out of the car, opens the rear door and leads Joshua down the grassy embankment. One dog starts to bark, the other remains asleep.

"This is your chance too, Ben."

"Don't have to." His face is pressed against the glass, watching Joshua. "He always has trouble with his zippers," Ben mumbles.

In seconds, Jacqueline is climbing back into the front seat and we're off again.

"Dirty sand and polluted water! Honestly, Dora Maar, you can be such a drag!" She laughs, her large, dark eyes sparkling. "I hope you're going to relax a little, Dora? Doesn't Nate ever tell you to?"

As a matter of fact, he does. But I won't admit that to my sister. My steady, responsible Nate. Despite his professional success, his seeming domestic content, now he wants change. Rather than appeal to my restless nature, this new development only makes me anxious. That's one reason I feel so uncomfortable with the idea of leaving him alone for three weeks. I hope this new R. & R. need doesn't involve something stupid, like buying a motorcycle and insisting I ride with him. His mother would have had a coronary. Wouldn't another trip to Paris be just as satisfying? As for me, Nate's decided the nuns of my youth surely had something to do with the seriousness doggedly accompanying me through life. Little does he know about growing up Catholic, or for that matter, London, Ontario.

"Did you hear me, Dora Maar?"

I turn to my sister.

"I hope you're going to relax, take it easy," Jacqueline repeats.

I nod. "Of course."

Jackie has sworn off men, at least for the summer. She's pretty, with straight, black hair and a slight face, but her breasts are awkwardly large for her slim body. She's only thirty-seven, so I figure she can afford to swear off men for a time, especially given her track record. Little Joshua's father is history, so, for that matter, are Paul, Roger and Sean. As much as I adore my sister, and vicariously enjoy her inevitably humorous, amorous escapades, I'm relieved that for three weeks, I won't have to listen to her adventures.

The cottage is a small, frame structure squatting in the sand. When Jacqueline said she got it on the water, she wasn't kidding. It smells damp and closed inside, but it's adequately furnished, even sort of comfortable, with rattan arm chairs and a large coffee table. The counters in the kitchen have speckled, green Formica, and there's a set of sticky tin canisters that have sea shells and small pebbles glued all over them. The crevices between shells and stones are filled with old flour and sugar, and something brownish that looks like molasses. I decide they've lost their charm and whisk them under the kitchen sink before the boys see them and fall in love. The boys are already out beside the picture window, their He-Man collection and sand toys spread around them. Around the back, behind the house, the dachshunds are checking out the small, wooded area infested with mosquitos and the last tenants' dog poop. A limp clothesline is strung between two pines.

If I get groceries, Jackie says she'll check out the waterfront with the boys. She's eager to rent some hand sailing equipment and see if there might be swimming lessons. I unpack first, inspecting the bedrooms and bathroom. The dresser drawers have sand in them, and the bath tub is orange with rust stains. For some reason, the beeswax toilet seal is exposed above the linoleum floor. All kinds of odd things have become embedded. I suddenly remember why it is I don't 'do beaches,' besides the sun, but I resolve to not let the cottage bother me. This is going to be a vacation. Later, after I return with groceries, Jackie has news of a pool, and that the boys are registered for a 9 a.m. beginners' class.

The next morning, in crisp air and a clear light, the boys and I walk along the empty beach to the lakeside pool. There's a small playground immediately beside the facility, with swings and slides and a fountain. The pier runs behind it, congested with a large cargo boat and several small vessels. The town, with its Victorian houses, is higher up and inland, just a few minutes' walk from the waterfront. Vanishing Point is so named because of that jutting bit of land along the shoreline that vanishes into the mist when seen from the water. After checking the boys in at the office and leading them to the change-room, I walk around to the front and find a place on the benches facing the pool.

Excitement and noise are at a high level. Mothers are chattering, babies in strollers suck pacifiers, demanding attention. I watch as Ben and Joshua are herded out of the change room, dripping from the obligatory shower, clinging to their towels. They're given a pep talk, and then told to slide into the pool and hang on. Small children in front of me press against the link fence, calling out to siblings in the water.

Despite the chaos and confusion, I see him immediately. He enters the pool area and reaches for the lifesaving pole. An Athenian athlete readying for the games. For a few moments my eyes settle on him with rapt attention. I could be at the Parthenon looking at horses on the friezes, or perhaps a lone, Greek youth, rendered in marble. The profile is classical—nose, lips, chin. The hair, blond and curly. The autonomy of youth marks his body. The solid neck, an entity of its own, is separate from the line of the jaw, from the torso. He's a kid, a boy, surely no older than my twin daughters. He has an easy gait around the pool, a sweatshirt thrown over his shoulders, a naturalness with kids. Clearly he's one of the instructors. The other is a petite, well-hinged girl with a shrill, relentless voice. For half the lesson I watch attentively as Ben and Joshua struggle to master their fears. When I finally turn away for a moment, tired of the enervating sight, our eyes meet. In motion, he's like any eighteen-year-old boy with a remote, but nice look. But when still, not moving, his face becomes energized with an almost psychic sensitivity, the sky before the storm. This must be the power of the maharishi, of the guru. The wisdom and pain that beckons souls who follow blindly, riveting themselves to the halos of their leaders. But then he moves, and all is lost. Standing at the edge of the pool, his weight resting on his lifesaver's pole, he smiles at me. His partner in the water shrieks out instructions to each child, flipping her head like a porpoise to remove the bangs from her eyes. There is sympathy in his glance, he understands my temporary anxiety over the boys' panic. I'm flattered. It's been a long time since I've been looked at like that.

As the days pass, I willingly wake up earlier than Jackie and take the kids for their lessons. We leave the cottage minutes before nine. I pad out across the sand with my coffee mug in hand, and take my place alongside the other mothers. I've gotten to know some of them. Pam is the one with the curlers in her hair. Debbie is a mother of twins, beautiful babies of nine months. With windbreakers zipped to our throats, we marvel at the children's bravery and spunk in the early morning cool. We speculate on the temperature for the day. We comment on the cleanliness of the pool and the pollution count of the beaches. There is discussion about which grocery store has the nicest produce and best pasta salad. I look forward to the early morning chatter; it leaves me free to observe, speculate and feel leisurely.

Occasionally there is talk of the male swimming instructor who doubles as a lifeguard in the afternoons. It feels quite natural that there should be gossip. After all, the women talk of everything else. The boy lives alone somewhere as a boarder; they say he hates his father. Every morning he comes to the pool early, before anyone arrives, and does laps. They tell of how his own mother struggled with cancer and finally died last winter. How his father, an alcoholic child-abuser, divorced her while she was ill and remarried a woman with many children. I try not to pay much attention.

I find my reaction strange. I'm usually interested in trivia. But somehow I don't want to know about his daily life, his family, the girlfriend he surely must have. I prefer him nameless and abstract; a Heathcliff, Michelangelo's David, Christopher Plummer—the storm and the calm—the man, for whom environment is irrelevant. The man, for whom peace is not easy, and freedom, even in the form of resurrection, is what he unknowingly lives for.

Ben and Joshua like him. They talk about him all the time. At meals, they chat happily about the things he can do underwater, as they pour ketchup on their hot dogs. For the most part, I ignore their talk.

"What are you after?" Jacqueline asks one night as we balance glasses of wine and drag our loungers over the sand to the edge of the water. "Really, Dora?" She stands for a moment looking at me.

I'd forgotten that Jackie came with me one morning to watch the boys' lessons. "I don't know." I dig my glass into the sand and settle back into the lounger.

"Maybe you want him?"

"Honestly, Jackie, doesn't bluntness ever get old for you?" I ask, tired out by the day in the water and sun.

"I'm serious, Dora, if that's what you want, go for it. Are you worried about Nate?"

"For God's sake!" I reach for my glass, sip the wine, and stare out across the dark lake. The smell of beach barbeques drifts toward us.

"Come on, TRUTH!"

"Jackie, the truth is, the lake is beautiful, the sky is dark and the sand is cool."

"Sure, but there are other truths, like your swimmer. I'll bet he's available. What do you think, Dora?"

The wine makes me feel lethargic, relaxed. Somehow I feel

secure knowing the boys are asleep in the cottage, seeing the occasional spots of cottage lights dotting the shoreline, knowing that what I'm lying on is indeed a lounger, and not a boat. It would be nice though, to drift out into the water. Further along the shore is the famous Vanishing Point with two pines and a huge boulder, pushing out onto the lake. We used to go to it as children. I wonder if I could find my way back.

"You're not even going to talk about him, are you?"

I can hear the pout in my sister's voice. I turn my head, I see her profile in the dark. She's bored. We've been at the cottage for a week and she's bored.

"They're still looking for that missing woman, Crystal Dunn, from Seaforth," I offer, reaching for my wine glass. "I heard on the news tonight that her family will give a reward for any information."

"Why won't you talk about him?"

"Jackie, there is nothing to talk about. This whole thing is beyond sex. I've tried to tell you that."

"Give me a break! Beyond sex! You're putting me off, and don't think I can't see through it. I know how you've been rushing off to get a glimpse of him every morning."

I ignore her.

"The boys' lessons?" Jacqueline adds.

"Shut up, Jackie."

"If I were you, I'd want him."

"Well you're not me. Thank God, because one of me is plenty." I feel angry and restless. I know it has nothing to do with Jackie.

The days drift on. In her boredom, Jackie abandons her vow to swear off men. Someone has caught her eye and she begins spending serious time with him. I don't mind at all. I can watch the kids and dogs, and still read or think or daydream. In the afternoons, I follow them out across the warm sand, lawn chair in one arm, the paper umbrella in the other. I know I must cut quite a sight in Nate's shirt, my protection from the sun. Fortunately, the boys are too young to notice or care what I wear in public. I speak with Nate every couple of nights. He tells me about work, and says I sound relaxed. I assure him I'm working on it. I don't tell him about the swimmer, and I don't ask what he does in the evenings. It's stupid, really.

"Joshua says he saw Portuguese-Men-of-War in the lake!" Ben is standing before me, taut, wide-eyed and dripping, pointing back to Joshua who has remained near the water.

"Really?" I shade my eyes and pretend to search the lake. "I can't see their boats. What color are they?"

"Mom!" His body eases, he shrieks with laughter. "They're not people! They're jellyfishes, with purple bags!"

"Oh yes, the jellyfishes. No dear, you tell your cousin that Lake Huron does not have Portuguese-Men-of-War."

"See!" Ben spins around, dashing off. "I told you! I told you!"

I watch them standing, facing each other, engrossed in conversation. Their arms wave, their heads turn, even their feet kick at sand. After a few moments they both shrug and slide down to their castles. I'm amazed at their five-year-old independence. Sand, water and sun seem to satisfy most of their needs. As for me, I find myself doing less and less every day. Sometimes I spend whole, blank afternoons sitting and watching them play with the dogs. I realize I haven't once thought about the next editing job, or the bills I've left unpaid. Occasionally I think about the girls, wondering how their summer jobs are going, thinking I must call them. But when evening comes, I never remember. Days ago I gave up wanting to do anything. I haven't touched the needlepoint or knitting I brought. Sometimes hours pass before I even pick up a book. I spend a great deal of time watching the sky through my glasses. I know about calm, hot days and how the warmed earth's surface sends up thermals of air that rise, condense, and thus those flat-based, piled formations of water droplets. The low cumulus clouds drift and shift, their tops and sides illuminated by the sun. A sharpness of blue and white and detail, a softness of light. In the early evenings, after dinner, the boys and I walk to the Marina; a fishy breeze picks up around the boats and we catch the late sun shattering like glass on the shore, where water meets rock.

The truth is, I've become obsessed with the swimmer. It's funny, isn't it? To think I was so worried about Nate getting itchy. Kindred spirits, soulmates, ships that pass in the night, call it what you will, there is an undeniable, silent, crashing of souls. I think about him teaching the lessons. I think about the day the boys and I arrived early, before anyone else. We sat on the bench and watched him doing laps; steady, long, driven laps. When he stopped for a few minutes to rest at the edge of the pool—unaware, I'm sure, of his audience—he threw his head back and released a loud, almost violent laugh. He seemed distant, determined, surly.

I felt uncomfortable watching. And yet … I want to soothe him for the loss of his mother, though he has the power to self-heal. I grieve that he must live as a boarder, though his family exists. I probably want to make love with him, though he's the age of my daughters.

No words pass between us, until the day, it happens to be a Friday, that I decide our silence is ridiculous. I am a mature woman. I will speak. I will break the spell. As soon as the lesson is over and while the boys dress, I stand up from the bench and walk toward the pool. Better still, I will pretend this is in my mind.

I stand at the link fence, my left arm raised, fingers thrust through the wire. "How are the boys doing?" I'm pleased to hear my voice sounding mature, confident. I raise my free hand to my hair whipping in a sudden gust of wind. He moves toward the link fence, turning his sweatshirt right side out.

"Nicely, but they need more work with the backstroke. Could they put in some practice time in the afternoons?" He pulls on the shirt.

Is he relieved to break the silence? "Perhaps," I say, brushing hair out of my eyes.

His face is close to the wire mesh, to my fingers. I can hear him breathing, I can see the oil on his torso, but our words do not break the spell.

"It's going to be a beautiful day," he says suddenly, throwing his head back, staring straight above at the sky.

I nod in agreement, turning to look at the water. There are already sailboats out. Bathers are beginning to arrive with their beach paraphernalia. The vendors are preparing their carts.

"Meet me at Vanishing Point, tomorrow night at nine." His voice is a low, hoarse whisper.

For a strange moment, the clouds stop moving. I feel myself shifting into low gear. I look back at him, but it's an excruciatingly slow motion. His words seem to hang in the air, waiting for me. He's turned away in motion, moving, bending in expectation toward a child, blue with cold and fear, clinging to the edge of the pool.

I blush. I feign. Smiling politely I turn around nervously, then hurry away. Walking back to the cottage with the boys, I can't help wondering if I've imagined what I heard. He couldn't possibly have said that.

"I dreamt last night," I tell Jackie the next morning, as I pour myself a cup of coffee. I slept fitfully, but dreamt fully and elaborately, not an unusual combination for me. It's Saturday, and the boys do not have swimming lessons. Fifteen minutes ago, they gulped down a bowl of cereal and dashed outdoors.

"I never dream," Jacqueline says, carrying her coffee over to the rattan chair in front of the picture window. She stares out at the water.

I think her boyfriend has returned to the city.

"What are we going to do today?" she asks.

"I was on a beach, a long stretch of white sand."

"In your dream?"

I nod. "I came back to search for something I'd left behind. At first I didn't know what I was looking for, then I realized it was Frannie."

"Frannie? Our sister Frannie?" Jacqueline asks, amazed.

"Yes. Mother sent me back. She was very angry that I'd leave a small child alone near the water. I don't know how or why I did it, it seems pretty stupid now. But at the time it was crucial that I leave. There was some conflict in the dream, and it was very urgent that

I go immediately, leaving Frannie. She was young, a small child. I had to walk along the shore for miles. I kept passing monument booths, like hot dog stands. You could wait while they made you a monument to order—a simple head stone, or a bust cast in bronze. They had all their foundry equipment behind the stands, half buried in sand. One place even carved in granite, to order. As samples of their work, they had an imitation of the Rosetta stone, and a huge postcard carved in the gray rock. It was from our sister, Olga, to her boyfriend Jerzy, telling him it was best not to come to visit. They had done her signature beautifully. You know how nice Olga's signature is. The thing was almost as large as a billboard."

"I need more coffee," Jacqueline interrupts, standing up and walking across the raffia rug toward the kitchen. "I'd forgotten all about Jerzy. What ever became of him? I was always sorry Olga didn't marry him. Why didn't mother like him?"

"Who knows. Mother didn't like a lot of our boyfriends. But about my dream. It was evening when I started back to find Frannie. I couldn't find anything. The monument stands were gone, everything was gone. It was as though there'd been a nuclear disaster; nothing was left, the sand had been raked clean. There was no sign of Frannie, except the plastic arm of her doll sticking out of the sand."

"That was some dream. Did it end there?"

"Yes, I woke myself up, I was terrified."

"So, what do you think, Dora? Are you going to abandon us, like you did Frannie?"

I look at my sister and laugh, but Jackie is serious.

"Listen, I'll take the kids for a walk into town. Take a shower and get dressed, Jacqueline. Maybe we ought to do something different today. It's Saturday, the beach will be impossible!"

An hour later, when the kids and I get back, Jacqueline is sitting on the front stoop painting her toe nails.

"Nate phoned!" She calls out, fanning her feet. "He's coming! He'll be arriving late, around 9, and he'll be able to stay all Sunday. He said something about waiting up for him, so the two of you could take a walk to Vanishing Point."

In the afternoon, Jackie takes the boys on a picnic. By the time they return, I've swept the sand out of the cottage, baked two peach pies, and made a tray of roast chicken. When Nate arrives, I take him out to sit in the sand with a bottle of wine, instead of walking to Vanishing Point. I don't tell him about the swimmer.

Sunday it rains. The first rainy day we've had since we've been here. Nate doesn't mind at all. He takes the boys for a beach walk in the rain. After Monopoly and comics, they build a miniature cottage with small beach pebbles and Elmer's glue. I read, and stand at the window, wondering if the swimmer went to Vanishing Point last night. Jacqueline looks through a Picasso book she's checked out of the public library. Jacqueline always thinks about our father on rainy days. It's a strangely quiet, calm day with Nate in the cottage.

That night Nate and I make delicious love, but I fall asleep thinking about the swimmer. I wonder if it's something similar for Nate.

Monday morning, and Nate leaves for Toronto at 6. I stand shivering in the cold air, still in my sleeping shirt. We kiss, and Nate says he'll try to get up some evening during our last week.

At ten to nine, we start out across the sand to the pool. The boys run ahead. I'm looking forward to the bench talk, the lesson, seeing him. The truth is, being near him makes me feel young. It really is as simple as that. For the moment, I don't care about anything else. I've never forgotten that picture of Dora Maar standing in chest high water with Picasso. She was clearly beautiful, vibrant, sexy. All my life, I've tried to forget that Picasso's Dora Maar went mad.

"We don't have a lesson today!"

I look up to see Ben running toward me, twirling his towel in the air.

"What? Why not?"

"Don't know." He's still twirling. "Something about the teacher."

"Stop!" I reach out to calm the towel, and myself. My voice is anxious. "Where's Joshua?"

Ben turns and points toward a group of mothers standing beside the pool. Joshua is wedged in between Pam with the curlers and Debbie, the mother of twins. He's looking up at their faces, listening.

I hurry over to the women, glancing at the vacant pool. A 'NO LESSONS TODAY sign is posted on the office door. "What's wrong?"

"It's the lifeguard," one woman volunteers.

"What?" I know my voice sounds high, clipped.

"He's in police custody."

"Police custody? Why? What happened?"

"They broke up a party late Saturday night. It was one of the kids' beer parties. They go on every weekend. It seems a woman claims the lifeguard attacked her, outside, behind the cottage. It's not clear what she was doing at a kids' party, apparently she's about forty. They say it was pretty messy, and she's sticking to her story."

A wave of nausea rises to my throat.

"Can you believe it!" Debbie says. "And to think." She lowers her voice. "To think he's with our children every day. Our little girls!"

"No point in sticking around here." A young, nervous mother pulls away from the women, anxiously drawing a sweater over her shoulders and turning to call her children.

"If you ask me," Pam says, adjusting the scarf over her curlers, "he probably had something to do with that Crystal Dunn woman from Seaforth."

All eyes turn toward her.

"Well, she disappeared didn't she?" Pam adds. "And clearly he likes older women."

Silence falls over the group.

"I guess it's possible," another voice says.

"More than possible!" Pam adds. "I'll bet anything they're going to find out he was involved."

"Do you think he …?"

"I wouldn't be surprised to hear the worst."

"Perhaps we're letting our imaginations get the best of us," I interrupt, weakly. But I'm ignored.

"How much do you want to bet they find her body down in an old well or something." Pam shakes her head, breathing deeply. "Maybe they'll get that crazy clairvoyant to help them. Any of you ever been up to Lamb's Way to visit with her? They say she'll read your palm for five bucks."

"Pam, stop it! You're scaring the kids!" Debbie says, nodding toward a cluster of wide-eyed children.

Shock and loss sweep over me. Anger, and finally, stillness. It's several minutes before I pull myself together to call Ben and Joshua away from the playground.

Later in the afternoon, I start off down the beach toward Vanishing Point, alone. It takes a good half hour, the walk and the climb up the hill. By the time I get up, I'm shocked to see how changed it looks. The two pines are still there, but now the boulder is perched dangerously near the edge of the cliff. I stand close and peer over at the rising lake that has eroded the cliffside, the precipice frightening and steep.

"Shame, isn't it?"

I whirl around, my heart in my throat. An old man is standing between the pines, lighting a pipe. He's wearing blue jeans and suspenders but no shirt. His barrel build and bald head remind me of my father. Clearly he came up the other side of the hill. I must look surprised.

"Didn't mean to frighten you."

I shake my head.

"I say it's a shame the way the lake is eating up our land." He waves his pipe toward the cliff and the water. "Was a time when this was a beautiful spot. Won't be long before it might just vanish completely."

I nod, collecting myself. I shake some pine needles out of my sandals.

"I sure wouldn't want to be out here in the dark. That's a nasty precipice now!" He cackles, taking off down the other side of the hill.

I walk quickly, anxious to get back to the cottage. Nervous and uncomfortable, I feel the familiar crawl of prickly heat on my back, my physical response to anxiety. I want to see Ben and Joshua, Jackie, right away. I want to call the girls. I want to talk to Nate. I start to run, thinking of the time Nate and I were caught in a Paris subway during an accident. Before we realized what had happened, there was a loud, shrill alarm that wouldn't stop, and a crowd of anxious people gathered near a car door. A small child was screaming hysterically. Panic rushed over me. The air was still and close and I was desperate to get out of the subway, to call home to Toronto, to make sure our children were safe and well. After several minutes of waiting, while time had stopped, a couple was led away by a subway attendant. The man was carrying a child, her hand bandaged in a bloody handkerchief.

I'm still running as I round the bend and the cottage comes into view. Ben and Joshua are playing in the sand. I stop to catch my breath, relieved, gasping, bending over, my hands on my waist. When I straighten up, I see the boys dashing toward me, laughing. After Sunday's rain, the landscape around them seems clear, clean. The sky looks promising. The tops and sides of my white, cumulus clouds are lit by the sun.

Ibiza, May 1965

W E TOOK THE BUS INTO town for things we couldn't buy in *Tienda Can Chocolate*—fresh fruit, vegetables and toiletries. The art store had basic supplies and I found typing paper and even 'white-out', both available in the *papelerías*, stationery shops. Every other week, we purchased *Time Magazine* in English. Waiting at a café for Anna, we'd order cold drinks and pastries and tear the magazine in half so we could read simultaneously. *Flaó* was Alan's favorite, a goat's milk cheese pie enhanced with *frígola*. I preferred *greixonera*, bread pudding made with yesterday's *ensaïmades*, the spiral shaped pastry typical of the Baleares. Anna liked everything.

Trips to town included queuing up at the main post office on the *Paseo Vara de Rey*. We wrote home at least once a week, often twice, a steady stream of aerograms and postcards, lifelines to our families. Postage was one of our greatest expenses. On one occasion we placed an international phone call from Barcelona. Only once, in all the time we lived in Spain. It ended up being a costly, tiresome ordeal involving a pre-arranged appointment at a huge telephone building, officious operators and waiting for an available phone booth.

Correspondence was the answer, and like the other expats and tourists on our busy island, we quickly learned *el correo*, the post office, required patience. Waiting in line one morning, I recognized a fellow ahead me—the crooked nose and smiling eyes, curly, sandy hair and easy manner. He'd been a print student when I was in high school.

During my junior and senior years, if a project kept me after classes until late in the day, I'd take the foot bridge across the Iowa river from U-high to the art school so I could hitch a ride home. Hanging out in the print area, I became acquainted with some of Pa's grad students. By then, we rarely saw them in our home. After decades of teaching, weariness had set in—the faculty meetings, the print room, the students. My father wanted more time alone in his own studio. They used to come, the post-war boys, gathering around our kitchen for the empanadas Ma would make. Pa was close to those first students—they shared a generation. He used to say those G.I.s were some of the most committed students he ever had.

"Elliot? Elliot Elgart?"

The curly headed American stopped talking to his friends and turned to face me. His smile easy, his eyes bright.

"No, but I wish I were!"

Tongue tied and blushing, I retreated to my place in line.

Going to town on my own and dodging lascivious advances, *estilo Español,* Spanish style, became the torment. I arrived home from those forays shamed and angry. There wasn't a lot to say, but *chanchos*, pigs, took on a new importance in my vocabulary, and Alan's. The subject was never discussed with José and María. We rarely spoke of difficulties. Their failure to conceive a child was mentioned only once in passing.

I wasn't tough or adventuresome the way my daughters would prove to be. Anna, self-defensively *groin kneeing disgusting dicks* on Parisian subways and her older sister, Rachel, breathlessly describing events in vivid detail. Recalling that trip to Paris, I'm stunned by our laissez-faire attitude and can only attribute our yielding to parental exhaustion. The girls were 16 and 14—gorgeous, energetic and confrontational. Daniel was 12, obedient and protective of his brother, Adam, a remarkably observant four-year-old. Fatigued or not, how could we permit our teenage daughters to take off on their own adventures? One afternoon, having taken a subway from the

Gare du Nord to the end of a line and parts unknown, they returned home wearing new boots. Rachel's red leather, Anna's teal suede. Flawless matches for their Université de Paris sweatshirts.

On Ibiza, I bore my embarrassment privately. Even Anna W. did not hear of my humiliation and anger. Remembering her personality, I probably feared she would dismiss the whole thing as harmless, or worse, me as fragile. My silence was self-preserving instinct.

Now it's called sexual harassment: same thing, different era. While it probably existed on the University of Iowa campus during my student years in the mid 60's, I never encountered it. And more recently, in the 23 years as synagogue administrator for Agudas Achim Congregation in Iowa City and Coralville, my workplace was safe and secure, except for the few instances of verbal and written abuse.

Lately, unpleasant Spanish memories have surfaced, undoubtedly because of the 'Me Too' movement and news-breaking sexual scandals. More and more outrages, every night, every news channel, yet, strangely, I've found a silver lining. Quite unexpectedly, I share common ground with the contemporary, American female. A refreshing truth, for in so many ways, I've struggled to connect with the women of my generation.

Having landed in Spain from Holland's well-mannered, Nordic culture, I was shocked by the rampant undercurrent of sexual repression in Spanish men, most evident on the street. A high proportion of the male population was stuck in the clandestine alleyways of archaic times and forbidden sexual urges. It may have extended beyond the street and been equally true of women, but that wasn't apparent. Was it possible the sexual revolution had not reached the Iberian Peninsula? Did they not know the 'Pill' was empowering women to manage their own sexual and reproductive lives?

It was considered unsafe for a young woman to travel alone. Tales abounded. The most disturbing we heard was about the American girl on a Fulbright, raped by an elderly guard in the Alhambra. Dorothy Dorf, our companion from the University of Iowa, also a Fulbright scholar, was studying painting at the University of Barcelona. Her nasty train experience, unavoidably having to share a couchette with five Spanish men, was sobering. She endured the situation, emerging whole and unharmed, but deeply shaken. When we returned to the States and I told Dorothy's story to a mutual acquaintance—a lively, not very feminine lady with flat feet and a limp—she humorously reported her own experiences with Iberian trains. Sadly, she'd run into no such problems, no advances from Spanish men.

Attempting to explain the sexual psyche of the Spanish male, Dorothy's Catalan boyfriend, an engineer in his late twenties, told us about his Jesuit-run elementary school. He recounted a playground event when the priest told the frolicking boys to promptly turn and face the school wall. The peeking boys saw their priest transfixed by the sight of two girls walking by on the other side of the school fence.

What was wrong with Spanish speaking men? In Barcelona, walking on the *Ramblas* with my left arm hooked through Alan's, I had to endure obscenities whispered in my right ear by passing yahoos. And what about that time in the Mexico City train station? As I exited a bathroom and started across the anteroom toward Alan waiting for me at a magazine kiosk, an overweight man hurried eagerly in my direction from across the vast, domed space. Smiling lecherously and rubbing his hands together, he came close enough that I could hear his heavy breathing and smell his salami breath. Following close beside me across the tiled floor, he turned away only when he saw Alan waving to me.

Raised in Iowa, I was appalled. Thin-skinned, perhaps. But I was worldly enough to see smiles accompanying Italian and French whistling and catcalls, unlike the solemn resolve of Spanish men, or alternately, their brazen grossness. Techniques of public harassment, especially on crowded Spanish buses, included 'unintentional/on purpose' prodding, touching and panting breaths at the nape of a woman's neck. On the narrow streets of Ibiza, besides the ostentatious display of male genital handling, women were accidentally shoved off the sidewalk. This made for an easy glance down the neckline, especially for the vertically challenged male. Daytime cleavages stayed home. If their visibility had been as acceptable as they are now, perhaps Spanish men would have been more civilized.

Ibiza's flourishing tourist trade witnessed an influx of construction workers from the province of Murcia, in southeastern Spain. María Chocolate's Ramón was a Murciano, though he'd come to the island long before his construction-working-compatriots. Native islanders considered most Murcianos coarse and unrefined. It hardly mattered if the 'street improprieties' were carried out by Ibicencos or Murcianos, I learned to cover up. On my solo shopping trips to Ibiza's main *mercado*, I donned a head scarf and long sleeves. In one of the photos Dr. Potts snapped of our house, I'm wearing my indispensable black cardigan. Sunglasses were essential; men were not to see my eyes. I eventually developed coping techniques to deal with the ubiquitous problem, but I never learned to take in stride the feeling of embarrassment and resentment. Without a doubt, the experiences fueled my cautious temperament.

By mid-May, surrounded by a landscape that had turned a magnificent yellowish hue from the ripe grain, we climbed our mountain to help the Palerms with the barley harvest. Butchering a hog or taking off the grain were communal projects with neighbors pitching in to help. José had an old-fashioned harvesting machine. As the men raked and collected, Alan and I followed behind with the women picking up the remains of grain. We worked until sunset. When darkness fell, we gathered in José and María's kitchen to share their evening meal. It was the same months later when we helped with the potato harvest. Leaving early in the morning for the *huerta* in Jose's cart, we dug potatoes until noon, stopped to eat, and continued digging until sundown. In preparation for the meal, María made a fire and set out her big *paella* pan filled with olive oil. We gathered under the *algarroba* trees and lunched on fried potatoes and green beans, *salchichón* and *sobrasada* sausage, olives, bread, and wine. Even at that age I found oil-soaked vegetables difficult to digest, but the physical labor was gratifying.

The neighboring families were eager to talk with us. Alert and curious, they had many questions about life in the States. Some of them had bits and pieces of information, mostly hearsay. None of them read well, if at all. We sat around the table talking for hours. They asked if the United States was a Catholic country, like Spain, but they ignored our explanation of many cultures, many religions. One outspoken fellow promptly answered that if it wasn't Catholic, it must be communist. The Spanish civil war had left its mark.

When *Time Magazine* covered the first American spacewalk, June 3, 1965, we shared the images with the Palerms. They were amazed, but insisted the astronauts' suits were for underwater exploration. The concept of outer space was simply too bizarre, and I'm quite certain they did not believe us.

With the approach of summer—visitors. At the beginning of June Dr. and Mia Potts came from Holland and stayed at the *Oliver*, the inexpensive, popular *pensión*. We were happy to spend time with them without having to interrupt our schedules. There were other guests, fellow students from Iowa and Princeton. In a letter to my parents, Alan complained of people casually camping on our *sala* floor. 'They're on vacation, we are not. So many days are an intrusion,' he protested. 'The studio is out.'

Having completed the Workshop course from Iowa, I was no longer receiving feedback on my writing. Alan was an astute first reader, but the only one. I sent my parents stories, but heard nothing. A year and a half later in Saskatchewan, I entered a literary competition requiring a pseudonym. That's when Nina Barragan, my nickname and my mother's maiden name—without the accent—came into existence. 'The Subway Car', written on Ibiza, did not win, but it appeared in *The Wascana Review*, the English Department's literary journal—my first published story. (R. Weinstein was credited as the author, but N. Barragan stayed on, eventually emerging in print and becoming my formal pen name.)

My father finally wrote. His advice was that I had to stop being an observer. He grasped something I still had not.

1. Top: *Luis and Pilar Barragán*, Buenos Aires, ca. 1912.
2. Bottom: *Ana & Abram Lasansky*, Buenos Aires, ca. 1908.

3. Top: *Nina* (age three), [detail].
4. Middle: Diego Velázquez, *Las Meninas*, [detail] 1656, Prado Museum, photo/Art Resource.
5. Bottom: Mauricio Lasansky, *Little Girl*, 1968, intaglio, photo/Lasansky Archives.

6. Top: *Pilar Medina Fernández Barragán*, ca. 1950, photo/Lasansky Archives.
7. Center Left: *Luis Barragán* 1933, photo/Lasansky Archives.
8. Center right: *Aurelio and Teodoro Barragán*, Buenos Aires, ca. 1945, photo/Lasansky Archives.
9. Bottom: Adam Weinstein, *Self-portrait at 18*, oil on canvas, [detail].

10. Top left: *Emilia Barragán Lasansky*, [detail] Iowa City, 1948.

11. Top right: *Emilia*, left, & *Roberta Myers*, Minnesota, ca. 1947.

12. Middle: *Mauricio Lasansky*, left, & *Malcolm Myers*, Minnesota, ca. 1947.

13. Bottom left: Mauricio Lasansky, *Mi Hijo y su Reina de Baraja*s, 1942, drypoint, photo/
    Lasansky Archives.

14. Bottom right: Mauricio Lasansky, *Hugo Manning*, Los Cocos, Hotel Sarmiento, ca. 1943,
    pencil on paper.

15. Top: Mauricio Lasansky, *For an Eye an Eye III*, 1946-48, intaglio, photo/
    Lasansky Archives.
16. Bottom: *On the Saturnia*, 1953. (10-year-old Nina behind Emilia).

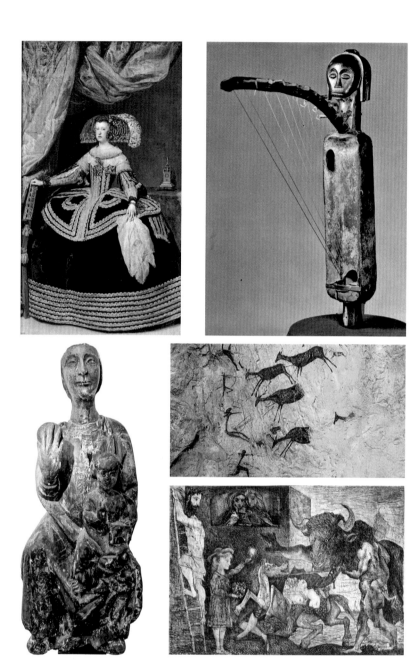

17. Top left: Diego Velázquez, *Queen Mariana of Austria*, 1652, Prado Museum, photo/Art Resource.
18. Top right: *Fang Harp*, Northern Gabon, Africa, photo/Lasansky Archives.
19. Bottom left: *Madonna and Child*, 15th century, Spanish, courtesy of Leonardo Lasansky.
20. Center: *Rock art from Cova dels Cavalls*, photo/Patronato Provincial de Turismo de Castellón, Spain.
21. Bottom right: Pablo Picasso, *Minotauromachy*, 1935, etching, photo/Art Resource & © 2021 Estate of Pablo Picasso/ Artists Rights Society (ARS), New York.

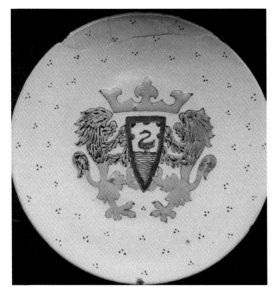

22. Top left: *Antique ceramic plate*, Spanish.
23. Bottom left: *Christ at the Column*, early Spanish panel painting, photo/Lasansky Archives.
24. Right: Unknown Artist, *Spanish Romanesque Sculpture of Christ*, late 12th century. Wood, 73 x 12, Cedar Rapids Museum of Art, Gift of Mauricio & Emilia Lasansky. 87.1.55 photo/Sue Bjork.

25. Top left: *Alan & Nina (in traditional dress), Ibiza*, 1965.
26. Top right: Alan Weinstein, *Portrait of Leonardo*, 1963, oil on canvas, courtesy of Amadeo Lasansky.
27. Bottom: *Nina & Alan's casa, Nina* left, *Mia Potts & Alan*, Ibiza, 1965, photo/Dr. Potts.

28. Top: *Medieval Tower,* Ibiza, photo/Jon Izeta.
29. Bottom: *Maria*, left, *José* and *Antonia*, Ibiza, 1965.

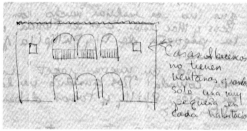

30. Top: *Finca near San José*, photo/Engel & Völkers, Ibiza S.L.
31. Center: *February 5, 1966, letter* [detail].
32. Bottom left: *La lavandera & Rita*, Ibiza, 1965.
33. Bottom right: *La Abuelita*, Ibiza, 1965.

34. Top: *Finca Can Cala*, photo/Rolph Blakstad, Ibiza.
35. Center: *Old Ibicenco bread oven*, photo/courtesy of www.Ibiza360.com.
36. Bottom: *Finca Can Pep d'en Salvador,* San Carlos, Ibiza, photo/Martin Davies, 1996.

37. *Albert and Elsa Einstein, and Konrad Wachsmann*, Caputh, Brandenburg, 1929-32, photo/Akademie der Künste, Berlin.

38. Top: *In the Age of Zhivago*, Regina, 1965.
39. Bottom: *Lasansky family*, U of I Museum of Art, 1976. Back row, *Alan, Jimena, Phillip, William, Leonardo, Terry* (Leo's wife) & *Mauricio*. Front row, *Nina, Emilia* & *Tomas*.

40. *Catenary arch kiln*, Teeswater, 1971.

41. Top: *Waxing pots*, Teeswater, 1971.
42. Bottom: *Dough mixer.*

43. Top: *Bitschy Pottery*, ca. 1880.
44. Center left: *Black chair*.
45. Center right: *Egyptian Man*, limestone.
46. Bottom: *The Huron Pottery*, Egmondville, photo/Huron County Historical Society,
    Goderich, ON.

47. Top: *Rachel, Anna, Daniel, Adam*, Saint-Brice-sous-Forêt, France, 1986.
48. Bottom: *Teeswater house.*

49. Top: *Vinalhaven Poor Farm*, ca. 1925, photo/Vinalhaven Historical Society,
    Vinalhaven, ME, & the Merrithew Glass Plate Negative Collection.
50. Bottom: *Poor Farm with privies*, 1956, photo/Lasansky Archives.

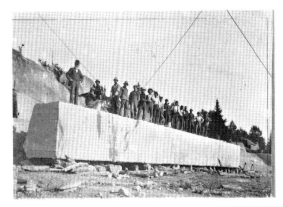

51. Top: *Block of granite*, ca. 1900, photo/Vinalhaven Historical Society, Vinalhaven, ME
& the Merrithew Glass Plate Negative Collection.

52. Center: *Lawson's Quarry*, Vinalhaven, photo/William Lasansky.

53. Bottom: *Granite quarry and workers*, Wells Lamson granite quarry, Barre Town, VT, ca.
1920's, courtesy of the Maurice Kelley Collection of the VT Granite Museum, Barre, VT.

54. Top: *Emilia, Nina, Mauricio*, 1986.
55. 56. 57. My Grandchildren: *Abraham, Johanna, Gabriel.*

'The Subway Car', 1966,
first published story,
under Rocio Weinstein,
The Wascana Review, 1967

AT LAST, THE ELDERLY GENTLEMAN on the subway train was alone, though his wife's talking still rang in his ears. His white suit, threadbare at the collar and tatty at the cuffs, was in its last throes; breathing peacefully, almost smiling, it hung limply from his slight frame. At breakfast, wearing her helmet of metal curlers, his wife Myra stood over him like a guard. Her short, plump body was lost under a new $4.99 Macy's special—a still stiff, sleeveless, pagoda-sprinkled cotton kimono with big patch pockets and brass buttons. The devoted gaze in her eyes had been enough to smooth his hair and press the creases in his grateful trousers. As every morning, Myra jabbered, carrying on incessantly about his health and his white suit. The man looked down. He could see absolutely no reason for buying a new one, and yet she bothered him about it every morning. His eyes drifted from the cuffs to the trousers. He felt the collar; he smoothed the front pockets. No, he could see nothing wrong. He stared at a spot of egg on his shirt and picked at it, slowly, methodically. Had his wife noticed, she would have made him change it. She was too busy talking. When finished about his suit, she began on the subject of his health. They all chatted about his condition—his colleagues, his friends, his relatives—somehow they found it a most interesting topic of conversation. The old man frowned and grumbled impatiently under his breath. Myra's fatty fingers had drummed out all those points again on the tabletop, all those reasons he shouldn't take the subway from his home to his office and laboratory every morning. "… an important, influential scientist, respected … so many prizes, awards …" She'd waved her arm dramatically pointing to the diplomas hanging on the dining room wall. Waiting patiently for him to crack his soft-boiled egg with his knife, she continued. "What's wrong with taxis?" He had nodded, squinting at his egg. "If you ever had an accident, if you fell, if you had an attack from the dirt and heat of the trains, we would never forgive ourselves," she said emotionally, packing his lunch attentively into his briefcase.

They would never forgive themselves—Myra, his colleagues, his friends, his relatives. The man was mumbling again. The red-headed lady next to him looked up, painted eyebrows raised. The young man next to her looked up. They exchanged knowing glances and looked down again.

After all these years, he still hadn't convinced them that he enjoyed riding the subways, that he enjoyed riding alone. When he told his colleagues, they coughed and smiled with embarrassment. He was an old man becoming senile. That was probably what they thought; in no time they might not allow him to enter his own laboratory. The incident that occurred three days before suddenly emerged. He was observing an experiment conducted by several of his assistants; they were taking too long and he was growing impatient with their cautiousness. Grabbing the test tube, he had wanted to show them how—but his hand shook and fumbled. Later, an assistant swept it up without a word. He wanted the incident to sink down in one of those crevices of his mind where it would not bother him again. His hand trembled as he pulled the briefcase up to his lap and opened it. It didn't mean a thing. So he had dropped a test tube … A hand-written note from his secretary was taped to the inside of his briefcase. He wiped his glasses and put them on. '… lecture at 11 A.M., lab. meeting at 2 P.M. with James P. McCawley, Alfred Rhines Jr., and two very important doctors from the French Academy …'

French Academy indeed. He shook his head, grumbling. She was perfectly aware of his friendship with … the man took off his glasses and closed his eyes, with … what were their names? He rubbed his forehead. It was strange that they should slip him so completely. When he received notice of their pending visit to New

York and his laboratory, he told his secretary about the last confer-
ence in France several years before, and how they had all spent a
week-end together. But how could he forget their names? Under
his breath he began to list French names. The red-head turned to
him again. To think that he had learned them so well—why they
had even congratulated him on his accent. He stared at the underlined words in front of him. What had his secretary felt as she
wrote and underlined? That wonderful sensation of importance
must have made her hand shake, her long red nails quivering like
feelers. Again he shook his head and replaced his glasses. Pushing
his lunch aside, he reached for the small note book containing his
lecture notes. He closed the briefcase and lowered it to the floor.
Amazing that he should forget. As he began flipping through the
pages, the subway train jerked to a stop and the doors flew open.

He looked up, he looked down. There was a sudden gush of hot
air, and then the crowd tumbled in. A girl with preoccupied dark
eyes walked on briskly. A scent of talcum powder followed close
behind her. With self-conscious sophistication she sat down on the
bench opposite the man. She seemed calmly aware that many eyes
followed every movement she made.

He took off his glasses and looked up again. At the same moment, she too looked up. His glasses and the book shook in his
hands. The scent of talcum tickled his nostrils. The girl dropped her
eyes to some school papers she had pulled out of her bag. He could
not take his eyes off her. How delightful, how marvelous youth was.
How intriguing that this girl, so beautiful as she already was, should
have her whole life to look forward to. Her thick, dark hair was
piled carelessly into a bun at the back of her neck, and so white and
soft a neck. Damp, moody wisps stuck to her forehead. His eyes wa-
tered; his thoughts faltered. A wave of giddiness rushed over him.
He leaned his head against the bench and closed his eyes.

Distance and time began to swirl and dissolve. He seemed
to be pushing through turbulent gray clouds of years that sucked
back into shape once he was out of them. Back, years and years
… back, until he was sitting in a field of poppies so vast he could

not see where it ended. A young girl, a familiar girl with a fair complexion and long white dress was rushing toward him. She reached him just as the train came to a stop, her black eyes brimming with eagerness, flooding her face. The crowds changed; the doors slammed. Then he saw her clearly. He saw the white skin of her raised arm vibrating with the train, the curlers bobbed, fingers drummed. He stared. Her white face and eyelids were overgrown with wrinkles and veins. He stared, startled, but calm. After all these years, how could he be shocked. His head shook with the train. In truth, it took effort to see her young. He tried to remember. Back, back through all those years. He tried to wipe his forehead with his handkerchief but his hand would not stop shaking. The red-headed lady squirmed on the seat and looked at him suspiciously. He wadded his handkerchief. What was it he was … yes, yes, there was no escaping the effects of time. He wanted to look at the girl sitting across from him, but he held himself back. He tried to concentrate on his notes, but the letters turned somersaults before his eyes and the heat had pushed through his suit to every inch of his body. The girl raised her face from her papers. His lips quivered and formed a smile. She looked away, head high, neck straight, pretending she had not seen. The red-head leaned forward enough to catch his eyes, a sneer curling her lips. He turned and stared blankly at the painted eye-brows.

If only her father could see her now. The girl smiled mischievously at the thought of her father's face when he saw people look at her. He would probably faint if he knew how many looked at her now. Her eyes sparkled. She thought of the time not so long ago when she would sit in the back seat of her family's car, her father eyeing her anxiously through his rear view mirror. Frowning, waiting, he used to watch for the expression on her face as they happened to drive by a group of young boys glancing at the car. Her poor father, she smiled knowingly. He probably knew very well what it was like in the city—he had been completely opposed to her going away. If she had not gotten that scholarship, he would never have allowed her to leave. A flow of old thoughts bubbled up;

impatiently she let them rush over her. Up until that last week he had tried, in all the ways he knew, tried to keep her at home.

She remembered the endless talks and arguments. With great emotion he told her she would not be happy. He had even resorted to stomping out of rooms, clouds hanging low on his face. But finally, she had won. She was studying in New York. For a few seconds, she smiled at her reflection in the glass. She smoothed her hair and shifted in her seat. How wrong he had been saying she would not like it. She loved the city—being lost in crowds, going to classes, crossing wide streets. It was hard to believe she had actually been nervous before leaving home. She blushed away the thought. Frowning impatiently, she recalled the disturbances that ruled her home the week before she left. Her mother, continually stopping in her tracks to nestle a small hand under the gray wave spilling out over her preoccupied forehead, her eyes tightly closed—there were so many things she'd never told her daughter. Her father, nervously pacing the house, the rose garden.

On that last day before she left, he moved through his roses, pipe and cane in hand, distractedly poking at the earth around the bushes. They were just beginning their last stretch of August glory. And she, she stood with her forehead pressed against the cool glass of her bedroom window, watching. Looking down through the large oaks, down, down to the sprawling backyard, lethargic with summer's end—she watched his every movement. Somehow she expected him to make violent, jerking motions with his arms, or clench his fists. But no. He'd puffed thoughtfully on his pipe, bent to examine a rosebud, straightened up and continued on through his bushes. She had been so nervous. The girl on the subway blushed again and re-crossed her legs. Up in her bedroom, moisture had glistened on her forehead as she fidgeted anxiously with the cord of the shade. Turning to glance around the room, she took in her trunk, suit cases, umbrella and rain coat. The book she would finish reading on the train lay by her purse, *Orlando*. Orlando! A huge, unexpected wave rushed toward her. Orlando with his white marble forehead pressed against the attic window, his unbearable mother, the peacocks in his garden, all bobbing in the foamy water. Thoughts began to thump in her head as she looked down again— her father's arm around her shoulder as they walked along a street, her feeling of pride with his occasional words of praise. But she held tightly to the shade's cord, and finally, the thoughts retreated. Breathing deeply, she watched her father walking calmly, coolly, but she knew the possessive feelings that must be surging, the self-nourished sadness weighing on his shoulders. And at that very second, that very second of possessive thoughts, she knew he would turn around in his path and look up at her window. Their eyes met (for she had not been quick enough to avoid them) and he looked away, seas of silent words in his sad, disturbing gaze.

The old man on the subway was entranced. What thoughts could possibly be rushing through her young mind at that moment? As much as he knew he should, he could not look away from her ravishingly strange gaze. Her head turned sharply. She looked at him quickly, coldly. His hands shook, his head throbbed. Again he attacked the perspiration with his handkerchief and fumbled for his notebook. He must read over his notes. She watched his nervous, awkward movements. A bored impatient look crossed her eyes and she looked away, eager to be rid of his old face.

Thoughts of leaving home uncovered a whirl of ideas clamoring within. All those times she hated the world and made promises to herself, came gushing back. Promises to be someone, to leave something behind, something for later generations. Her eyes glowed, her hands played with her school papers. Was it meant that only a handful from every period would be the markers of truth and guides of future generations? Was it meant that most should live in their niches of contentment, and that in the end, if they had never lived, it would not have mattered at all? She frowned. Her neck straightened, her chin became firmer. There was one thing she was sure of. Her eyes scurried across the subway car. She would not be like the rest of them. She would not be undistinguished like that bored, old man with the insipid face who insisted on staring at her. What had he done with his life, what had he left? She watched as he fumbled with his handkerchief, as he picked at the spot of egg on his shirt. He inched forwards, sideways, and then, the red-headed lady snapped around, impatience glowing on her face, little puffs of disgust forming around her mouth. Coarsely, crudely, she jerked her skirt out from under his thigh. The old man turned. Nodding, smiling with embarrassment, he edged away from her on the bench. The girl smiled, her eyes sparkling. She almost giggled. The young man on the other side of the red-head laughed aloud.

The gentleman fumbled with his book, his hands shook. The laughter splashed and broke against his ears. He looked down. He was a senile old man who shouldn't be allowed on the subways. His colleagues were right; his wife was right. His eyelids fluttered; the egg stain vibrated on his shirt. He was so feeble that someday he would have an accident. It would be better if old people did not exist. Wasn't that what they were thinking? He looked up.

No doubt now she is thinking she will not be like the rest of us, all the common, dull people surrounding her. She looks at me with boredom, impatience. Her eyes tell me that she will not be like me, like all of us who are kept going for a life-time merely by the daily challenges of our small lives. She will go beyond this, beyond us. She will find truths, many truths, and she will crystallize them. Now it was his turn to stare out the window. The giddiness left him and his head stopped throbbing but his face took on a greyish pallor. Isn't this what we all promise ourselves when we start out? Surely we are all convinced, as she is, that we are one of those des-tined—his mouth formed a tight, narrow smile, a shiver skipped across his back—destined to "crystallize truths." But she is right to ask herself why it is that those of us around her, no matter what we have done, can only see our lives as failures when the time is up.

Again he saw his wife's arm raised toward his diplomas, prizes, awards, and he shuddered. He was famous; he was well known, and Myra was happy. But what did she know about his work? What did she understand, what did she care? Myra would never under-stand that only now, now after a life time he was prepared to begin working. Only now he would be able to get beyond ... but why should she understand, not even his colleagues understood. And you, the man looked up. The spell of youth and beauty, shattering like a mirror, reflected on his face. What will you make of your young, beautiful life? Quite suddenly, a foolish, wonderful thought crossed his mind. He felt he could jump up and kiss the back of her white neck. Only a little of course, and quickly, as if nothing had happened.

The girl arranged her books and papers into her bag. Her stop was next, and if she wasn't quick enough, she would be late to class again. In a few seconds she was off the car and walking briskly along the long platform. It was a relief to be off the train. She smiled at the thought of the red-head and the old man. She glanced at the movie advertisements and pushed past unfamiliar faces. Six, seven, her car had been the eighth one away from the exit that morning. As she passed under the neon exit sign and was hurrying up the set of stairs, two chatty young girls who had seemed in a great hurry to get down, abruptly stopped a few steps above her. Their mouths froze, they gasped. It took her an instant to realize they were staring beyond her. She spun around as they sped past her. A maze of people were entering and leaving the subway cars. Trains rumbled above. A maintenance man with a blond mustache was refilling a gum machine immediately to her right. Beyond it all, she could see that a crowd had formed at the subway car door she had just stepped out of. People pushed and shoved and hurried on and off the cars. Most of them did not even realize a crowd had gathered at one of the far cars. Through all the movement and noise, she could see the crowd clearly. She saw silent women clutching their collars, mouths open. Men stared down, arms hanging uselessly at their sides. The two girls who had stopped a few steps above her were already there. She felt her heart leap to her throat and her body become weightless. Past the mustached maintenance man, past the first car, she hurried. The second, did these people not realize what had happened? The third car, the fourth, her throat was tight, her heels clacked with every step. She ran the length of the last few cars, and finally, she was there. A choking stillness hung over the crowd. Like some huge beast, stirring, turning over in its sleep, the crowd swayed, gasped. It pushed forward, closer, mumbling, "It happened so quickly. I saw him …" Mumbling, "he just stepped out and …" Whispering, "horrible … poor man …" Whispering, "… heart attack …" She too pushed, she had to see—the white suit, the handkerchief, the briefcase. But if she didn't hurry, she would be late to her class.

As the girl walked away from the crowd, she threw back her head and raised her shoulders. A slight, damp breeze had passed the back of her neck and made her shiver.

Ibiza, summer 1965

M Y SMALL STUDY IN OUR Ibiza house had a tiny, west-facing window in the thick, stone wall. Late afternoon light bathed the round wooden table, my green typewriter, the piles of paper. Very little came easily. I wrote, re-wrote, cut and pasted—common stuff before computers. My manuscripts were messes of crossed-out, scotch-taped paragraphs on yellow newsprint-like paper. When the feeling of swimming against the current overwhelmed me, I became more determined not to be pulled under. I was 22. Despite having few interruptions beyond the activities of daily life—we were not interested in the Ibicenco party scenes—I did not work hard enough, or long enough hours.

But I read. Literature was my chief obsession. The Russians, and a great deal of Virginia Woolf, all by the glow of our Coleman lamp. The books, purchased in London, accompanied our belongings from Holland to Ibiza.

That month in London we divided our time between the National Gallery and the British Museum—long days of visual confirmation and discovery. The year before, university art history classes bolstered my interests but made clear the massive amounts to learn. The British became our second home. In her vast galleries, Egypt, Mesopotamia and Greece came alive, while poster size signage, black lettering on white, brought history and geography into clear focus. Purchasing post cards of choice works, we recouped in the museum's Tea Room while writing our families. The British Museum carried me into past worlds and two significant encounters—one with Virginia Woolf, the other with Queen Tetisheri of

Egypt. The story surrounding Tetisheri eventually linked my writing and Alan's work in a joint project.

One afternoon in the British, Alan left me to visit the impressive reading room while he went off to explore. After inquiring if the library had original manuscripts by V. Woolf, I was told they had *Mrs. Dalloway*. At twenty-two, I expected no less. After all, I'd already encountered MacKinlay Kantor's original manuscript of *Andersonville* at the University of Iowa libraries. In my last year of high school, Dr. John Haefner took his senior Social Studies class on a tour of the Rare Book Room.

I waited patiently for the Reading Room librarian to return from the archives. Presented with an ordinary manuscript box, the only request was that I take notes in pencil, rather than pen. Daunted? Not really, just very pleased. Now I'm amazed thinking about it. How was it that a 'non-credentialed' young woman—not a scholar, not even a 'bookish' grad student with the backing of a respected University—was permitted to walk off with *Mrs. Dalloway*? It was like the first time Alan and I visited Stonehenge. We descended the bus and walked right up to the stones, circling in and out, touching them gently. By the time we took our children twenty years later, it had become a restricted site, roped off and protected. As it should be. (Prior to 1900, visitors were handed chisels so they might take home a souvenir of the 5,000-year-old monument.)

At the reading table, carefully turning onion skin, typed pages, I read through hand written corrections, the confident cross-outs, the notes scribbled onto margins. V.W.'s changes made complete sense. I understood and recognized the manner of working. But my writing, with so many alterations, so much cutting and pasting, never looked like Virginia's manuscripts, clean and self-assured.

Recent inquiries have turned up disturbing information and I've had to accept that my memory has probably failed me. It turns out the library's holdings include three hand written volumes of notebooks for *The Hours/Mrs. Dalloway*, but no typescript of the work. Apparently the MS, typed by Virginia and mentioned in her diary, was sent to the printers in Edinburgh, and shortly after the book's publication, the pages were lost in a fire. That would have been in 1924-25. So what did I see that afternoon in October of 1964? Could it have been different draft of *Dalloway*, or another of Virginia's typed manuscripts? I've researched the scholarship on *Mrs. Dalloway*. I've checked into the archives of both the British Museum and British Library. (In 1973, the library was separated from the museum but wasn't moved to its new location in St. Pancras until 1997.) Nothing. There is no record of such a manuscript. Could it have been stolen? For decades I've lived with the memory of studying the typed *Mrs. Dalloway*. The experience of that hour, the feeling of camaraderie, the opportunity to observe Virginia's re-working, became a star in my sky.

The Tetisheri story began a couple months after we were married, the day a man entered *Things, Things and Things*, a popular Iowa City hippie shop. He was interested in selling several boxes of antiquities that had been in his garage for years—they'd belonged to his archeologist father who had been in Egypt in the 1920's. The shop owners, former art students at the University, finalized the purchase and placed a call to the art department. The faculty, my father included, dropped their work and hurried to town. Word spread. By the time Alan and I heard about the cache of artifacts, one of the few remaining pieces was a twelve inch high limestone figurine of a young Egyptian seated on a bench, a braid adorning the right side of his head. The twenty-five dollar expenditure was a big deal at the time, and we gave it careful thought before writing the check. When we asked Pa why it wasn't included in his selection of several smaller objects, he said the piece just didn't feel right.

The following year, while in Toronto to bid Alan's parents farewell before our departure for Europe, we took our ancient friend over to the Egyptian Department at the Royal Ontario Museum. We had to leave him for a couple days so he could be studied. During that interval, the ROM insured him for several thousand dollars. We were impressed, and so was Alan's dad.

In the end, his authenticity could not be confirmed. Winifred Needler, Egyptian expert and Curator of the Near Eastern Department, had never seen baboons carrying lotus leaves like the ones incised on his bench, and the hieroglyphics didn't make sense. Our curiosity piqued, we packed a couple photographs in our luggage, left our Egyptian friend on my parents-in-law's living room mantel, and departed for England.

Convinced our limestone youth must have a history, we were determined to discover his provenance. The British Museum seemed the perfect place. The baboon business did not deter us— Ms. Needler admitted being perplexed. A search through the upstairs Egyptian rooms finally led us to his mate, the delicate Queen Tetisheri—same size, same feeling, surely the same hand. Scantily attired, serenely holding court in her glass case, she appeared oblivious to the unheated gallery.

Some years later, leaving our toddlers in the care of our Teeswater neighbor Wilma G.—of the black chair story—we embarked on a 10-day trip to Paris and London. Eager to see Queen Tetisheri again, we were stunned and disappointed to find her glass case empty. A posted sign included details of a published article, available in the gift shop library, as well as an explanation. Having recently been found to be a forgery—the clumsy hieroglyphics, the wig's design, the style of her dress, specifically the shoulder straps— Tetisheri had been sent to storage. Shocked, I stood before the empty case, remembering Pa's comment that the piece just didn't feel right.

In time, I wrote about our friend, flash fiction for a 1,000 word competition, and in 1988, it became a joint project. *The Egyptian Man*, a large format book with my narrative and six of Alan's etchings. The story? The owner must sell his beloved figurine to pay for his son's gender reassignment surgery. He's still with us, our seated Egyptian, and still loved, unconditionally.

Back to Ibiza and that small room with the western light and my green typewriter. Decades have passed, but writing can still be agony, and I allow it. The pain eases when I think of Thomas Mann's quote:

> *"A writer is someone for whom writing is more difficult than it is for other people."*

With the summer heat upon us, Alan and I purchased two used bicycles for the ride out to the ocean near Sant Jordi. We wore hats and loose, long sleeve shirts. Neither of us could tolerate the sun. We swam, but rarely remained to stretch out on the sand.

We made an exception for the poet, Paul Oppenheimer, Alan's Princeton classmate. He came to visit with his girlfriend, Ginger—a tall, stunning redhead, a sweet girl with weak Spanish language skills. That afternoon we did linger on the beach, enough to get sunburned and fuzzy from the red wine Paul brought in his knapsack. When Ginger noticed the sentinel medieval defense tower further down the coast, she asked what it was. Without missing a beat, Paul said it was the 'exit'.

The following evening, when they arrived for dinner from the *Oliver*, Ginger told us she'd had trouble on the beach that morning. While sunbathing in her bikini, several men came to ogle and pester.

"I told them to go away—*Vámonos!*—but it made thing worse and more men gathered around."

"*Vámonos* means let's go. *Váyanse*, go away, might have worked better." I'd seen Ginger in her bikini. Nothing she said would have made those men go away.

By the end of July, after weeks of corresponding with printers and engravers in Barcelona, we finally located an old press. We hurried to make ferry reservations. With the hordes of seasonal tourists visiting Ibiza, crossing to Barcelona in the summer months was impossible without advance booking.

Buenos Aires, 1923

A S A SMALL GIRL IN Villa Devoto, Buenos Aires, Emilia could be found occupying the front steps of her family home. A petite child with dark eyes and black ringlets, a starched pinafore and white socks bunching down her legs, she could sit for hours caring for her dolls, attentively watching the neighborhood goings-on. Her parents were perplexed by the insatiable curiosity, veering toward nosiness. Nevertheless, it was an innocent enough pastime, and seeing no reason to end it, they gently acquiesced. My grandmother, Pilar, adjusted her apron and returned to the kitchen. My grandfather, Luis, cigar and hat in hand, stooped to kiss the curly head on his way out the door.

Emilia was born the second of three and the only girl, pretty and indulged. Her father was in the grocery business in Buenos Aires—wholesale and retail, with partners and without. There were multiple bankruptcies, but he always resurfaced. At the prime of his life, it was barrels of dried codfish and vats of olive oil imported from Spain, biscotti from Italy, coffee from Brazil. By the end, he was dealing in extracts and tinctures—the essential oils of today.

Traveling to his clients on bicycle, the tiny bottles were carried in a leather shoulder bag. In a snapshot taken of me before we left Argentina—a blond toddler bundled in my grandmother's knits— I'm sitting on the bicycle's handlebars as my grandfather prepares to pedal off to his clients.

During the depression, *Comestibles Barragán,* the Barragán Grocery, kept the family in relative comfort. My grandmother was a diligent housekeeper; quietly steadfast, she tended to her own and any neighbors in need. Too busy and too private to be out and about, the neighborhood soup deliveries were relegated to the affable Emilia. Everyone was happy with the arrangement.

Comfortably middle class, the family extended to include aunts, uncles and endless cousins on my grandmother's side. My grandfather's two bachelor brothers, the spiffy dressers, Aurelio and Teodoro, both musicians, moved to Chile as young men. The family's Spanish heritage endures, though not as tenaciously, and the striking white manes of the Barragáns continues. The *Abuelo Luis* had a fine head of hair in his youth, but eventually he too went bald, as both his brothers. The trait of snowy locks has been linked to the Barragán name, but conceivably that DNA information traveled the maternal Fernández/Medina line, rather than the paternal Galgo/Barragáns. Music, art and hits of rebellion moved up and down those Iberian double helixes. Two of my mother's uncles were cobblers.

"Anarchists ..." my father told me one evening, *sotto voce*, index finger tapping the side of his nose—a sign of irrefutable information.

"That's why they were shoemakers, so they could work independently and not have to tolerate a boss."

He must have known I'd just studied Sacco and Vanzetti in my tenth grade Social Studies class. His dialogue included none of the usual embellishments. It was the same in 2001 when I was doing research for *Losers and Keepers*. Asking him about the white slave trade that plagued Buenos Aires for more than five decades, he told me his old man had called it a curse and pestilence, a disgrace. He was ashamed of being a *lantzman*, countryman, to those scandalous Polish Jews. Leaders of the *Zvi Migdal* network, they controlled the organized trafficking of Jewish women for prostitution. I was fascinated that Pa willingly revealed such intimate words and feelings. He didn't often speak of his father, but he clearly agreed with his sentiments. Hearing those cries of *shanda*, disgrace, attributed to my grandfather, an exciting urgency possessed me. No matter how private and separate we considered ourselves—the Lasansky gene pool overflows with determined independence—we were, nevertheless, three generations tied to community, to causes greater than our individual lives, to values of dignity and humanity beyond our personal worlds. I was proud of both of them, and proud to be daughter and granddaughter.

from May 12, 1904: THE RIFKE CHRONICLES
Losers and Keepers in Argentina,
A book of fiction,
published, 2001

THE OTHER NIGHT, MY INTENTION was to write about Bela Palatnik, a remarkable young woman. Bela is struggling with a shocking reality that most of us cannot begin to comprehend.

On the evening of May 9th, when we arrived at headquarters for our usual printing work and union meeting, we were told that Moses Soltansky, Marcus's son, would be bringing a visitor to speak to us. I assumed it would be yet another representative from one of the anarchist cells or some other group wanting to convince us to join forces with them. They come around so often now, and they're exhausting with their commitment and almost violent zeal. At about half past nine, while we were busy cleaning the press and assembling the flyers, our work was interrupted by the code knock at the back door. I unlocked and opened. Moses stood smiling shyly in the doorway; beside him, a pale, young woman with determined eyes shivered in the dim light of the alley. She seemed too frail to be an anarchist. Moses is a tall, burly man of twenty with a head of thick, curly red hair. His friends call him Big Moses. He did not follow his father into the tailoring profession. His large, rough hands could never hold a needle. Moses is a metalworker. On the evening of May 9th, he seemed as meek as a lamb beside this strange, young woman.

After Moses gently led her in, he introduced Bela and announced that she had come to tell us about the white slave trade and the misfortunes she encountered arriving in this country. Bela's slight figure was wrapped in a dark woolen shawl. Her attire was drab, devoid of any indication of the life she had been forced to lead for nine months.

Bela began speaking in a quiet voice. Slowly it took on more volume as her story progressed. She was anxious for us to know there were more girls like her, trapped in a nightmare existence with nowhere to turn and little hope for escape. Determined to help the others, she kept repeating that she was one of the lucky ones, she got away. Bela's dark eyes and small, pretty face displayed a dedication that overwhelmed us all, and her tale held us transfixed for the duration of the evening. She spoke eloquently—her voice and story softened hearts in our drafty warehouse full of toughened, young revolutionaries.

Bela Palatnik landed at the port of Buenos Aires a year ago. She arrived on a ship from Germany, destined for the Clara Colony in Entre Rios where she had an aunt and uncle. I was struck by how similar her story was to mine, even though I was older and had arrived earlier. She too left her parents and family behind, she in Vilna, I in Tomaschpol. She too traveled alone, except for the friend she made on ship, another young woman also headed for a colony.

"We were met at the pier by a well-dressed, well-mannered couple. The woman, stout and friendly, announced that she too had come from Vilna. In a soft-spoken voice, the man explained that he represented a hotel for newly arrived young women, a haven where we might stay for a few nights before proceeding with our journeys. Exhausted from the voyage and frightened by the strangeness of our new surroundings, we eagerly accepted the couple's invitation to lead us to the hotel. Not until we arrived at the 'hotel' was the true nature of the situation revealed to us. The man was paid by the owner of the establishment, a Mrs. Guttman, for delivering us. It was horrible. In all my days in Vilna I had no idea such things happened. I had no idea that it was possible for a woman to be 'sold' for her body. Until I arrived here, I did not even know the word 'brothel.'

"I see from the look on some of your faces that you are wondering how my friend and I could have been so innocent, so naive as to follow strange people across Buenos Aires. You are right, we were naive. But the important thing is that we were no different than so many of the young women who arrive here alone. It happens every day. More and more Jewish women are being forced into prostitution and most often by Jewish perpetrators."

Bela Palatnik dropped her head. "My parents in Vilna know nothing, nor do my aunt and uncle in Colony Clara. I have never written them." Bela remained silent for a few moments. "I prefer to have them think I am dead."

I stood up and moved to sit beside Bela, to be near her, to offer support. Another woman in the audience followed my lead. Bela continued with her story.

"If you had known me a year ago upon my arrival, you would understand. I was a pleasant enough looking girl, but young and with no great reserve of nerve, and certainly no sense of commitment to anything in particular. I was journeying to the Colony Clara to live with my aunt and uncle in this new country. Like most young girls, my greatest concern was finding a husband and having a beautiful dress for my wedding. It all seems a lifetime ago. I can hardly believe I was ever that girl." Bela closed her eyes for a few moments, clearly drawing on inner strength. "I intend to dedicate myself to helping girls in distress—to fighting this horrible evil that is plaguing our women."

There was quiet clapping in the room. A quick smile passed Bela's lips. She no longer looked quite as frail as she had shivering at our back door. As she spoke, she became energized with dignity and strength.

"If it hadn't been for Moses Soltansky, I might still be in that awful place. It was Moses who helped me escape." Bela looked in Moses's direction. He acknowledged with a shy nod.

"How did you manage to get away?" Someone asked curiously from the audience.

"Moses happened to be walking beside Mrs. Guttman's 'hotel' when I threw a small rock out the window. I had tied a note to the stone, explaining the situation and the nature of the place, asking for help. The timing was luck," Bela said softly. "Moses promptly returned the next day with several large companions." Bela grinned for the first time. "After some discussion, I was permitted to leave the establishment without much problem, although Mrs. Guttman stood in the doorway jeering at us as we departed."

"As for my friend," Bela's smile disappeared, "I don't know where she is. We were separated only days after our arrival at the brothel. I heard people whispering that she was taken to another establishment in another city."

"Maybe the owners of the place should be forced to reveal where they sent your friend!" An angry voice called out from the back of the room. "There are plenty of us who wouldn't mind marching over to that address this very evening!" Cheering began in the warehouse.

"No!" Moses Soltansky jumped up. "That's not the way!" He took a few moments to collect himself.

I've always known Moses to be a shy young man, a reticent speaker. But that evening, he became an orator. Driven by his obvious feelings for Bela and his disgust for white slavery, he quickly overcame his shyness.

"We must be systematic, organized," he continued. "It's the only way. Violence will only attract the police, and the police are involved in this terrible ring of prostitution. The white slavers are referred to as the *tmeyim*, the unclean ones, and they've become a powerful organization. They have enormous control and they're steadily gaining. Politics, law enforcement, the business world, the theater."

Here Bela interrupted. "They've even formed their own synagogue and benevolent society. Last Yom Kippur, I actually saw a Madame taking her 'girls' in for services!"

"My father can tell you," Moses said, glancing at Marcus. "He can tell you of how they have not been allowed to bury their dead in our cemetery, although they've certainly tried."

Marcus Soltansky spoke slowly and articulately. "As many of you know, I am on the board of the Congregation Israelita's burial society. A few years ago, in 1899, the *tmeyim* wanted to donate an enormous sum of money to the synagogue—to insure their people proper Jewish burials—but they were turned away, thank God. I understand they have finally bought their own cemetery, and that the Moroccans have bought a piece from them with a meter strip of land separating the 'pure' from the 'impure'."

Moses raised his arm. "Perhaps some of you don't know of these things because you do not frequent their establishments. But I tell you, they are a pestilence. We must work to rid our community of them."

Applause broke out.

"What's to be done?" Aaron M. asked quietly from the shadows of the headquarters.

"Many things," Moses said. "We can write home to family and friends in Europe, warning them of the dangers to their daughters, sisters, and yes, even wives. Many girls are brought under false pretenses. Dealers go to small towns in Europe, collecting girls by promising to bring them to Buenos Aires where jobs and husbands await them. The girls are usually violated during the voyage by the dealers themselves. By the time they arrive in Argentina, they have no choice but to enter a brothel."

Bela stood up. "We can patrol the port when ships arrive," she said eagerly. "We can make sure girls are not led away in the manner that I was, and my friend. At times the girls are lured with offers of candies and perfumes. We can send women onto the ships to warn the girls and to encourage them to be very cautious. The Jewish Association for the Protection of Girls and Women has been working with Scotland Yard, helping to track down missing women who traveled to Argentina by way of England. Posting warning signs in the port buildings is a good idea, but I'm afraid that won't help much because so many girls can't read. Then, of course, you men can actually rescue women from brothels, the way I was. By pretending to frequent these establishments and keeping your eyes open, you can help many escape. Then there's the problem of where these girls go after. They are no longer considered respectable for marriage," Bela's voice quavered, but she continued, "and many cannot return to their families or continue on to the families they were joining." Bela turned to Moses.

He nodded and began speaking again. "As for how you deal with men who knowingly sell their wives and daughters into prostitution, I don't know." Moses stared out across his audience. His large figure with the shock of red hair was an enormous presence in our suddenly hushed warehouse. It was as though everyone had stopped breathing. "I've heard," Moses began again. "I've heard of this happening with a family bound for the Colony of Moisés Ville. Once they arrived at the colony, things seemed so very bleak, the husband—to his wife's horror—turned around and sold their eldest daughter to the white slave 'trader' who had pursued them all the way from Buenos Aires. That 'trader,' that disgusting piece of garbage, was a Jew."

When Moses and Bela had no more to say, the atmosphere in the warehouse was heavy and still. I felt as though I might choke. We were left speechless and shocked by this story. I, like everyone else in the room, felt only grief. One never likes to hear of the existence of evil amongst your own, and in the place you call home.

Buenos Aires, 1927

"WHEN YOUR MA AND I were kids in Buenos Aires, if you were Spanish or Italian, and a shoemaker, everyone knew you were an anarchist."

Then came the story about a certain Villa Devoto shoemaker and his collection of Italian art books. The impressive volumes stored under his cobbler's bench were a draw for the neighborhood's aspiring, young artists. Pa was one. My mother's brother, Luis, another. They were 13 and admiring images from the Italian Renaissance when Sacco and Vanzetti were executed in Boston in August of 1927. While those neighborhood boys thumbed their way across pages of Italian painting, oohing and aahing and wiping noses on sleeves, I wonder if the anarchist shoemaker held his tongue about Boston, out of respect for the youthful dreams in his midst.

In May, immediately after the Sacco and Vanzetti death sentences were announced, the US embassy in Buenos Aires was bombed. In July, the statue of George Washington in Palermo Park was blown up. After the executions in August, a 24-hour city-wide general strike was called in protest. The Italian born Argentine anarchist, Severino de Giovanni, along with his comrades, was responsible for the chaos and violence. Over the next five years they continued committing acts of aggression, many against American organizations in Buenos Aires: The Ford Motor Company, Citibank and the Bank of Boston.

In December of 1928, Herbert Hoover, who was visiting Argentina as Secretary of Commerce (he would become the 31st U.S. president the following year), narrowly escaped an attempt on his life. As Hoover's train moved down the Andes from Chile and across the pampas, the bomb plot Severino de Giovanni planned was foiled. Hoover was safe, as was the extraordinary 2,000-year-old Paracas textile given to him in Peru, one of several scheduled stops on that 1928 South American goodwill trip. It's conceivable the ancient piece was shipped back to the States from Lima, but I prefer thinking it was carefully packed and intentionally retained with the personal luggage, to be strictly guarded.

President-elect Hoover's successful visit to Peru was reported in the *New York Times* on Dec. 6, 1928. The citizens of Lima witnessed parades and heard speeches enthusiastically announcing hopes for closer ties between the two countries. Hoover was presented with the king's mantle by Peru's President Augusto Leguía and Professor Julio C. Tello, a leading Peruvian archeologist and Director of the Museum of Peruvian Archeology. There were other gifts, including a solid gold Inca mask, but the Paracas textile, spectacular for its size, artistry and age, was surely the star.

The incredible weaving, 12 ft. long and 5.5 ft. high, eventually ended up at the Herbert Hoover Presidential Library and Museum in Hoover's hometown of West Branch, Iowa.

On a visit to the museum, Alan and I heard an intriguing anecdote from a curator, but I've found no evidence to confirm it. His theory was that Hoover's 1928 visit included a trip to the National Museum of Peruvian Archeology. Shown the many artifacts gathered from the newly discovered necropolis at Paracas, he admired the king's mantle in a display case. President Leguía ordered Tello to open the case, and the textile was gifted to Hoover, then and there.

I liked the story for its multiple implications. During an official State visit focusing on political and economic ties, a tour of the national museum of art was deemed imperative. In addition, the story speaks of an era when a leader's positive—if somewhat maverick—actions, could override accepted conventions and conduct of his time. And finally, as Herbert Hoover paused before that display case, momentarily captivated by the mantle's perfectly preserved technical and artistic accomplishment, hopefully he was both mindful of the historic achievement and visually moved by the ancient weaving. I'd like to think our mining-engineer-future-president left the museum empowered—his aesthetic acumen heightened, his emotional response more passionate. Both assets that would surely stand him in good, presidential stead.

As a kid, we used to take family drives into the countryside around Iowa City, but the Hoover museum did not open its doors to the public until 1962. After my adult visit, I told my father about seeing the amazing textile. He was not aware of it and I don't know he ever visited the museum.

If he did go and stand before it, would he have connected the wool knots of its creation with those events of his youth—the Villa Devoto cobbler, Sacco and Vanzetti, Severino de Giovanni, Herbert Hoover's near fatal train ride? Or is such a thought the farfetched machinations of a daughter, eager to seek such ties, finding solace in linking the comfort of fabric with the tough realities of life?

EXCERPT
'Whatever Became of Robin Bender?', 1986
No Peace at Versailles, and other stories,
published, 1990

WHAT, ROBIN WONDERED, WHAT WOULD she have been in her other life? Amongst the Paracas, she might have been trusted with the embroidering of a great mantle for chief. Sitting in her niche of a dusty, ochre Peruvian landscape, chewing coca leaves to ward off the cold, she would labor for years on the same task, eagerly interpreting and recording the Paracas Gods that her eyes and coca-leaf-psyche understood. Human-headed serpents, cat-like creatures holding trophy heads, birds and whales—the spirits of nature. Would a feverish determination eventually take control of her senses, or could a calm prevail until the last creature showed its articulate, colored outline?

Buenos Aires, 1931

AURICIO AND LUIS WERE 17 when the anarchist Severino de Giovanni was finally captured, tried, and summarily executed by Buenos Aires police.

Turbulent times. What was it like to circumvent trouble in 1931 Buenos Aires? Did those two young men want to demonstrate against injustice, or did they see themselves as apolitical? Luis and his younger brother, Julio, both painters, remained in Argentina all their lives. From conversations I had in Buenos Aires, it was apparent my uncles learned to protect themselves and their families, especially during the political repression and state terrorism of *la guerra sucia*, the dirty war of the mid 70's and early 80's. As much as possible, they distanced themselves from turmoil, escaping to the privacy and safety of their studios.

Society's difficult periods, the Perón era in Argentina, the Depression and 1930's in the States, typically witnessed outspoken activism from the ranks of artists' wives—alert, intelligent women frequently more interested and better informed than their husbands about current events. This was true of my uncle Julio's wife, Nieves, a three-newspapers-a-day anti-Peronist, a gifted sculptor, a devoted wife and mother. I hope there's been research conducted and PhD theses written about these resolute women, many of them artists. Their own creative lives regularly suffered, because of the times, because they were daughters, wives and mothers, and often, because they were constitutionally incapable of the commitment creativity requires, nearly to the exclusion of all else. With energy to burn, they became devoted political and social activists. A global phenomena that knows no borders.

If my father had remained in Argentina, he might have become more politically active. It was fortuitous that his Guggenheim fellowship took him away to study in New York, just when his condemnation of Perón was at its height. For him, there would be other statues of George Washington to replace the one blown up in Palermo Park. America would soon be his new home.

We've had no cobblers in the family since my mother's uncles. In college, while studying Russia's revolution and the push for a classless society, I would have happily claimed an activist from any of the Left's movements, those intriguing fellows with good hair and brooding eyes, their scruffy tweed jackets, scarves and wool turtlenecks. Italian surnames and striking faces leapt from my textbooks and I fantasized we were related, or at the very least, soulmates. With gullibility on my side, I conveniently ignored the reality of anarchists' bombs and the Left's repudiation of the individual.

In the end, I had to make do with my family's other form of rebellion. Artists—swimming in the gene pool, walking across it like holy men, flying and falling like Icarus, resurfacing. Artists. My mother's two brothers, my father and one of his brothers. Three of my four brothers and numerous cousins. My husband, one son and several nephews. All artists, most apolitical, all pacifists. No bombs. As for the negation of the individual, possibly it's a concept no longer remembered, a country no longer visited.

So, there sat my mother, tiny Emilia, an inquisitive, sensitive child, keeping tabs on Villa Devoto. Though her parents regularly pampered her, she was continually afloat in fear. Morbidly counting and re-counting, as only a small child does, she held tight her neighborhood's instances of misfortune and grief. The small boy squashed by a trolley as he runs after a ball; the old lady felled by a daydreaming-tree-pruner; the one-legged organ player who cannot catch his runaway monkey.

Constantly re-visiting and re-telling her collection of woeful events, especially as she played with her morning porridge, the young Emilia carried on until her mother finally turned from the stove, waving the wooden spoon. *¡Basta, Emilia, vete a jugar con las* *muñecas!'* Stop, Emilia, go play with your dolls! Happily abandoning her breakfast, she skipped off to the front steps, eager to add to her wardrobe of calamitous happenings.

Demise was the ultimate tragedy. When she heard the clomping of hooves on cobblestones, her small heart filled with dread. Familiar with the hearse wagon drawn by dray horses, the somber parade always passed when she was alone on the front steps, very much alone. Her mother was tending tomato plants in the back garden, her father gone to the store, her older brother in class, poised before his easel. She knew he stood contemplating his subject, the plaster head of Alexander the Great, or maybe a sphinx or winged beast from the gate of Xerxes. She knew because he brought home his art history book to show her. Turning pages, his serious voice cautioned her not to touch as he rubbed his thumb over the images. It made her crazy with envy.

Alone on the step, she nervously pulled up her socks and watched the funeral procession pass. Alone, she learned the unfortunate's identity. Slipped into the ornate brass pocket at the front top of the hearse, a simple card announced the calligraphed name of the deceased.

Obstinate nightmares inevitably followed and she awoke in terror, convinced she heard the hooves, certain of what she saw in that brass pocket.

Pilar Medina Fernández Barragán

Rounded black lettering and intertwining circles of infinity captured her mother's name. When her heart stopped pounding and the fear eased, she sat on the side of her bed reaching for the warm milk and honey Pilar had hurriedly prepared.

Who generated that calligraphy of death Emilia wondered, sipping the warm milk? Perhaps that sickly, wheezing clerk from the undertaker's office. She'd seen him coming and going, a dark handkerchief pressed to his mouth. Had he already created his own announcement, storing it in the undertaker's vault so it would be ready when his moment came?

Iowa, 2009

"TIME FOR HER BATH!" *La Jefa* shouts out, entering the sliding glass door at the top of the staircase.

One of my brothers calls her an Amazon. A tall, ungraceful woman in her mid-fifties, she originally came to my parents as a cleaning lady. It was better in the beginning when she wasn't also a caregiver. As a housekeeper of sorts, she thumped about whistling in her high-pitched voice, clanking cooking pots, kicking furniture out of the vacuum's way, mixing colored laundry with the whites. The worst was her distracted swatting at the sculpture and prints in an effort to dust.

Hearing her voice, panic sweeps my mother's eyes as she reaches for me, tightening her grip on my arm.

"Bath time," *Jefa* repeats, moving in for the kill. "It's always the same!" She elbows me as though we're partners in crime. "You've seen it … your Mami doesn't know if she's coming or going." She cackles, shaking her head, her forehead damp with perspiration.

Cleaning the steps, dragging up the vacuum, emptying the bucket of water—physical exertion, I acknowledge, glancing at her bandaged leg. Her varicose veins bleed through the wrappings, but she doesn't trust doctors. She's told me she takes care of herself with home remedies. It could be that she doesn't have medical insurance and refuses to go to the free clinic. Or maybe she really believes in herbal cures. Who knows?

Moving in closer, obsequiously stroking my mother's cheek, *Jefa* whispers sweet nothings in her ear. Ma does not respond.

I've disliked *La Jefa* since the day she told me, in all seriousness, that *Don* Mauricio deserves complete respect because of his fame and importance. Whereas Emilia, *la pobrecita, siempre está sacudiendo un trapo.* The poor little thing is always shaking out a rag.

If it was a teasing attempt to provoke me, she succeeded. After that, I could no longer abide her voice, let alone her manner and foolishness. A *ferd*—a horse, as they say in Yiddish—had clomped up the stairs and entered my parents' home.

Jefa gets nowhere with her whispering, so she gives up and heads to the bathroom. I hear the water running. Ma is left clinging to my arm.

I'm upset about my parents' care. My younger brothers claim they're getting more personal attention than they would in a nursing home. They may be right, but I can't bear how rough *La Jefa* is with Ma, and how she claims to know more than the doctor about treating Pa's bedsores. Painkillers have been prescribed—and rightly so, I've seen the frightening lesions—but she insists pain medication isn't necessary. Besides, she says, he could become addicted, like Michael Jackson.

I try not to show my shock. Instead, I attempt to convince her that, given his advanced age, we shouldn't be concerned about dependency. My father is 94. His tolerance for pain may be high, but we've all heard him moan as he's turned on his side so the sores can be dressed.

Addiction? Does *Jefa* want to talk about addiction?

I can do that.

A writer once told me, 'All fiction is non-fiction, and all non-fiction is fiction.'

'Self-Portrait in a Cautionary Tale', 2010
from a story collection in progress,
This I Can Tell You

THERE WASN'T A LOT TO say about the apartment on Elm Street. One of three above a row of small shops, it was sad and unattractive, but a roof over one's head was better than no roof, and she was grateful. The trees were gone. Dutch Elm disease had moved through years before.

Though the building was of little consequence and easily ignored, it was not old and had been well constructed in its day—red brick, shingled roof, and a decent number of windows. At the front, facing Elm, a simple veranda spanned the shop doors. Around behind, on both sides, metal staircases with wooden steps led up to the apartments from a paved parking area. Considering the shifting stream of tenants, things had been well maintained over the years.

She often sat in the car waiting for their son. She'll call him D. Watching the traffic moving along Elm, the same thought frequently crossed her mind. It would be wise to buy the building. Sometimes she'd step out onto the pavement to stretch or do a few neck exercises, glancing up at the brick structure, squinting in the sunlight. It was long ago. She was younger, with lively honey hair and a determined demeanor, and she was accustomed to caring for him. Naturally, her husband did too. They took turns. He did some things, she did others. He was more realistic, she, more hopeful.

Anyway, for this fantasy to work, the business of buying the place, she had to 'make-believe'. No offended, old parents continually saying there was nothing wrong with D., insisting, indignantly, that the doctors were wrong, all of them. How dare did her parents pretend mental illness was news to them, that it hadn't existed in Argentina? What about Villa Freud in Buenos Aires? What about their close friend in Córdoba, the psychiatrist, Gregorio Bermann?

What about all those compromised art students her father had dealt with: the depressed and anxious, the addict, the suicidal, all of them, gravitating to their professor for help. Endeavoring to create a 'make-believe' world, she could not have those parents, or her committed husband, or their three other accomplished children—D.'s siblings.

She had to imagine they were alone and she alone was responsible for D. There could be no other distractions. He consumed her; that part wasn't a fantasy. The three apartments could be converted into two—she could live in one and fix up the other for him. They'd rent out two of the downstairs shops and the third could be his studio. Their boy was an artist; he painted and wrote songs. He was good.

The truth is, mothers of these sons, even the most resolute, self-possessed women, habitually rely on fantasies to get by. They'll go to any length searching for ways to help their boy.

After a painful past, D. returned to town and moved into apartment #1. It was the first one at the top of the left staircase with the loose step three down from the landing. Downstairs, there was an antique store in the first shop, a blade-sharpening business in the second, and a shoe repair establishment in the last. The proprietor of the collectibles shop was an enormous, handicapped man with a shy smile, a large heart and blue striped overalls. One icy day he took in a forlorn, hungry beagle. The skinny pup slept on an old afghan thrown over a pressed-back rocker and he became the shop's mascot. D. was fond of the dog and named him Joey.

D. enjoyed hunting for treasures and was regularly in the shop browsing. He tended to obsess about his acquisitions—purchased, traded or found. Important finds possessed impressive provenances, supernatural powers, or mystical destinies entwined with his. A jawbone pulled up with a fishing pole belonged to an extinct water creature, not a drowned rabbit. A black rock was never a black rock but a meteorite. The object found in the creek bed was not someone's trash, but an Indian relic. Disappointing realities rolled off him like water and he continued to believe what he wanted—the signs and symbols connecting his perplexing existence to a place he continually sought.

The owner of the building, a fat little man with a camel hair overcoat that was too long and a face that was too red, likely from high blood pressure, regularly came around to check on things. Given the population he had to deal with, how could he not? She happened to be in the shop the day he tried explaining that the dog could not live there. It wasn't easy, especially with the handicapped man smiling and repeating over and over that the dog's owner would come soon, or someone would, to take him home. No one ever came. D. would have taken the dog up to his apartment but the man in the long coat with the red face made it clear pets were not allowed, the way smoking wasn't.

There was something wrong with everyone associated with that place of little consequence. Besides the big man in the antique shop, the cobbler next door was missing a leg. The shop's blinds were generally pulled down, but he managed quite well in the dimness, wheeling around the crowded shelves of old shoes and purses, the scraps of leather piled on the dusty floor. D. enjoyed the smell of leather and the sound of the stitching machine, but he didn't linger because the cobbler was a taciturn man and didn't like having people around. Upstairs, felons continually moved in and out of the last apartment, and aging addicts, in and out of the middle apartment. D. calmly watched the progression, reminding himself that he was an artist and a musician; quite possibly, a genius.

In the beginning, he was happy—painting self-portraits and composing songs on his guitar, cooking and cleaning his dishes, keeping his art books and painting supplies neatly arranged on his table. Putting seeds out on the windowsills, he sat on the top step of the staircase, smoking and watching the birds come and go. He had soulful, tan eyes, a fine, straight nose and curly, brown hair. In the past, there'd been girlfriends. D. wrote poems, love fragments, on an old manual typewriter someone had given him. She never knew if he intended them for a specific girl. He left them lying around and she found them in strange places: wrapped around the toothpaste tube, buried in the grounds at the bottom of his coffee tin, tucked in a shoe.

In the beginning, taking the pills was not a burden. He had a couple friends, the birds chirped, and early mornings seemed very bright. Soon, he felt better. So much so, that one day he woke up convinced the medication was no longer necessary. It was not the first time; the situation was familiar. She tried talking to him, explaining, but he would not listen. The pillbox remained untouched for days.

D. dropped his clothes on the floor and stopped cleaning his dishes. She knew his mind, the dashing and speeding. Thoughts and words and images must have come and gone so rapidly, he probably wasn't sure if he was asleep and thinking, or awake and dreaming. Confusion overcame him. Perhaps he would have liked keeping some of the ideas whipping by, but taking hold was impossible. She was certain he began laughing aloud when he was alone. She used to hear him when he was younger—when he thought no one was around. He grew a beard to hide his bemused smile. He shaved his head. What she could not see, she imagined. She was haunted.

She came around more, almost daily, always with a good excuse. Food he liked—cold roast chicken and banana cake—some days, the clean shirts and jeans she'd carefully washed, mended and folded. Really, she came to count his pills.

D. stopped going outside to smoke. He lined cigarette butts around the bathroom sink and dropped them into coffee tins filled with stiffened paintbrushes. One night when insomnia set in, he cut a hole in the plaster wall beside the bathroom doorframe with his bread knife. It must have taken forever before he could feed through the rope attached to one end of his hammock. At the far end of the bedroom, he bore a hole in the wall beside the window and cut out a piece of screen for the rope at the other end of his hammock. Afterwards, did he climb into his hammock and lay very still staring at the ceiling fan, the way he had as a baby? When he finally fell asleep, he must have dreamt about the man in the camel hair coat with the angry, red face.

As the days passed, she could see him worrying. He complained about ants, telling her he followed some on his hands and knees. They moved from the base of the toilet, down the hall, passed the kitchen and into the main room, disappearing over the baseboard at the edge of the carpet. Pulling up the corner of the carpet, he decided the darkness on the plywood was black mold. The spores were confusing him, causing the insomnia. Insisting he was being watched, D. stuffed clay into his laptop's web camera so he couldn't be seen. The bulb in the kitchen would not turn off. Dragging his mattress out from under the table, he shoved it into the bedroom closet.

Fine, she thought. He shouldn't sleep with mold. Lots of people like to sleep in small spaces. Perhaps it wasn't that peculiar.

Sometimes he got hold of a baggie of weed. It helped him forget about everything, until the next morning, when his tan eyes looked like a distant sea, glistening with worry. How would he get more?

Everything started again: the doctor and therapist, talks about why his brain couldn't cope with 'substances', the visits from nurses. D. acquiesced and returned to first base. He didn't say anything, and she didn't either. They both knew first base was shrinking.

One day, after washing dishes left in the sink, she painted the kitchen walls. Just to freshen up, she told herself. Lots of boys make a mess when they cook. Lots of boys leave rotting sardines and dirty dishes in the sink, drop coffee grounds on the floor, eggshells and orange peels. Lots of mothers help their sons.

She painted the walls of his two rooms. Just to freshen up. Clean house, clean mind, or something like that. Anyway, it didn't bother her. She pulled her honey hair into a ponytail and got busy. Being a hard worker, it felt good making things clean and tidy. She painted around the hammock holes in the wall, and as for the cut-out window screen, well, anyone might do such a thing if …

During the following weeks, the nurse came around daily to dispense his meds. D. soon felt better. His curly hair was growing back and his eyes seemed nearer. He felt so good and spoke so calmly, he convinced everyone he could take his medication alone.

He did, for a while.

Then it all began again, the worries and headaches, the insomnia. One sleepless night he could not find a large enough piece of canvas, so he painted on the walls. Letters, numbers and symbols moved above his faces, marching around windows and doorframes, their colors dripping like neon blood.

Again, she painted. To freshen up, she told herself again.

Another night around midnight, he called and asked her to bring him some crazy glue because he was converting his classical guitar into an electronic instrument. He had a small, battery-operated contraption that would function as a sound box. It just had to be attached.

He could not expect her to go out at that hour. She worried that her voice betrayed her anger. Then she was angry that she worried about it. When she arrived the following morning, D. was asleep in the closet. He had smashed his guitar with the large mallet from his carving tool case.

The following night, convinced a solid wooden floor was necessary for sculpture projects, he used a razor knife to slice the dirty carpet in neat rows. The pulled-up strips of carpeting and padding exposed the stained, plywood underlay. With a little varnish, it could become a studio floor, he may have reasoned. As for the wood burning stove he'd always wanted, knocking a hole in the outside wall would suffice for the chimney pipe. But first, it would be good to have an opening between the bedroom and the main room and that could be done with his mallet and one of his chisels. He began.

A few hours later, when D. stepped out on the landing to smoke, did he see the streaks of color starting to show behind the rooftops? Yes. He never missed a thing, visually, and she'd seen his energetic paintings of the ocean and sky. He told her the colors of a dawn are so much more intense, so much more remarkable than a sunset's.

It had rained at night; the air was cool and smelled clean. As he flicked his cigarette on the staircase railing, did he see Mount Olympus in the distance? He'd said he could live on a mountaintop, and he once wrote a song about lifting into the clouds, floating with the air.

When she came around, her son was sleeping. Weeping softly, she moved silently around the rooms, picking up pieces of guitar and chunks of plaster, pushing her honey hair out of her damp face. She'd always kept everything, all the people and words, the bits and pieces of her life. Keeper that she was, she'd never destroyed or lost anything. Staring at the hole in the wall, she dried her tears. Anyone might have done such a thing if … but it was huge, not like the small hammock holes. Looking around, wondering what more could be done, she left to call the doctor.

When the addict with a gray ponytail stepped out of the middle apartment for a smoke, and the big man from the antique shop returned from his walk with Joey, and the cobbler wheeled himself out and leaned over the veranda to reach for the mail, they all watched a white van with lettering on the side pull into the driveway.

D. waved and smiled as he was helped into the vehicle. He told the big man to take care of Joey and he asked the addict with the gray ponytail to feed the birds.

The next day, she came by again. There were pills to count and walls to paint, just to freshen up a bit, in that place of little consequence.

Iowa, 2003

OCTOBER 23, 2003, HARD TO forget, and harder to write about. By now, have I learned to take our situation in stride? Hopefully. Have I learned to stay away from disappointments and expectations? Easier said than done. But I'm consoled that optimism never completely disappears, at least not for me. Hovering appropriately out of reach, it sends out occasional, encouraging flashes, like a lighthouse guiding ships and souls. For better or worse, I have a clairvoyant's inclination to heart quickening flashes of crushing awareness. Awakened, sitting up in bed, I know something is terribly wrong. And he's so far away, our son, so out of reach.

A friend once referred to those nighttime warnings as '*the mother thing.*'

Our youngest child, our son, waits in the lobby while the psychiatrist sees us alone. After, the three of us together. When we made the appointment, the doctor asked if we could meet the following day, the 24th, but that was out. We would be busy. Our daughter was scheduled to deliver her first baby by cesarean.

Rain the night before and the autumn sky is a crisp blue. Rays move down through branches and leaves splashing large, hopeful patterns on the hospital grounds. The psychiatrist's office is a pale yellow box in the original psychiatric complex, a layout of buildings mirroring the old children's hospital. The compound seems so familiar, the *moment* carries me back to my brother's hospitalization as a little kid. It was something contagious. Mumps? Leo stood at a ward window, his sad little face pressed to the glass as he waved to us down on the hospital lawn.

The psychiatrist tells us he feels comfortable giving a diagnosis, based on the three visits they've had. He always hopes it's youthful 'angst', or one of those bubbles that can unexpectedly appear on a young man's path—trapping and holding him captive until he finds the exit—but unfortunately, in our son's case, it's neither.

How can he be so sure, so soon?

Without turning in his chair, the doctor reaches to the shelf above him and pulls down the *Diagnostic and Statistical Manual of Mental Disorders*. Reading aloud from the list of schizophrenia indicators, he wants us to consider how many apply.

Yes, yes, no. No, yes.

So what? Can't some of those indicators, as he calls them, be true for most people?

He speaks about us, the parents—an artist, a writer. Obviously, our creative personalities explain the unusual patience with aberration. He says we're used to stretching, that we have a high tolerance for deviation. Most parents would never have accepted our son's eccentricities.

Hearing him speak, it wouldn't surprise me if he said we walk on our heads and live in trees.

The doctor asks what he was like as a child. We tell him. And his three siblings? We tell him. And us? We tell him.

What about our use of substances?

Of course. Aren't all artists and writers *users*? Especially those coming of age in the 60's, with the flower wreathes and communes and drugs.

"He didn't learn it from us, we never did that shit."

The psychiatrist stares at me, listening in disbelief. "Not even pot?"

"No, not even pot."

"Really?"

"Seriously."

He considers my words, smiling and shaking his head in amazement.

I look around, taking in the mess of his office.

Promptly pulling himself together, he apologizes for the disorder, explaining they've just moved him again. University bureaucracy.

There are several bulging briefcases on the floor, leaning against walls. How does he know where anything is? Would he like help organizing?

I'm good at that. What about his shirt collar trapped under the rumpled jacket? If I'm nervous enough, and the situation is ripe enough, I tend to put my hands on men I don't know. It happened with Leo's divorce attorney, when I went up to be a witness at the trial. Unlike this psychiatrist, that lawyer was incredibly tidy and well-turned-out. Limey aftershave, striped tie, dark blue suit, and just the tiniest speck of white lint on his polished lapel ... gone. There I was, witness and groomer rolled into one.

Aberration, high tolerance for deviation, eccentricities—what kind of words, where is he going with this? I know, I know. The road is familiar.

Even before the shrink's formal diagnosis, we've witnessed our son navigating the waters of his addiction and psychosis, the relentless vortex of compulsions and narcissism. We've faced his renegade equilibrium, his frequent sleepless nights and fugitive tranquility, his battle to remain sober. In the beginning, we stood at the rim of that void, an abandoned well, lowering lifelines, one after another. We felt him grab and hang on, until the weightlessness of line and our hopes smashing against stone. Peering down into his darkness, we called his name, but heard only our echoes.

After the appointment, as the three of us walk silently toward the parking lot, something under a tree catches our son's attention. Dropping to a crouch, his hand gently moves the grass around a flash of whiteness. Does he think about the 'incompletes' of his university courses? Does he worry about last semester's Italian fiasco? Studying in Florence was never about studying in Florence—maybe at most, a bicycle ride to classes. It was all about pot and drugs and girlfriend craziness. I watch our son on the grass. What preoccupies him at that moment?

I don't remember the lot being this empty when we parked. Maybe Thursday isn't a big day for psychiatric appointments. Reaching our car, I turn. Is it my destiny to confront every event, every moment of my son's life, because he doesn't?

I see my husband pause on the walk, preoccupied by the psychiatrist's words. He glances up, shifts his stance and focuses on our son examining his find in the grass. I think of the unusually cool evening only weeks before—the end of summer in Teeswater.

He came in from the studio carrying his bucket of paint brushes, finished for the day. A wind had picked up after sunset and he was wearing his black felt hat with the wide brim, his down vest.

Sitting at the kitchen table, reading, I told him he had to hear an incredible passage from the Leonard Woolf biography he'd bought for me—Virginia in Freud's London greenhouse. I read aloud while he stood at the sink filling the bucket with warm, soapy water. He listened attentively, swishing his brushes. It was those few minutes in the Hampstead greenhouse when the aged and ailing Freud presented Virginia Woolf with the famous narcissus, the afternoon the Woolfs arrived for tea.

Pausing, I glanced up to see Alan's right hand raised high above the sink, a favorite paintbrush poised between thumb and fingers. My husband, certain in his visual world, vulnerable to the urgency of the written word. As he pondered Freud's narcissus, did that brush want to continue an unfinished thought from the studio?

By the end of August, astonishing landscapes crowded his studio walls. Wind pushed those daring strokes, green and blue, through dense pines at the front periphery of his woods. Dark sentinel trunks, lifting, marching from orange pine needle floors. And when the branches swayed, parting for the sky, rose clouds lingered, before drifting on.

I felt the hovering energy in those bold fingers and suspended brush, the stillness of his left hand resting on the bucket's rim. He understood Virginia's weakness—the mind incapable of clarity when needed most, incapable of keeping madness at bay. Did

Virginia acknowledge the white narcissus she shyly accepted from Dr. Freud? Or did she leave its message for Leonard—to analyze, to apply, to ignore, as he saw fit?

I saw the fingers relax and paintbrush drop to the bucket of soapy water. Whooshing, tapping his brushes clean, I knew the fixated thoughts, despite his calm, reflective mind. Even the most stable of minds can be ravaged by the act of contemplation.

He hasn't moved. Still fixed to that spot on the walk, he watches our son gently moving the grass. In that second, is he permitting a strange memory from our young son's life—an odd moment of loneliness and hope. "Dad, if we'd been children at the same time, do you think we would have been friends?"

My hand on the car door, I'm overcome with frustration; we have to get home. Tomorrow our baby will be born. I have things to do, things to be joyful about. All the diagnosis stuff will have to wait.

What's keeping them?

He's still on lawn.

I open the car door.

'Common white button,' he calls out matter-of-factly, as if all is right with the world. 'I'd like to find an orange oyster, or chanterelle,' he adds, as if requesting we swing by Starbucks.

We aren't in the woods near dying elms, boggy ground and mossy mounds—*ubicate!*—we're on a groomed lawn of the old the psychopathic compound, and there are no orange oysters or chanterelles.

Ubicate! Gather yourself, get your bearings, get aligned. English doesn't have a word like the Spanish *ubicate*.

I want to shout this, and more, other things … but I don't.

At the end of the meeting, the psychiatrist asks why we had to reschedule. What is the *important procedure* taking place the next day?

The birth of our first grandchild, I answer.

Buenos Aires, 1923

B ACK TO THE CHILD SITTING on the stoop of her home. If it'd been acceptable for little girls to jot down their observations on legal pads, the young Emilia would have. Straightening up to see over the garden wall with the CASA BELLA tiles, pushing curls out of her face and licking the tip of her pencil, she would have documented her neighborhood's activities. At that early age, did she already want to write? She once confessed a desire to record her stories. And did she already want to paint, like her brother? By adolescence, that obsession would be firmly rooted, but the closest she came to paint was as an errand girl for her brother. It was expected she'd go off to the neighborhood art supply store for a tube of vermillion, or ultramarine blue.

It would be more than half a century before she had her own paint set-up and easel. Tomas tended to her, as he would at the end of her life when he braided her hair, when she was given that respite from dementia, when she felt safe. He brought the wheeled cart up from the basement to my parents' bedroom, set out the tubes of paint and brushes, the spatulas and small tin of turpentine. All neat and tidy, ready to go. I can imagine his shy smile as he whipped off the drop cloth in presentation, shaking off some of his own white dust in the process. I appreciated that Tomas took charge and made it happen, but it saddened me that my mother was never given a room of her own. Late afternoons before dinner, everything had to disappear into the corner. The cart of paints, the easel with a drawing or painting, the rolls of paper and canvas, all of it, as though nothing had been going on.

My parents' 1880's commercial building in downtown Iowa City was huge. It included a basement, three floors and an industrial lift. The converted ground level became my father's gallery and printing studio. The second floor, his drawing studio and display area for the African collection. The top floor, my parents' open living quarters. There was no privacy. No walls separated the living room from the kitchen, the dining area from the bedroom. Surely somewhere in that vast building a small area could have been designated my mother's private workspace, but no. It still distresses me that it was never a priority.

She painted still lifes and portraits of herself as a girl. We all accompanied her journey, and I'll always be grateful to Alan for his attentiveness and gentle manner. Ma knew she was catching the tail end of a dream. There weren't enough hours and years. Dedication and skill, the complexities of reality and imagination, all of it, demanding the kind of devotion it takes a lifetime to give. When she stopped painting, maybe she was done. Or perhaps her self-esteem simply surrendered, struggling to understand why the paint cart and her work deserved to be pushed into the corner.

Though my mother was wise and worldly in so many ways, primal terrors clung, fear was entrenched. Her anxiety was made worse by the overbearing protection that accompanied her life. In the beginning it was her parents' doing, then my father's. She was never given a chance or reason to drop her feigned innocence; independence was not a possibility. She was taken care of. Driving a car was out of the question. Topics that frightened her were avoided.

During shopping trips into town, if we passed the retarded newspaper boy happily swinging his dirty canvas bag and drooling on his shirt, she'd panic and grab onto my sweater. I could feel her shaking behind my back, urgently pushing me to hurry beyond him. Physical defects, visible handicaps and mental instabilities frightened her. She dreaded the chemicals in toilet bowl cleansers and was so afraid of sharp knives, slicing a tomato was nearly impossible, not to mention carving a roast. Incapacitated by the reality of death, burials sent her into a state of panic. During her life time, my mother attended only two funerals.

The first was at the age of five or six, when her three-month-old baby cousin died in the middle of the night. It would have been in the era of her front-step-neighborhood-watching. More than once I heard how she was awakened at dawn and hurried off to the corner store to buy the dead infant a pair of white stockings. Crazed with grief, her Aunt Rafaela pushed her out the door saying the baby could not meet his maker in dirty socks. In her haste to the store, Ma fell and scraped her knee. Distraught, she sat on the stone walk hugging her knee, weeping until her father came searching for her.

I've wondered what role my grandmother, Pilar, played in this story. How could an overprotective mother permit her little girl to be burdened with such a task, and in the semi-dark, no less? She must have been completely wrapped up trying to calm her sister's anguish. I never knew Aunt Rafaela, but I can visualize her flying through the sleeping streets, wailing and tearing her hair as she arrived at my grandparent's door, breathless, hysterically announcing her baby's death and falling into her sister's arms. Ma said it was such a tiny, white coffin, they could have been burying a doll.

The second funeral was her father's in 1954, when we were in Spain. William was the only grandchild to attend the funeral. The rest of us were sent away for a few days to stay with our parents' friends, the sculptor Ángel Ferrant and his wife. When we returned home, my father took me aside and explained I wasn't to mention our grandfather because it would make Ma very sad.

Barcelona, July 1965—
no printing press

THE PRINTING SHOP, SITUATED ON a side street in one of Barcelona's old commercial districts, had been in the family for several generations. The owner was a bespectacled little man, kind and forthcoming. He led us through a maze of rooms to a storage area where an old letter press awaited our inspection. Black cast iron, a 19th century workhorse—it would have laughed out loud printing my delicate pamphlet of poems for Professor Duncan's class—a stunning piece of equipment, but wrong.

Alan and I stood in disbelief and disappointment. A short discussion followed as we described an etching press for intaglio printing. The kind that once produced calling cards from small copper plates, the kind of press no longer used, the kind of hand-printing no longer done. Listening to our clarification, the shop proprietor removed his glasses and cleaned them with a large, crumpled kerchief. He understood, although he had not seen such a press for ages. He replaced his glasses. Those obsolete pieces of equipment generally became scrap metal, but he promised to keep a watch.

We left the shop in silence. Alan's plans to set up a printing studio would have to wait.

We'd scheduled a week's stay in Barcelona, assuming there would be arrangements involved in crating and shipping the press to the island, as well as purchases of necessary supplies and equipment—copper plates, burins, ink, paper. Instead, we found ourselves stuck in the city during a heat wave, our hopes dashed. It was impossible to change our return reservation to Ibiza. The ferry was booked solid.

Regardless of the season or weather, the country or city, our custom was to arrive at museums first thing in the morning as doors opened. Besides the Picasso, the Mares, and our favorite, the National Museum of Catalan art on Montjuïc with its overwhelming stone staircase and cool, domed rooms of Romanesque frescoes, I don't know how many other museums we visited that week. We spent lunch hour in the department store, *El Corte Inglés*, and late afternoons on the *Ramblas*. Side street shopping usually turned up necessary items unavailable on the island, including a second, hard to find, Coleman lantern.

By four or five we'd return to our small *pensión* for a nap, but it was impossible to sleep in the heat. If we opened windows on those still days, a fetid stench drifted up from the street. Barcelona's antiquated sewer system accounted for the reeking air in its older neighborhoods. (The city underwent a 'master drainage plan' for the 1988 Olympics, long after we left.) It took only a few days away from the island to miss the cool of our little house with its thick stone walls and pebble cement floors—the garden, thymy with *frígola* and the prospect of nearly ripe figs.

The week dragged on. With time on our hands, I contacted my old schoolmate from the *Colegio Británico* in Madrid, Nina Martí. We'd intermittently kept in touch over the decade. Alan and I were invited to lunch with Nina, her mother and two sisters at their apartment. Her family's move from Madrid to Barcelona had something to do with her father. He wasn't mentioned over lunch so we never knew what happened—if he'd passed away, or left them, or what. I recall that Mrs. Martí had relatives in Barcelona. In my letter home I describe the three sisters as attractive, enlightened young ladies searching for Spanish husbands, all three employed by Pan American Airways. Though the reunion was enjoyable, we found little common ground and lost all contact after that visit. It could be that our bond was strongest as 10-year-old best friends sharing a name, memorizing and reciting the poetry of John Masefield, and indulging a mutual infatuation for our classroom teacher, Mr. Phillips.

The next day, Alan and I boarded the ferry back to Ibiza.

During July and into August, dry conditions continued on Ibiza. Though cisterns were seriously depleted, there was an abundance of corn, grapes, melons, and the almonds were almost ready to harvest. In August, another visit from a Princeton classmate, Michael Leiserson. We did not realize the extent of Ibiza's magnetism. By then we could offer our guests a small cot, serving as our *sala* couch, instead of the floor. Alan made the base and legs from bamboo canes and rope, similar to the three panel screen he'd constructed to serve as a closet. Purchasing a felt mattress in town, we rolled it up and carried it home on the bus. I covered it with a blue striped ticking fabric.

It became our norm, climbing onto buses and planes with bulky parcels wrapped in brown paper. Usually, ceramics, but once—such craziness—a raffia baby bassinet purchased at an outdoor market in Oaxaca and transported to Ontario. I was pregnant when we took the girls to visit my parents in Mexico. Months later, the infant Daniel slept in his red gingham-lined-basket, dreaming sweetly of the orange tree he would climb in his grandparents' Cuernavaca garden.

The afternoon before Michael left, I made an apricot pie from the tree in our backyard, baking it in the tin box camp-oven on our two-burner hotplate. We had the same oven in Maine for blueberry pies and hot days not suitable for the wood stove.

Michael's reservation was for an early morning flight out of Ibiza. At three in the morning we awoke, ate more pie, and left for the airport on foot. Alan and I accompanied Michael across the Ibicenco fields by a full moon.

After Michael left, we continued our work with few interruptions. Alan brought new energy to his painting as he temporarily put aside thoughts of printmaking—demonstrating, even in his 20's, a desire to make the best of things, to let go the disappointments. An acquaintance once told me that life has the A problems, those you can solve, and the B problems, those you can't. The ability and desire to distinguish between the two did not come naturally to me. I wanted to solve all obstacles.

Alan's early inclination to move beyond situations not in his control, shaped how he would deal with complications, and my tendency to fret can still dictate my handling of difficulties. Reading those aerograms written to my family, I realize very little has changed. Buried in descriptions of our daily lives and interactions were exposés of determined self-protection veering toward self-righteousness. Our 'birth gifts' of serenity and the instinct to hold to our cores, to nurture our dreams, were true even then. The same could be said of our contentment with rural life. Like our personalities, that too would not change.

EXCERPT
'Emma and Max'
from *ONE APRIL AFTERNOON*
in the time of Silberman and Gould,
unpublished novel, 2010

"TELL THEM," MAX SAID.

Early that morning, in a moment of peace before breakfast, before their talk of Noah and how her family needed to be told, Emma watched from bed as Max got up and began moving around the room. He stood before the window to determine the weather, to stretch, to see if the old jay was in the birdbath beside the flowerbed. Then on to his dresser, barefoot on pine boards, to sort, to organize socks and underwear, T-shirts, a silent exercise in preparation for the day.

A bit of gray shows in his curly, dark hair, but nothing else has changed. Emma moves about the kitchen, preparing for lunch. Though not an athlete like Ben, their eldest son who thrives in motion, Max has the posture of a young man with a healthy spirit. Certain of himself in his physical space, his large frame moves with such confidence and stands so straight with promise, heads always turn.

Max, Ben, Noah. These are the men in her life.

Opening the fridge, Emma takes out the cheese and cold meats. Occasionally she permits an alluring thought to move into her consciousness, out of its sleepy alcove. She doesn't give birth to her sons—no pain, no hours of labor. Instead, she cuts them from cloth, the way she used to make dolls when she was young.

Ben's pattern pieces run parallel to the selvage, a straight shot. When all his sections are joined, they hang true, in line with the grain, no question of the fabric's right side.

Noah's pieces resist the straight edge. Giving in, Emma lays him out on the bias, diagonally, so he can feel the call from all directions. Predictably, he favors the wrong side. When his sections

240

are gathered and sewn (with difficulty, the bias is always hard to work with), they possess amazing elasticity along with accompanying uncertainty. If not carefully handled, the diagonal can prove disastrous, pulling totally out of shape. But in the end—please God the end should be as it is in her mind, probably her most accomplished and important sewing project—in the end, the completed work hangs with the economy of line and fluid elegance known only to a good, bias cut.

When Emma permits these images, she thinks of her daughters and wonders how she would lay them out on cloth. Complications. Unlike the boys, the girls' pieces must be created wearing clothes. Girls will be girls. The chest/yoke might be placed either on the straight or diagonal of the fabric, as well as the inset for a pleat, allowing the knee to bend. She would have to match the plaid and choose the shape of the arms/sleeves, while considering piping and cording of the same fabric, or different. The project weighs heavily and she encounters a wall of difficulties. She has only to turn her head to see the white tiles of the delivery room—lights, nurses, doctor—and the baby's tiny pink fist in her mouth, as both her daughters first greeted her.

Max looked remarkably cheerful in that moment he bent to pull on his socks, his eyes reassuring, steady, despite the worries and uncertainties about Noah.

"You'll feel better if you tell them. Do you want me with you?"

Waiting in the early morning peace of their bedroom, he moved to kiss her forehead, to rest his hand on her shoulder.

"I always want you with me. But I'll tell them, when the moment feels right."

He smiled, running his finger along the shoulder seam of her sleeping shirt, turned inside out.

After, pulling on her pajamas in the dark, it's not something she considers, the right side or wrong. Maybe Noah's preference for the wrong side of fabric isn't so surprising.

She stayed under the covers a few minutes longer listening to the water run in the bathroom, the cabinet door open. He's always shaved with a razor. Electric things are to be avoided: shavers, knives, can openers, even drills. Lying in the warmth of bed, she thought of the rainy afternoon they met—the bus in Keswick, England, the hand-knit Norwegian sweater, his damp hair. He'd leaned across her to point out the ancient rock fences crawling up that English mountain. He spoke about those stones with such excitement, they could have been an archaic, proud race—their noble heritage, their strength, their ability to withstand. She could smell the lanolin in the damp wool of his sweater. She could feel the intense warmth from his body. At that moment, Emma knew she would spend her life with this man.

"What are you thinking, Emma?"

"What?"

"What are you thinking about?" Apple asks again. "It's something lovely, because you're smiling. I can't see, but I can feel your smile. Am I right?"

Anger miraculously evaporates from her sister's voice. She's standing at the kitchen deck door, her forehead pressed to the glass. Has the headache lifted?

"You're right. I was thinking about the afternoon Max and I met."

"The Lake District in England, the bus and that wool sweater you talk about. Whatever happened to that famous garment?" Apple's words are animated. She turns, the hard edges of her face shifting into softness.

"Max reluctantly gave it up. It had gotten ink and paint stained, moth eaten, and accidentally thrown into the washing machine. It shrunk down to a tight, unyielding little thing, unsuitable even for a Norwegian dwarf." Emma knows Apple's elation is temporary and her talkative mood will soon pass—her blindness will shroud her again.

"I've been waiting for that story to appear in a book. When Emma?"

"I guess I've never thought of using it."

"You and Max," Apple hesitates, "why do you think some people know how to fall in love and stay there, while others just lose it all?" Her smile vanishes. "I wish…" Her face harbors a complicated tale: the anger of having been neglected, the guilt of being neglectful.

"I don't know what I wish for." Apple turns back to the sliding glass doors as if she can see out to the patio and beyond, as if she isn't blind. "I wish things could be the way they used to be, for Reyna and her memory, for me and my eyes." She leans her forehead against the glass again. "Abe hasn't planted his roses yet, has he? I haven't planted anything either, that is, my assistant hasn't." Apple nervously rubs the back of her neck. "We're so much further north my garden is still soggy and cold. Is it here, as well?"

"I think spring is late everywhere," Emma answers, wondering how she will tell them about Noah.

Ibiza, September 1965

IN THE FALL, FOLLOWING A flurry of letters back and forth, scheduling and travel arrangements, we were finally re-united with Alan's parents. They arrived on Ibiza in September, an ideal season. After spending a few days in our *casa*, the four of us left the island to tour the south of Spain before continuing on to Israel, Greece and Turkey.

The night before their arrival, rain. It rained so much, we awoke to brown streaks running down our freshly whitewashed interior walls. With Ibiza's yearly rainfall averaging just over 16 inches, it felt as though most of it fell that night.

Typical of the island's country *fincas,* a layer of fine clay and ash had been used in the construction of our flat roof, designed to collect and channel rainwater to the cistern. The clay sealed with the first rains, theoretically creating an impermeable surface.

Such facts did not interest me—potter's clay had not yet entered my life. I was attracted to flowers in *punto Mallorquín,* the *Mallorquín* style of embroidery, and blooming in the fields. Bunches of wild sweet peas regularly adorned the arched recess in our *sala.* Blossoms and curly tentacles stretched happily in that whitewashed niche, the Virgin's confiscated alcove. My need to bring the outdoors in, surprised and delighted María and Antonia. It was not their custom, but how easily embraced in their desire to please.

After that winter in Saskatchewan where Alan diligently committed to his first university teaching job, we eagerly returned to Ibiza for the summer. We'd made plans to rent an apartment and studio from a friend of Anna Wachsmann, a painter returning home to Scotland for the season. José, María, Antonia and Anna W. all met our arriving plane at the Ibiza airport and three days later, the Palerms invited us to a welcome back dinner. The table was proudly adorned with a huge bunch of roses and lilies from a *huerta* in Sant Jordi.

Similarly, our Teeswater neighbors, green-thumbed-farmers with remarkable, blooming gardens, wouldn't think of cutting flowers for their kitchens but they do for mine.

I've since become more curious about things that eluded me when we lived on Ibiza, including Ibicenco roof construction and the dead leaves of the *posidonia oceanica* plant, known as Neptune grass. Harvested along the shores of the Balearic Isles, it served as roof insulation, along with clay and ash. We also saw it used as a commercial wadding product. Setting up house in the spring, we collected two free crates from an Ibiza liquor store to use as shelving. They still had their Neptune grass packing along with a bottle of cognac, inadvertently overlooked by the shop owner.

Alan recently reminded me of a key fact. When building a house, the Ibicenco farmer had only to purchase the imported beam used to support the *sala's* ceiling. Everything else came from his own property or the surrounding countryside. Stone, sand and whitewash for the meter-thick walls, juniper logs and slats, bamboo canes, ash, marine plants and clay for roofs, pebbles for cement floors. Although there was no glass on the small openings, the finer homes had purchased, indoor shutters.

We were soon speaking of staying on the island, of not going back, and the idea of acquiring an old *finca* presented an exciting and serious possibility. José became our enthusiastic guide, his horse and cart, our transportation. When hearsay brought him news of available properties, we were off to the races. José and his family wanted us to stay forever.

Why couldn't we? Plenty of expats had done it over the decades. Despite the alarming stories we'd heard about doctors and schools, not to mention we'd never held 'real' jobs, it had to be possible. Properties were cheap on Ibiza, the cost of living was incredibly reasonable and we were frugal. But in truth, besides not having money, life had not given us reasons to escape, reasons to make new, distant existences. If we hadn't wanted children, then yes, and if we'd been willing to expatriate, yes. But we wanted kids, and we had our families and homelands.

Not long ago, I was very moved reading about a young Canadian couple, Rolph and Mary Blakstad. In 1956 they boarded a boat in Alicante destined for Mallorca. Sailing into Ibiza's harbor at dawn, the Blakstads disembarked for the short stopover but never returned to the ferry. They stayed. Blakstad, an art student who'd won the Emily Carr scholarship and studied painting in Florence, went on to become one of Ibiza's well known architects. His wife, Mary, founded an international school.

We never met the Blakstads, but our paths crossed with Gisele Broner, wife of Blakstad's fellow Ibiza architect, Erwin Broner. Broner, originally from Germany, had settled permanently on Ibiza in the 50's, painting in his studio and designing houses inspired by the Bauhaus. Gisele, a weaver, was responsible for 3.5 yards of 30-inch white, Ibicenco wool fabric, replete with tiny twigs caught in the handspun yarn. I placed an order for the yardage when Anna Wachsmann recommended Gisele's weaving services. Later, that first fall in Saskatchewan, I made a *CHANEL* suit from a vogue pattern. After carefully cutting and interlining the fabric to prevent sagging, I faced the collar and lapels in Thai silk—a deep teal, to match the shell blouse. Meticulous top stitching followed. The skirt was straight and fitted with a back slit for easier walking. Neckline labels were the final touch—one with my embroidered name, the other with *CHANEL*. I wore the suit for several seasons until it slipped out of fashion, eventually ending up in the Goodwill bag out in the garage. Months later came the excited phone call from an acquaintance who frequented secondhand shops. It was in her possession should I change my mind and want it back.

That Ibiza encounter with Gisele Broner later resurfaced in an anecdote involving her brother-in-law, Paul. Escaping Nazi Germany, both Broner brothers left Munich in the 30's, and both eventually ended up in the States. In America, both—separately—anglicized their name. Erwin Heilbronner became Erwin Broner, and Paul Heilbronner became Paul Laporte. Paul was a painter and art historian at Macalester College in St. Paul, Minnesota, when my father wrote to him in August of 1953.

Having been given Laporte's name, Mauricio reached out for advice on where he should settle with his family during his Guggenheim fellowship. Paul promptly responded, saying he knew Italy, not Spain, but a friend of his, Erwin Broner, had a painting studio on Ibiza and might be able to help.

Friend, not *brother?* Were family issues showing their face, or was it the immigrant's habit of wartime caution? Conjecture aside, the Broner name in Paul Laporte's letter raised a flag of recognition and serendipity. When I was 10, my family might have gone to Ibiza instead of Madrid, but it was not preordained, *bashert*, as they say in Yiddish.

The Blakstads were a decade before us, living and working on the island, raising and educating their children, doing exactly what we were seriously considering. Vessels that pass in the night. We saw our friends, the Palerms and Anna W., but we did not mingle in bars or cafes, making conversation and acquaintances. Permitting few outside forces to penetrate our world, there were things we never explored—the fishing villages along the coasts, Ibiza's salt flats, lime pits and potteries, the inside of her cathedral, the remains of a synagogue and the island's ancient history of conversos. Our lives were enriched by Ibiza, but now, so long after, I think about all we missed.

If we'd stayed, how would our lives have been different, beyond the ancient *finca* and studio on a mountain? An expatriate lifestyle with friends dining *al fresco* under the bougainvillea. The extensive herb garden to supplement an obsession with homeopathic remedies. Stomach ailments to explain my cotton-shift-thinness— though 'childless by choice', the more likely culprit. I might have indulged my love of pottery and outdoor bread ovens. And Alan's fascination with chairs? Those raffia-seated old timers gazing down from hooks on Ibicenco walls, would they have replaced their kindred spirit Amish cousins of rural Ontario? Would our own work have consumed us, or perhaps other causes, to replace the children that would never be?

Decades have passed, but photos of her old *fincas* still tug at the pit of my stomach and do the heart-in-the-throat pulsing dance. While we lived on Ibiza, I had little historical or architectural knowledge and certainly wasn't aware of Blakstad's premise that the Ibicenco style of building was 1,000 years old and a direct descendant of Phoenician constructions—a theory held by others who came to the island. The Austrian Dadaist, Raoul Hausmann, spent from 1933 to 1936 studying and photographing Ibicenco dwellings and their inhabitants. His striking images focus on light, form and volume in Ibicenco architecture—the simple modular structures expanding into statements echoing ancient certainty and universal dignity. Each family member performs age-old roles connecting them to the natural world and the household's needs.

The agrarian societies of Ibiza and the Amish of rural Ontario communities share more customs than the storage of unused chairs. Both stretch beyond the nuclear family, growing their dwellings with add-ons to accommodate the newly married son or elderly parents.

The more unassuming the arrangement of whitewashed cubes, parapets and balconies, the more primitive the bread oven and primeval the olive press, the more visceral my response—an affinity so strong, I felt myself melding into the whiteness and simplicity. My identification was complete and unwavering, as though in a previous life I'd been born to one of those dwellings, some having housed the people of those mountains for centuries. With entrances facing south and backs to the mountain and north winds, the whitewashed walls remained protected. Only structures facing the sea were traditionally painted subdued earth colors, cutting down on their visibility to seafaring pirate enemies. Farms with adjacent watch towers, like the one Ginger asked about that hot day on the beach, can be found scattered across the island. Some are marked with white crosses to ward off evil spirits.

I wrote in detail about our house hunting adventures. One breathtaking *finca*, far beyond our immediate neighborhood, prompted José to say, '*Aquí, sí que había plata y oro*'. If ever there was a home of silver and gold, that was it. Nine rooms, an inner court-yard, a kitchen with a 12 ft. high, 4 ft. wide, screw-type olive press, a mill stone, earthenware amphorae still filled with oil, animal corrals, and even a fancy old buggy.

On February 5, 1966, I described our favorite old *finca* near the town of San José. On the onionskin letter, Alan drew a tiny sketch of the front façade. I mention its asking price of a million pesetas, $16,000 US, and how it was in such fine condition, one could live in it tomorrow. Tucked in the side of a mountain, the *finca* was surrounded by terraces of tillable land and old fruit trees. A date palm, the height of the house, stood in the courtyard. Peace echoed through its abandoned rooms. The old patio and arched bal-conies—composed, dignified.

I recently got online to find the finca. A farfetched idea, but worth the try. Amazingly, there it was, palm and all, gussied up and posted on an Ibiza realtor's site. The listing describes it as being on the highway to San José and available for rent—tennis court, swimming pool, satellite TV, Wi-fi, staff on location and accom-modations for 17 guests. Price upon request.

I've toyed with the idea of taking our grown children and grandchildren to Ibiza. Many old farms have been refurbished into spas and Airbnb's, like the one in San José. The internet provided quick information regarding the availability and costs of villas for rent—by the night, week or month. (It was not out of the ques-tion, we'd done it before with the kids, one July in a village near Paris, the following summer, London.) Not out of the question, but seeing those contemporary pergolas and king-size white lounging couches stretching out around modern swimming pools, their side tables sparkling with swizzle-stick-drinks, I felt distressed to the core. What happened to the grace and poverty? The idea of an Ibiza vacation was rapidly abandoned.

On the morning Alan's parents were to arrive, we discovered our *finca* roof was not impermeable. Barely awake, we quickly mixed up whitewash and hurriedly painted out the muddy streaks before heading for the airport. José insisted on taking us with his horse and cart, though we hired a taxi for the return trip with my parents-in-law. The driver agreed to pick us up three days later for our early morning flight to Barcelona.

I had prepared for Alan's parents' visit by making a second mattress so they could have the comfort of our bed. The cotton sack sewn on María's machine was similar to the fabric I'd used for our *sala* couch. We filled it with José's fresh straw. It was plump and inviting, but after two nights, I was covered in fleabites. Alan was spared.

When we met Anna W. at a café in town to introduce her to Alan's parents, I related the flea story. She merrily assured me the same thing happened to her in Marseilles, while she and Konrad waited for a ship to New York in 1941.

During my twenties, something about me invited older women to identify with my 'braided-hair-immigrant' core, skipping generations in the process. Before I was born, Anna found herself in a shabby Marseilles *pensión* with fleas hopping over her lover's flesh to settle on hers. Outside their window, the city teemed with European refugees eager for assistance from the Emergency Rescue Committee. Intellectuals, artists, writers and doctors, most of them Jews escaping Nazi Germany, some hunted by the Gestapo, all waiting for visas and passage to America.

Like Anna W., my mother-in-law, Bess, was drawn to my first generation aura. Hearing stories of the old Poor Farm on the island of Vinalhaven, my family's vacation place, Bess made the leap from her 1920's childhood kitchen in Rochester. In the mid 1950's, electricity had still not reached the abandoned Poor Farm, so we made do with an icebox until midway through that first summer and the advent of power.

The decade was not important to Bess, what mattered was our shared experience with sawdust covered blocks of ice. I was flattered she willingly traveled through time to secure our bond.

Vinalhaven, 1958

I WAS 15 THE SUMMER HE wanted me to pose. It was an August afternoon and they'd come for tea. I didn't know Raphael Soyer was a famous New York painter. I figured he was just another artist passing through. The Soyers were older than our parents, both gray and diminutive, about the size of my mother. Raphael was thin and tensely alert. Rebecca, calm, with a round face and gentle, brown eyes. Her tie-up walking shoes, perforated white leather repeatedly swabbed with liquid polish, looked uncomfortably tight, even for her tiny feet. She lugged a huge, damask knitting bag with wooden handles.

On the rare occasions we had guests—socializing was never a priority for my father and Ma typically acquiesced—we entertained in the big room with the Franklin stove and painted, white floor. Open windows let in the sea air.

Our summer place in Maine was Pa's baby, the cape cod cottage and its colossal afterthought. I don't know how he convinced Ma, but I believe it had to do with the memory of their 1945 visit to the island. Newly arrived from Argentina with two small children, they were invited by friends, fellow artists, to leave the heat of the City and spend a month in a cottage by the sea. With trains to Rockland and ferries across West Penobscot Bay, Vinalhaven had long been a favorite vacation spot for Northeasterners, especially folks of modest means. The others went to North Haven or Bar Harbor. My parents would always remember those days, idyllic and perfect.

Our acquisition of the Poor Farm happened more than a decade later. There must have been significant coaxing, despite Ma's compliant nature. In the end, it was hard to challenge Pa's enthusiasm. First, there would be the satisfaction of fixing up an old place, an important lesson for the children. We were being raised on a strict diet of self-reliance. Next, peace of the country, the sea air and woods of Maine. Finally, freedom, my dad's freedom from the University and teaching. A summer retreat for his own work, his own creative time.

Who could argue? Not Ma. Her mild temperament and genetic makeup did not include markers for debate and disagreement. Years ago, when there was all that talk of men getting in touch with their 'feminine side', I realized a 'masculine side' doesn't exist for some women. That was my mother, so serene with her femininity, she had no desire to be a fireman or astronaut, head of the family or leader, and she never wanted to carry the household keys as her Spanish matriarchs had, proud bearers of an indisputable tradition. Ma didn't even drive a car. I don't know if she lacked motivation, or if it was Pa's impatience. He tried teaching her, but those country 'rides' around Iowa City didn't last. His need for control had him squeezed in beside the partly open driver's door. Half hanging out, he held on to the door handle with his left hand, his right arm wrapped around her shoulders, fingers itching to grab the wheel. He was the opposite of easygoing during those driving sessions, and there were frequent, nervous outbursts—*'FRENO!* BRAKE! *FRENO!'* It's not surprising he sought out those country roads, not surprising she never learned. If a car passed, he signaled politely—he would have tipped his hat had he been wearing one—while Ma struggled to control her laughter. Generally reserved, our pretty, petite mother occasionally erupted like Vesuvius, a spontaneous laugh bubbling up from her depth. She didn't have an innate sense of adventure, and that was fine. Pa had more than enough for everyone.

The Poor Farm entered our lives during the summer of 1956, changing everything forever. Instead of traveling from Iowa to Minnesota for our usual two-week vacation—by then our family had grown to five children—my parents rented a cottage on the island. One evening, instead of searching the beach for old glass bottles, we walked into town for ice cream. The *'For Sale'* sign posted on the Town Hall's façade included the 1925 photograph and a short narrative. My brother, William, read aloud, ice cream cone in hand.

> ... *the Big House was added to the existing cottage in the early 1900's to accommodate the indigent. The Poor Farm and accompanying property will be sold 'as is'.*

Wasting no time, the next day Pa and William went out to inspect the place. Though abandoned for years and in shocking disrepair, it was impossible to ignore the proud, lonely structure, tenaciously clinging to its by-gone status. My father—probably bored with the seashore and in need of physical adventure—decided the least he could was replace the shot-out windows. With putty, panes of glass and the lunches my mother packed, Pa and my brothers made several trips to the property.

By the time we attended the Town Hall meeting, the councilmen were duly impressed. What kind of man would take on the job of repairing windows on a house he didn't own? The high ceiling fans turned the warm evening air as my parents' bid was considered and quickly accepted, followed by the aldermen's restrained pronouncements of *good luck*. Those 'salt of the earth' New Englanders may have long known the appalling state of their Poor Farm, but they were just getting to know my father.

With more window glass, barbed wire, *Private Property* signs, mosquito repellant and brooms—all of us were promptly put to work. Sweeping the wooden floors from one end of the Big House to the other, I easily imagined the feebleminded lingering in the empty halls, the bedridden pleading for help. Fortunately we didn't know it at the time, but according to lore, the place was haunted.

It was ours—the crumbling structure, salty breezes and swaying grasses flanking stone outcroppings. Standing on our front yard facing northwest, we could see Calderwood's Hill dotted with jack pines, rising from its granite bedrock. The east side looked out over the meadow and a ledge of evergreens separating it from *Seth's Place*, Smith's Cove and the ocean. The winding Poor Farm Road accompanied our land like an old friend.

When we closed on the property, *Seth's Place*, the 'other' house, was not part of our world. I'm not sure how my father learned of it, or when he knew it would become his studio. He may have been standing in the waist high meadow when he first saw the small farmhouse in a thicket of trees—the orchard and garden's ghost, the field down to the cove and the 'Point', that outermost granite formation where gulls gathered. Or possibly, someone mentioned in passing that old Seth Norwood would likely respond to inquiries because it'd been his parents', and they were long gone. We kids were never surprised by the occasional 'Seth sightings' in the or- chard. One of us was often at the studio helping out when he would suddenly materialize under an apple tree—dirty overalls, pipe and that toothless grin. Never a bother, he just wanted a look at the old place, vanishing as surreptitiously as he'd come.

Whenever that little house entered my father's imagination to the moment it became part of our holdings, was my mother involved in the process? If Ma felt we'd chewed off quite enough with the Poor Farm, it didn't matter. Pa generally did what he wanted, when he wanted—if possible—and after so many years, she'd learned to remain calm, if possible. Signing that deed of purchase in the Town Hall, she had no idea that the next summer, when the real effort was to begin, she would be eight months pregnant.

The following June, as soon as university classes were over, Pa, William and two grad students took off for Maine, the car loaded with tools and supplies. My younger siblings and I remained in Iowa with Ma—my parents' sixth and last child was expected at the end of August. The renovations to the Poor Farm that began that summer continue throughout our youth. Accustomed to painting his own walls, Pa was ready for anything. What he didn't know about roof beams and floor joists, load-bearing walls and sagging foundations, he made up for in self-confidence and hard work. He was a quick learner and his enjoyment of manual labor was contagious.

In the room with the white floor, my mother gently encouraged Raphael and Rebecca Soyer to take cushioned seats. After some fussing and discussion about her back, Rebecca finally picked a small rocker. Our collection of chairs included a few parlor pieces with turned legs and cane seats, but most were the old pressbacks with their giraffe-like presence—height, finial horns and splayed back legs. I'd painted them white, sky blue or yellow, embellishing their pressed designs in a rainbow of colors. Assigned a room at the back of the Big House for rainy days, in good weather, the wooden veranda pictured in that 1925 photo became my workspace. Chairs, commodes and night stands came under my brush, any abandoned piece of furniture I could find in the back of the Big House, the studio attic, the barn. I was determined to give those sad Victorians a second chance. Raphael picked the tallest chair, my favorite of the yellows, its swirls and curls carefully executed in a range of autumn browns.

Both my parents were considerate and patient with the self-effacing Rebecca, the solemn Raphael. Pa was rarely concerned with societal norms of etiquette, so his moments of social graciousness, his bells and whistles, were unexpected and entertaining: the quick smile, lively eyes and jovial voice. That's how he was with the Soyers. That alone should have piqued my curiosity, but it didn't. I was an introvert—a reader, a project-oriented daydreamer who preferred painting chairs to socializing.

When we arrived that June, there was no electricity or running water, just the icebox, the one my mother-in-law, Bess, would later hear me talk about. No amenities, and we were eight: five kids, including a toddler and baby, *La Bobeh*, cranky and suffering from sciatica, and my parents. William remained in Iowa to attend University summer classes, joining us when they were over, and in August, my best friend, Alice, arrived.

Our lack of conveniences presented a pioneering adventure. As the eldest daughter, I helped cook on the cast iron wood stove that required firing up hours before dinner. On rainy days, I'd sit on the bench between the wood box and the stove, reading and tending the fire. The sawdust covered block of ice was replenished every other day. Kerosene and Coleman lamps provided light. Well water was pumped into pails for bathing and cleaning up after meals, and we washed clothes in a wringer-washer beside the rain barrel. Our sheets smelled of sea air and tasted of salt. Despite the east side's pleasant meadow, it was impossible to ignore the attached privies on the big house. They extended out like a condemned elevator shaft.

Before bed, we took turns deciding which facility to use, the first or second floor, as if it was the 'Vinalhaven Grand Hotel'. On those nightly expeditions down the halls to the hanging latrines, *La Bobeh* insisted on many stamping feet in her joking attempt to scare off mice. Those were the lighter flashes in her disengaged silence. The island was not her world.

I remember a heartbreaking moment for both my mother and grandmother. One afternoon, *La Bobeh* was staring forlornly out the multipaned kitchen windows—it had become her habit. I was doing something with the kids and my mother was starting preparations for dinner when *La Bobeh* called out that a man was walking along the road toward the Poor Farm.

We all hurried over. Though the occasional car passed, we rarely saw anyone out walking.

"I think he's a *Yid*," my grandmother said confidently.

My mother, who'd been having a bad day, was unusually silent. Hearing *La Bobeh's* words, she burst into sudden fury.

"Why do you say that, here, in the middle of nowhere? Why do you assume such a thing?"

Old, residual anger abruptly emerged, filling the room with suppressed misery. I led the kids into the other room while Ma and *La Bobeh* remained beside each other, two mute women, incapable of repairing their fractured relationship. In fact, *La Bobeh* was correct. It was our neighbor, Mr. Stone from New York. He didn't come often to his cottage further along the shore, so we rarely saw him. What were the chances of a *Yid* walking on the Poor Farm Road, in the middle of nowhere? Apparently, pretty good. *La Bobeh* was not all-knowing, she just missed her people.

At the end of hot days, if Pa was in a good mood, we'd head to our favorite abandoned granite quarry for a swim, eliminating the need for baths, much to Ma's relief. Without running water, it was a major undertaking getting the children washed and ready for bed. Hurriedly packing the station wagon with towels, fins, inner tubes and a folding lawn chair for *La Bobeh,* we were off to the gravel side road. A path from the parking area cut through wild juniper and stone-hugging blueberry bushes, passed the cigarette butt stubbed in the sand, a discarded grocery list, a forgotten article of clothing, grimy with mud. We knew it well, that walk to the clearing, yet the thrill of discovery met us every time—our own paradise, breathtaking in its serenity.

Though my sister and brothers would have enjoyed playmates, and *La Bobeh,* a bit of socializing to escape her loneliness, I was content having the small quarry to ourselves. Sometimes we took a picnic supper, packing a thermos of boiling water for the *maté* and a tea bag for *La Bobeh.* Before leaving the house, Ma filled the *maté* gourd with *Cruz de Malta yerba.* Sipping their *maté* and enjoying the granite's warmth, my parents relaxed—hushed words, a private laugh—their children never out of sight. If we went too far, too fast, wading out on those submerged ledges, the water clear and inviting until that unexpected drop to darkness, their anxious voices called us back to safety.

When William was with us, we followed his lead. Examining the sliced off cliffs, their cutting lines marked by drill holes and embedded chisels rusting in stone, his habit was to analyze and surmise. Recounting the history of granite quarrying—massive columns for St. John the Divine in New York, blocks for carving eagle gargoyles, stone for bridges, custom houses and state capitols—he brought us the past. As the western light through pines dappled our tranquil world, we listened to his explanations: galamanders, steam driven versus pneumatic drills, the mineral composition of Vinalhaven pink granite, and finally, how the advent of steel and reinforced concrete brought an end to the industry.

While my brother was busy with stone and technology, I would have worried about those immigrant laborers, had I been at all informed. Coming to the island in the mid-1800's, the Italians and Spanish spoke no English. Representatives of the granite companies met the ferries, prepared to billet the men in boarding houses and private homes. Ideally, they were treated humanely and not thrown into temporary sheds. Cold in winter, hot in summer. Some stayed, making the island their new home. Others re-crossed the ocean to find what they'd left.

As a chill moved in and Pa called out that it was time to go, we packed up the *maté* and towels and *La Bobeh's* folding chair.

When my father proudly announced that I was the painter of chairs, Raphael Soyer turned to me—an old man immersed in his world of white and gray, the wisps of hair, the baggy pants, his thick, coke-bottle glasses fixed in my direction. He was not interested in painted chairs. Settling back, he ignored peripheral distractions, accustomed to being alone with his model. His thin, serious face scarcely moved as his eyes narrowed in scrutiny, abruptly opening wide, then closing again in a squint. I felt my familiar blush. The chair dwarfed him. Avoiding his eyes, I focused on the Franklin's chimney rising behind him, watching as it grew into an African acacia tree, watching as the yellow chair became a giraffe, stretching to eat the leaves above his head.

As Ma re-appeared with the tray of tea, Soyer swiftly straightened up, tilting his head toward my dad. "Would the girl pose?"

A frown moved across Rebecca's forehead as she nodded, opening the knitting bag on her lap.

Pose? Heart pounding, I turned to my mother. How could she remain so calm at that moment, so proud? The afternoon light illuminated her beautiful face as she lowered the tray to Rebecca. What? Did she want me to pose?

Rebecca pulled out a sock in progress. Raphael continued staring. Embarrassment blocked my empathy, and I did have some, even at 15. I knew about the slide into privacy, the altered state that runs alongside the mind in contemplation, the eyes in study. The voices around him, the scraping of a chair, the breeze rustling a blind—they were not happening. Those around him did not exist. The clocks stopped. Rebecca was still unwinding the ball of speckled wool.

By the middle of July, power. Lights and a flush toilet, an electric pump to produce running water. A new gas refrigerator replaced the icebox and a two burner hot plate appeared for those warm days when we didn't light the wood stove. The Poor Farm was approaching the 20th century. We could use the shower apparatus installed above the tub, but baths were out because of our compromised well. One Sunday, when our grandmother's sciatica pain was especially bad, Pa drove the station wagon down to the 'Point', parking as close to the water as possible. Like firefighters, my siblings and I formed a chain, passing along the filled pails and loading them into the car. The water took forever heating on the wood stove. When the bathtub was full, *La Bobeh* was finally happy. She had her own 'saltwater cure', just like the old country.

Our well was an ongoing concern that made Pa incredibly uneasy. We were programed with apprehension. I hated those underground springs for holding us hostage, for threatening to run dry at any moment, so we were told. A broken record of vigilance played continuously. When it was a bad day in the studio, a wind began in the orchard and blew across the meadow. By the time it reached the Poor Farm, it had gathered menacing strength and was no longer about Pa's work, but always about the well. Too much water was being used. The pump was overheating. We weren't being careful. Turning like anxious whirligigs, we learned to weather the challenge, knowing better days would follow. They always did.

Every season we arrived with our big family noise and excitement, our on-going efforts to establish our vacation home. Resourcefulness is in the nature of the artist, at least the ones in my family. We enhanced the eastern wall of the kitchen with a row of multipaned windows looking out to the sea. Horsehair plaster walls were knocked down to enlarge rooms, new putty run on old casements, trim and window frames painted. In the evenings after dinner, accompanied by crickets and black flies, we took turns pushing the mower through the meadow grasses, creating that path to the sea. Yet regardless of how much was accomplished, the Poor Farm's agony of abandonment, like the smell of old wallpaper and damp plaster walls, was nearly impossible to eradicate. And when the fog lifted off the creek, approaching for its melancholy embrace, the sorrow was worse.

On sunny days, Alice and I stood on twin extension ladders, scraping, painting and gossiping, occasionally swatting away bees. In the late afternoons, we drenched our arms and legs in kerosene to clean off the paint. The times were pre-latex, pre-sunscreen and pre-OSHA. Our skin and complexions survived kerosene, the Maine sun, the sea air. I doubt it would be considered a safe work environment, up there at the top where the ladders ended, but it was truly perfect. I had my best friend beside me, sun on my back, salt on my lips, and I wielded the paintbrush. Freedom. We would have used trapeze ropes and swings, without nets, without an audience. Going back up after dinner, we watched the sun drop behind the far pines circling the creek.

The two of us painted the entire exterior of the Big House, as we children referred to it. Chatting with islanders, my dad continued calling it the Poor Farm. He preferred conversing in the original, a language some might remember. And some did. *Seth's Place*—a burial ground for the artifacts time passed by—spoke the same language. The discovery of a wrought iron door latch, a thrown pot with the remains of molasses, or a crooked milking stool, never failed to amaze. Any find that could momentarily stop the onslaught of mechanization was a confirmation of man's ingenuity.

By the time that little house was refurbished, the men in my family had become ingeniously skilled at repairing abandoned farmhouses. Gone was the aroma of apples cooking in the kitchen, the scent of lavender drying in the attic, the organ's hymns floating from the parlor. When that little house was re-born as Pa's studio, the smell of turpentine and printmakers' ink filled the air, tins of rosin and hard ground replaced sealers of apple butter, Vivaldi played from the turntable.

After breakfast, with toothpaste breath and jeans hitched to suspenders, with his walking stick and thermos of coffee, he left for the studio by way of the old gravel road. Other mornings, the path through the field. If the day went well—the burin's job pushing out curls of copper, the inking and wiping and pulling of proofs, the breaks on the deck to smoke his pipe—he was satisfied. I knew his habit of observation as he stood checking the landscape. Those visits to the Prado were still vivid. He'd hold up two horizontal fingers at arm's length and close one eye, blocking out a mass in his line of vision. The sea at the bottom, distant pines at the top, or something in between. I knew the blues and greys of the ocean, the tide rolling in or pulling out, the stretch of grasses and goldenrod undulating toward the shore. But I could not know how his eyes processed, though we stood together on the deck, the same landscape before us.

Now, a lifetime later, I wonder why that Soyer event has surfaced with such urgency. I suppose the nature of memories is their entitlement to float, coming, going, and under no obligation to clarify uncertainties that often accompany them. Because of that reminiscence, so loaded with a young girl's emotions, so shockingly devoid of facts, I recently listened to a 1981 interview conducted by Milton Brown for the Archives of American Art. The intimacy of the Soyers' voices was mesmerizing—Raphael about his work, Rebecca about their life. I was astonished by our common realities. If time played no role, our ships could have passed in the night on that ocean of creativity: the same obsessions, disappointments, elations, the same demands of imagination.

Had acquiring models become an awkward challenge for Soyer, age making the transaction more problematic? It was easier when he was younger. Encouraged by Brown, he spoke about the Depression and how it wasn't difficult finding destitute women willing to pose. Soyer gave them a cot in his studio, a place to sleep, in exchange for modeling. At times, a number of women together. Was Rebecca remembering those occasions, as she nodded to his request that I pose? Nothing had changed. The painter still needed his model and the painter's wife still loved him, still worried.

When Rebecca raised her eyes, the sadness lifting, she responded softly. Yes, her back was feeling better, and she would take her tea with one sugar.

She knew he'd want me to pose, even before he asked. She didn't say anything, knitting four, slipping one, hardly glancing up from her needles. She saw how he looked at me, as if we were alone. Only seconds passed between his request and my response, but she knew my answer before I gave it. Stillness flooded the room.

Was the situation familiar? Was she hoping to spare her husband? It was apparent from the Milton Brown interview she'd had her own life: their child, her teaching, her dedication to the Party. Like my aunt, Nieves, it seems Rebecca was more committed to *causes* than her husband. Ostensibly Soyer joined, helping to establish leftist organizations for artists, but fundamentally he was apolitical. Rebecca encouraged him to stay the course. Without her, hard to know.

The dealers and critics labeled Raphael Soyer and his twin, Moses, social realists. But Raphael wasn't interested in criticizing society, or advancing those *causes* with his drawings and paintings. There were plenty of others making societal statements with their art—artists he respected whose work he admired. Raphael just wanted to paint humanity. In the last stretch of his life, when asked by his dealer what was going on in his studio, Soyer said he was still painting disheveled girls.

My heart skipped a beat as I read that statement. When Raphael Soyer died in 1987, I was a mother of four, a wife, still a daughter, a writer, and I often felt disheveled. I know many posed for Soyer: Allen Ginsberg, Gorky, Chaim Gross, Edward Hopper, Diego Rivera. Even if I'd known it then, and who they were, I feel certain my reaction would have been the same. I know the young Raphael Soyer loved literature as I did, and I know we shared a heritage. His town was Borisoglebsk, more than 12 hours by train from Vilna and Grodno, my ancestral connections to Russia.

I know things now, but that August afternoon in the room with the white floor, I just wanted the moment to pass. Why me? We sat in a circle around the Soyers, the kids scratching mosquito bites as they waited to be excused, waited for Pa's cheerful command to scram. Why not them, or Alice?

I shook my head.

Rebecca was offended. How often had she gone through this? How many times, helping to find a model? She looked tired.

Ma disappointed, Rebecca upset. But I heard Pa's involuntary gasp of relief. Had I agreed, I know he would have permitted the posing, despite his discomfort. He respected Soyer and understood the desire for a model, a muse, an inspiration. Even at his youthful stage, he understood the negation of old age, the finality of death. It was his vocabulary. Mine was body language, and I saw his relief when I shook my head.

If my answer had been yes, 'Girl with Braid' might have been standing at the dresser with the flow blue pitcher and bowl, washing her hair. Or sitting at an open window staring at the sea, or maybe lying on a couch in the voyeuristic style of Balthus.

The painter of women shows us what he sees that we do not. Perhaps the placement of hands and crossed legs, the tilt of the head, the clothes, the chair rising behind. But does he journey beyond the physical to step foot on that 'dark continent' Freud spoke of? In the end, even if I'd agreed to pose for Raphael Soyer, it's possible the shore of my continent would not have been reached.

Later, after the Soyers' visit, an unknown tribe of jabbering earth girls moved single file in the meadow, eager for warm stones and chilly water, the salt to sooth bites. I led, Alice followed, then my sister—our long, terrycloth ponchos, billowing red sails in the wind. Traversing the narrow path, the lawnmower's width, we carried sundries for the seashore and young brothers on hips, clinging like chimps. Missing were baskets on our heads, the graceful, tanned arms, flying buttresses of support.

Genetics and family dynamics are not the only forces to forge a personality. During those Vinalhaven summers, the certainty of the island's isolation taught me the gift of seclusion and its inevitable result—autonomy.

Iowa, April 2009

MA'S BATH DOES NOT GO well. Although the water temperature is comfortable, getting wet frightens and confuses her. There's a lot of crying and whimpering. I dry her, whispering that I've brought a treat, while the caregiver goes for a change of clothes. The truth is it takes both of us to bathe her.

When she's calm, I lead her to the table for a cup of tea and the box of candy. *Jefa* checks my father sleeping in his chair and announces she's off to the drugstore. I'm always happy to be alone with my parents.

Slowly sipping her tea, Ma distractedly folds and re-folds the piece of wrap from a chocolate. Holding onto the foil, her eyes turn to my sleeping father. Frowning, she squints, straining to bring him and her thoughts into focus.

"I remember," she whispers, reaching across the table for my hand. "That man." She nods toward him. "That man wouldn't let me go." She turns back, breathing deeply. "Maybe he thought I would forget, but I remember. It was winter … lots of snow … he stopped the car in the middle of the road and said, *No!*"

I marvel at her certainty. Confusion, her usual companion, has momentarily stepped aside. I think of the saying that God gives us many gifts, and slowly he takes them back, one by one. My mother had many gifts, and she's been remarkably brave about giving them up. She's never indulged in histrionics because she can no longer speak or observe, as she once could. And she can no longer read or walk or reason, as she once could. She has courteously accepted her losses.

"I was finally going to see my Ma, but he wouldn't take me to the airport. I'd waited so long. You remember how my brothers called, week after week, telling me how sick she was, telling me to come, to hurry. Your grandmother was holding on, waiting for me … but the man said *No!*"

Considering all the things that have fallen by the wayside of her memory, why hasn't that incident? It was the one event I hoped had melted into that abyss. Disjointed pieces of the story had occasionally surfaced in her conversations, fragments she could barely piece together. I understood. It was unspeakable.

At some point, inquiring about the incident, both William and Leo confirmed the event. Leo said he'd heard it from Ma, and William, who was on that road trip, said they never made it to the Chicago airport. Somewhere in Illinois, Pa stopped, turned the car around, and headed back to Iowa. Ma told me how shocked she was, how sickened that he would change his mind at the last minute, and finally, how she despised herself for not fighting back, for being weak. But as Leo said, what was she to do? She had no family to turn to for help, she was alone, and Pa wore her down until she acquiesced.

Young and not really aware of the circumstances, I have no memory of the facts, not even who looked after us when they left. It must have been our first winter at 404. My grandmother in Buenos Aires had been ill for months. She was dying of cancer when my mother was finally allowed to plan her trip. At first, Pa had to have been willing because he got a bank loan for the ticket and made sure Ma's passport was in order. Everything was set.

On my first visit back to Argentina, I was told about Pilar's last days, how she waited, how she called out for Emilia every time the white curtain around her bed was pulled back. The equivalent of a generation had passed, yet all the family—brothers, cousins and one remaining aunt—all of them expressed bewilderment. The incident was still painful, as if it had happened yesterday. What kind of man would not let his wife return to her dying mother? Ma must have phoned to tell them she wasn't coming. In that period, my uncles' homes did not have telephones. Incoming international calls were received at the neighborhood tobacco store and an errand boy was sent to fetch someone in the family to take the call.

During that trip, for the first and only time in my life I had to defend my father, a fiercely independent man who'd never needed anyone's protection. There were explanations and excuses, and although my relatives listened to me, their opinions were formed.

Even Mauricio's brother and sister expressed their disappointment that he never returned to Buenos Aires. They told me the money he'd been sending to help support his mother was appreciated, month after month, year after year, but what *La Bobeh* wanted most was to see him. Didn't he understand?

Of course he understood, but he couldn't go back, so my mother couldn't either. The reasons were deep and murky. He implied it was about politics, but there had to be more. Whenever correspondence arrived from Argentina with descriptions of family problems and complications, he'd shout out his impatience with the lot of them, followed by impossible bragging. 'If I ever make up my mind to return, I'll show them, I'll fix all those problems in 15 minutes.'

That was my father at his know-it-all worst.

Neither of my parents ever returned to Argentina. For Mauricio, leaving behind country, friends and family was essential. Conceivably he felt hanging on to his past would compromise his present and future. I believe he wanted a clean slate for the New World. For Emilia, not going back became a residual ache she learned to live with. It was what it was. Yet she never gave up hope, even in later years as they sat together sipping their *maté* and reminiscing. Her desire to return to her country was always close at hand, and my own trips back to Argentina were a great comfort to her. Each time I wanted to take her with me, but there was no way. Occasionally I heard my father become emotional as he tried to pacify her, saying they would go back, they could do it. They never did.

I've wondered what irrational panic seized him during that winter drive to Chicago. Did he worry about my mother traveling alone? Did he fear she would not return, abandoning him and their four children? Or was it that he would be out of the loop and not in control?

It would take another twenty years before my mother straightened to her full five-foot height, expanded her chest, *pecho afuera*, gathered her strengths. Twenty years before she was able to say to my father, 'I am going, please make my reservation.' On that occasion, it was not to Argentina, but to snowy, rural Ontario, where I was about to give birth to our first child. My mother and I had planned it and she was coming. *Punto final.*

I've wondered if Mauricio had ever encountered such fierce determination in his own backyard. Backing off, perhaps he consoled himself thinking it was a mother daughter thing, finally accepting it was one relationship he could not be in charge of.

The day of my mother's departure from Cedar Rapids to Toronto, I went into labor. She tried calling us before leaving for the airport, but we were already at the hospital. She wasn't worried. Where else would I be? As arranged, Alan's brother met her Toronto flight. Philip assured Ma that Alan had called in during the day—the labor was progressing and he would be waiting at the station. After dinner and a family reunion, noisy and exciting with the children and dogs, Philip took my mother to Union Station and she boarded the train for Wingham, the hospital town fifteen miles south of our Teeswater farm. I needn't have worried about Ma being shy with Philip and Diana. Of course they'd met at the wedding, but I was always in a protective mode with my mother. Later, they told me she was bright and chatty, funny as could be, and wonderfully attentive to the children. I came to realize my mother was a different lady on her own.

It was the third week in March, still snowing and cold. I heard the whole story—how after an hour on the train, apprehension set in. How the sky was pitch black and the fields covered in snow. How she worried that Alan might not be able to meet her. What would she do in the middle of the night, in the middle of nowhere? Then Pa, and her feelings of guilt. Would he manage, alone, without her? She had never left him before. And why were there so few passengers on the train? People got off at the small stations along the route, but no one got on. It felt as though she was traveling to the end of the earth. When the train finally pulled into Wingham, she was the last remaining passenger.

Alone, she descended the train into driving snow. Looking up from the icy metal steps, she saw a single lightbulb hanging above the station platform and could just make out a tall figure with outstretched arms.

As Rachel was being taken from the delivery room after 18 hours of labor and a forceps delivery—bruised, healthy and weighing in at almost 9 pounds—Alan rushed off to meet the train, only blocks away.

"It's a girl … a girl … a girl …!"

Ma delighted in describing the moment—Alan's voice echoing from the station platform, the falling snow and his cold, smiling face, her sheer relief as she sank into his huge embrace.

In those years, the hospital stay for birthing moms was close to a week. After a couple days I was anxious to get home but Ma was beyond happy. Free to keep me company for hours on end, I'd never seen her so lighthearted, so talkative, interrupting herself only to change the baby or to assure me my milk would come in once I got home.

The night before Rachel and I were discharged, we were hit with another blinding blizzard and it took Alan and Ma hours to get home from Wingham. The visibility was so bad, they had to ride with the passenger door open so Ma could keep an eye on the edge of the road to guide them along. Later, she admitted it was the first time in her life she wasn't sure how the story would end. They had to abandon the car at the end of the snowed-in lane and walk to the house across our frozen field—Alan sinking below the surface of crusty snow, my tiny Ma walking on top. Much to her delight, they were the same height. Shaken by the harrowing experience, those two non-drinkers settled down to tumblers of cognac and our wood stove.

The next morning, blue skies and stillness. Our lane was plowed and we brought Rachel home to bright sunshine and blooming geraniums in Bitschy pots. Throughout my mother's time in Teeswater, she cheerfully tended to us. Cooking, bathing the baby, singing lullabies and bringing me glasses of milk while I nursed. Ma's reassuring presence was everything I needed—for myself, my husband, and our miraculous infant.

'The Assimilation of Solomon Teper', 1991
Losers and Keepers in Argentina,
A book of fiction, published, 2001

THIS TIME, SOLOMON TEPER FLEW to Argentina via Chile. As United Airlines flight 985 crossed the Andes, Sol's forehead remained pressed to the window, his eyes riveted to the mountains. How long had it been? How long forgotten, the majestic stones, the ancient stillness? The simple realization that his mind and eyes could so easily lapse, so easily forget, triggered an immediate and profound sense of loss.

Sol was shocked by his reaction. For years he had made this annual trip home to his mother, and never had he felt so emotional. Could the sight of mountains really create such confusion, pressing to expose other things forgotten? Could stone demand the taking of inventory? Bewildered, Sol turned from the glass. He had never been one to dwell and mull over the details of his life, and the uncharted territories of introspection were not his terrain. His habit was full steam ahead, looking back only to see where he was coming from, and never long enough for nostalgia, or analysis.

He knew that the separation from his wife, Faith, was partially to blame for this chaos of doubt and frustration. But it wasn't just Faith.

Why an inventory of his life? Sol smiled, remembering he still had his sense of humor. Why not? He could manage it.

A brilliant, so it was said, cardiovascular surgeon. Good start. Plus. Forty-five, and in somewhat of a slump. Minus?

Sol turned back to the stone landscape below him—the Andean shapes and shadows of prehistoric beasts and female figures.

A wife, two daughters, a stylish house. Plus, plus, bobkes.

270

The colossal stone silhouettes of hips and fecund bellies and breasts, dipped and swelled in the clouds. The white, veiny roads scratching the foothills, all led to the sea.

Now the girls were teenagers, and Faith wanted a divorce. She was bored with him, tired of being the 'primary parent'. Without question, a shitty minus.

The deposits of iron ore, copper green and something acid yellow, stain and streak the rock. From heights and out of stagnant thoughts, he saw those colors, in beautiful, organic shapes. Strewn stems and petals.

He ran five miles three times a week. Another minus, it should be six. But his small frame is still wiry and fit. Plus.

"Dr. Teper, would you care for a drink?"

Solomon pulled away from the glass and turned toward the steward, shaking his head.

Blood pressure good, cholesterol count excellent. Plus, plus.

The flight wasn't crowded and he was grateful no one was sitting beside him. He adjusted his seat to tilt as far back as possible.

He'd become an American. Plus. More than that really, an Iowan. It was love at first sight of her shape on the map. Iowa, planted so solidly in the middle of the country, so certain of her straight Minnesota and Missouri borders, more allowing to Nebraska, gentle to the curves of the Mississippi River. Her farms and campuses, her bankers and library volunteers, she became his America. On her part, love took longer, not like his impetuousness. A slow respect developed, steady and committed, until he felt himself taken to her heart and core, claimed forever. He hadn't intended such a love affair, nor had he ever imagined that love would change him so. That part was sad. Except for his accent, not much remained that reminded him of his village in Santa Fé.

There was little that made him different from his colleagues at the hospital. They wore the same clothes and built the same kinds of houses, with whirlpools and Italian tile floors. They had the same kinds of wooded lots, the same cars, even the same friends and memberships in the same athletic clubs. Plus? Minus? Who knows. Those were the things he had never cared about.

How many other beautiful things, like the mountains, had he forgotten in his life time?

Inventory complete, so soon? No, his mother. She was old and lived in Argentina. Plus. She could be old and living with him in Iowa. Minus. She still thought he was a genius, and gorgeous. Plus.

One more thing. Sol sat up straight.

He wasn't balding, like so many of his American colleagues. His thick, curly dark hair was rapidly turning gray, but he wasn't losing it. Plus.

Now it was done. Surely, Faith, surely these are all the makings of a desirable, contemporary, North American male? Sol felt the tightness in his chest again, tense and swift, burning. He knew he shouldn't think about her, he knew he should let her go. But why, Faith, why?

"Your sarcasm, for starters."

He could hear her voice, he could see her long, slim body leaning against the stone wall beside the fireplace. She had just showered. Underneath her loose, white sweats, he knew her shoulders were tan and lean, fit from the months of tennis. Despite her usual calm, her body had tightened nervously as divorce crossed her lips; the high, cool forehead and fine nose on the cutting edge of concentration. She had up pulled her blond hair, away from her face, still so incredibly beautiful. Years ago, when Faith met the department's legendary, retired surgeon at a cardiology cocktail party, she'd blown him away with her slim physique, her cool, Norwegian looks. Although teetering at the brink of senility, crackers and cheese crumbling down his tie, the old surgeon was still preoccupied with ancestry, physical delineation, and of course, racial characteristics. He was not at all surprised to learn that Faith was from Decorah. Carefully he explained to Sol that the Scandinavian immigrants had gone north in Iowa, while the others, the Italians, the East Europeans, had remained in the south. For in Decorah, he added—this stalwart of surgical innovation, this pillar of scientific knowledge—in Decorah, the streets are wider and the people are taller and fairer.

It had been a rainy, damp evening. Sol could still smell the spring earth outside the living room windows, the scent of Faith's shower as she pulled away from the fireplace wall and walked past him toward the piano. He knew there had been stress, now and then. But never before had she mentioned divorce.

"Seriously Sol, we've grown apart. What more can I say?" She ran her fingers along the keys.

He had watched her face in silence, not taking in her stupid words. Even the new freckles seemed intense. She had spent the weekend at the cottage with the girls, closing up for the season. He would do anything for her, absolutely anything.

"You know it as well as I do. Surely I don't have to stand here and make a list!"

"Faith, you're asking me for a divorce. I want to know why."

"For God's sake!" She walked over to the window. "I'm tired of this marriage, Sol, tired and lonely. I'm sick of being the primary parent. I'm sick of competing with the hospital for your attention." She stood with her back to him, looking out at the wet hostas clustered along the walk. "Then, when I get your attention, I'm bored," she said quietly. "You bore me. Do you understand?" After a few seconds of silence, her shoulders drooped, she turned around. "Sol?" her face had softened. "I didn't mean it to come out that way … but surely you've known? Surely you've felt it?"

She'd never put it quite that plainly, that he bored her. But she would not wound him, he would not permit it. "Do you think I'll just give you a divorce? The way I've given you other things you've wanted, with love and affection, and no questions asked?" At that moment, he'd felt like a surgeon gearing up for the operation. The cool determination, the energy, the control. "You really are a spoiled bitch, Faith."

"Really?" Her voice became crisp, mocking.

"Yes, really. And I'm fed up hearing about your primary parenting!"

"Don't make me lose it, Sol!"

"My darling, you knew I wasn't going to stay home and change diapers and make peanut butter sandwiches. You knew I was a surgeon when you married me."

"What about me!" Her face suddenly contorted, her clenched fists pressed into her chest. "ME!" She moved quickly around the room—window to fireplace, fireplace to couch, couch to piano. Her body taut, like a fine, pacing lioness. Finally she dropped down onto the piano bench. "I just want out, Sol," she'd said quietly.

"And what if I don't?"

[EXCERPT]

They had been 'Faith's girls' from the beginning. She had made them in her image, and it was no one's fault but his own. He had permitted it, because he loved it, and them. Perhaps he should have listened to his mother and occasionally brought them to Argentina. She'd always said it would be good to bring them, to teach them Spanish. But clearly he had not cared enough, more than that really, he had not wanted it. Yes, he had not wanted it, and it had been through choice. His past had been his past and his present was his life. When the girls were young, the excuse was the long trip. He'd convinced himself he was doing the right thing by sparing his little, blond daughters. And Faith had supported him, saying, 'all that way, to spend a dusty week in Moisés Ville?' Faith had been to Moisés Ville only once, and once had been enough. In the early years, he'd sent his parents tickets, so they could visit their grandchildren in Iowa. His own visits to Argentina had been sporadic events, when guilt suddenly weighed on his shoulders. But since his father had died five years ago, he had returned, conscientiously, every year.

[EXCERPT]

Finally, on Saturday afternoon, wanting to escape the noise and commotion of his mother's house, Sol walked over to the old Brener Shul where he had attended *cheder*. It was cool and quiet inside. Someone had cleaned and repaired, painted. Sol sat down on a bench in the front row. Nothing had changed, he realized, looking at the simple green walls and the wooden railings of the women's balcony. He saw the same trees through the two large windows flanking the carved, wooden ark. It was still there, the ark, with its painted lions and cornucopias of fruit, still as he remembered it.

Sol suddenly stood up and quickly left the synagogue. He did not need to sit there and confront his ghosts and the ghosts of his town. He did not need to hear the old voices. It was enough that his village was dissolving. It was enough that he had not given to his children—never mind his heritage, his language, his culture—but he had not even permitted them a piece of his own clear, ringing childhood, peaceful and nurturing. Had it been through good intentions? Or neglect? Or perhaps fear, fear that his two, blond daughters might stake their claims, and that his past would no longer be his? It was enough that he'd been so self-involved he hadn't known, honestly hadn't known that Faith was tired of him. It was enough that it took his mother to make him realize the divorce would affect his children, too. And were they all better off for it? He, the girls, Faith, his mother? Were they better off, because for whatever reasons, he had not shared?

Madrid, winter, 1954

TOWARD THE END OF DECEMBER 1953, the Barragáns arrived, our Buenos Aires relatives—my mother's brother, Luis, his family, and the *Abuelo*, our grandfather. It was an emotional reunion for Ma. She hadn't seen her family in a decade. Her own mother had died of cancer the spring before so that time with her father was especially poignant.

While Luis and Isabel searched for *pensión* accommodations, we were one big clan. Our overflowing flat was lively with talking, laughter and storytelling that continued from one meal to the next. The sleeping arrangements were tricky. Leo and Andrés, our youngest cousin, shared a single bed, one at each end. Bed-wetting was an issue and it was never clear who the offender was. Mornings found both boys sitting up in bed, bright-eyed and bushy-tailed, each pointing a finger at the other. Museums, sites and outings to Segovia, Avila, Toledo and beyond, were ongoing. The car was small and we were five adults, two teens and four children. We took turns, the trips carefully choreographed. When my uncle, aunt and the boys moved to their new lodgings, it was like the Yiddish folktale about the farmer who complains of going crazy because his dwelling is too small and his large family too noisy. When the Rabbi advises him to bring in the chickens, goats and sheep, things go from bad to worse. Finally the Rabbi tells him to let the animals out, the chickens, goats and sheep, and at last, peace. Only our grandfather remained with us in the apartment. Serenity reigned.

After so much time apart, my mother was delighted to have her father. They sat together in the small parlor dining room, the *Abuelo* reading while Ma repaired his garments. She darned socks, mended worn coat sleeves and cleverly removed and reattached shirt collars, frayed side down. The shirt was given its 'second chance', a Depression trick she learned from Pilar. We all enjoyed our grandfather's company. For Mauricio, his father-in-law was '*Don Luis*', a term of affection and respect. For William, he was the long-lost *Abuelo* from his first five years, before America. The plan was to have *Don Luis* accompany us back to the States in June. My parents were hopeful that Iowa would appeal and he'd want to stay.

He went for long, daily walks and on Sundays, he took one of us with him. It was an exciting event when he returned from a bookstore with a specially ordered volume. A voracious reader, he occupied his days with leather-bound volumes on the lives of Spanish painters. His custom, while reading, was to sit backwards on a ladder back chair. As he rested his heavy book on the top slat, his legs embraced the chair's hind legs. I was fascinated that the pages of those tomes required a slicing open with his pen knife before they could be turned, a task he completed with finesse and satisfaction. He was not in a hurry, on the contrary, he relished the pause, a further moment to contemplate the preceding page.

While we were busy with homework or drawing, the *Abuelo* sharpened our pencils with his silver pocketknife, methodically marking a neat groove around the six yellow sides before shaving away the wood. One of his great pleasures was ridiculing Franco. More than once he held up a copy of the newspaper *ABC*, with a photograph of Franco on the cover. 'Mauricio, where should I give it to him?' He asked gleefully, penknife poised.

The Madrid reunion proved challenging for my father and uncle, though they both had positive memories of growing up together. They struggled. Despite visits to Madrid's museums and evenings of *maté* drinking and recollecting, too much water had passed under the bridge. Buenos Aires and their close camaraderie of youth was irretrievably lost, at least for my dad. Their differences were ideological. Like so many Argentines, my apolitical uncle had become accustomed to life under Perón, and my highly opinionated father was personally stung by the political apathy.

Intense discussions, mostly Pa's voice, broke the calm. One evening he called out asking me to fetch one of the Lincoln books he'd been reading. I knew he meant the volumes of Sandburg's biography that lay stacked on his bedside table. The atmosphere in the dining room was taut with discord. I placed the book on the table and cautiously opened it to the frontispiece with the photograph of Lincoln. He slapped the book closed and pounded on the cover, emphasizing to my silent uncle, some point about the United States of America, democracy and freedom.

In the midst of this family unrest, the *Abuelo* suffered a heart attack. Recovering enough to return home from the medical clinic, he required continuous attention and his convalescence was slow. My mother tried to make our surroundings comfortable and happy, but she was exhausted from worrying and caring for her father. In April, it was decided a seaside vacation to Alicante would provide a needed rest. Luis and Isabel moved back to our apartment with their boys and took on the responsibility of the *Abuelo's* medications and diet. If I'd been 15, or even 13, I might have been more attuned to the pressures at home. But that spring I was still a child, navigating those Spanish seasons with good spirits and youthful curiosity.

Alicante was my first memorable encounter with the sea. When we'd first arrived in the States, there was that month on Vinalhaven in a cottage by the water, but I was a toddler and have no recollection. My experience with Alicante's bluish white sky, water and sand became long-lasting and deeply personal. The evocation of large bodies of water, waves and the quality of light repeatedly appear in my fiction. Not a unique theme, but it began in eighth grade with my dramatic story, The Cruel Sea, about a lost fisherman—the summer island of my youth a residual influence, Hemingway, a new one.

We boarded at an old, rambling hotel facing the ocean. I don't recall the length of our stay or the number of rooms we occupied, but I retain vivid memories of playing in the waves, the delicious antipasto arrangements with marinated vegetables, and the piano in the sunroom. That inviting space had a wall of small windows looking to the water, books and magazines piled beside armchairs, children's toys in the corner. A real place that would eventually mesh with my fiction. The narrator of 'Wasn't Hemingway at Enghien?', the final story in my collection, *No Peace at Versailles*, sits in the *Pavillon du Lac Café*. Its curved windows hang out over the vast lake like a fish bowl. France or Spain? It's unclear where one glass enclosure ends and the other begins, where reality fades and fiction jumps in.

A piano. I was continually on the lookout in Spain, despite not being musical, or accomplished. Nevertheless, I desperately wanted to play and missed my Iowa City lessons with Mrs. Robbins. The apartment below ours at 77 Francisco Silvela had a baby grand and at some point the tenants moved away. In the interim, before the new occupants, I was permitted to go down to the piano. It was only a couple times, but what bliss. My parents must have spoken to the concierge of the building.

The Alicante hotel not only had a piano, but a piano-playing-guest, a red-headed lady my father called the Polish Woman. A huge *Señora* with an ample bosom, loose fitting, flowing garments and thickly accented Spanish. It was my good luck that she willingly sat with me at the piano. She taught me a polka I still play, though my fingers can't retrieve the simplest minuet from all those lessons with Mrs. Robbins. I loved my Polish lady and our encounters in the sunroom, just as I had the gypsies at the *Hotel Zaragoza*.

While my friend took long naps after *la comida*, the main meal, I waited in the sunroom, picking out tunes on the piano or flipping through magazines. Everyone rested after the traditional late lunch, including my family. They weren't concerned about my whereabouts, though occasionally William was sent to check on me. Some afternoons seemed incredibly long before she finally swept in, refreshed, face powdered and painted and a hefty perfume thickening the air.

The two of us remained squeezed together on the piano bench until the evening meal. I thought her pianistic command amazing: the crisscrossing of hands from one end of the keyboard to the other, the imposing foot maneuvering the pedal, her performer's humble nod and smile when someone complimented her performance. Speeding up and dramatically slowing down, melodies floated in the air above her.

Years later when Pa was cultivating those waxy, white gardenias down in his studio on Summit Street, their *déjà vu* scent brought back the sunroom's sea light and my friend at the piano.

Everyone was pleased with our Alicante days. They restored my mother and the air and sun kept us all happy and healthy. It had been a perfect vacation and I was sorry to leave the ocean.

ALICE'S WHITE PIANO WAS BEYOND hope. Of all the keys to harden like an old artery, why middle C? Alice was certain that her teacher had suspected the declining state of her piano, but she had the decency not to ask, and Alice did not have the heart to tell her of this recent development. Until then, the damages had not been that serious. Perhaps a lifted ivory here and there and a few jammed keys at the very ends of the keyboard, where Alice neither took interest nor had occasion to play. That stoic piano withstood a great deal of abuse from her brothers—they banged on it, sometimes with their fists, sometimes with anything they could find.

Alice's mother continually looked embarrassed. And the whiteness, the whiteness, when had that happened? Exactly at what point the piano was given that coat of white, latex paint, Alice could not remember. One hot July the back half of the house was repainted and unfortunately there was left over paint. Clad in shorts, paint splatters, and that knotted handkerchief on his head—looking like some kind of Arab's head gear—Alice's father wielded his brush until the paint was gone. Everything that couldn't run was subjected to his enthusiasm for the new, water base paints.

Medina del Campo, 1925

WHEN THE *ABUELO* ARRIVED IN Madrid, he brought a large envelope he said Emilia should keep. He may have known he would die in Spain, or maybe it was his wish. Castilla, home of his ancestors, land of his birth. He'd left as a young man to make his fortune in Argentina, but that never happened. A grocer his entire life, he was too compassionate to expect payment when impossible, too smart to attempt squeezing water from rocks. My *Abuelo Luis* was not known for his business acumen. His grocery career saw several bankruptcies, but he weathered his misfortunes with a cigar in his mouth and a happy-go-lucky temperament, non-complaining and easily satisfied. Except when his wife was ill. Then he worried. Life in Buenos Aires had been good, but the return to his native land offered a final peace unmatched in the New World. He was home.

One winter afternoon in Madrid, when the apartment was unusually quiet with everyone away on an outing, I sat with Ma at the dining table studying the contents of the *Abuelo's* envelope. Letters, documents, and a pile of pictures. That's when I first understood the importance of photographs for my mother, her profound need for family. Eagerly pointing out aunts, uncles and cousins, she became a consummate storyteller. Though still bright in her memory, many of those relatives had passed. Ma's rambling free associations transported me from her reserved present to an emotional past.

Recuerdos de Medina del Campo was stamped in gold, cursive lettering across the bottom of a postcard featuring The *Hotel Balneario de las Salinas*. Southern light flooded the red brick façade and elegantly balanced windows trimmed in white brick. A pleasant solarium awaited guests, as well as outdoor tables, carefully arranged. I was amazed to see my grandparents, Luis and Pilar, standing beside the fountain. As a child, I couldn't understand how they'd gotten into a commercial postcard, nor could I make out the reluctance emanating from those two startled figures. As an adult, I still consider it a miracle the moment was captured. On the card's back, '*España, 1925*', in the *Abuelo's* neat script.

Just as Luis was hurrying Pilar back from their walk, the hotel photographer waited beside his camera, smiling. Pilar had gotten too much sun. Again, she wasn't feeling well, and again, Luis was considering the doctors' recommendation to take her to the rheumatoid specialist in Burgos. The pain was worse, and her troublesome fatigue, more apparent. He tried shaking off his irritation with the photographer, but the camera caught the squint of annoyance as he proudly straightened to his 5'2" height, his right hand still resting on the small of Pilar's back. It was his habit when they walked. Luis Barragán was a compassionate man, so despite his preoccupations, he would have noticed the photographer's well mended suit and antiquated equipment, far behind the cameras used by Buenos Aires newspaper men, with their slicked hair and big flashbulbs spritzing the air. He would have understood the poor man was only trying to make a living.

It won't take a minute, the chirpy fellow assured them, pulling out a kerchief to mop his face. A memento of Medina, no? A souvenir to show your children and grandchildren, yes? Only a minute, he repeated, ducking under the dark cloth.

As winter snow fell on that Madrid afternoon, I searched the glossy, sunny image, hoping to draw out my grandparents, hoping to understand their hesitation. It was hard visualizing our *Abuelo* as that young man. And what was the small box tucked under his left arm?

"A watercolor paint case," Ma responded, smiling. "My parents were married ten years when they went to Medina for the waters. The Buenos Aires doctors advised visiting the renowned specialist in Burgos and taking advantage of the hot springs in Castilla.

The waters at Medina del Campo were said to be exceptionally healing, especially for rheumatoid arthritis …" Her fingers traced the gold lettering at the bottom of the image. "Pilar always knew how to make things better, even in pain. It was never difficult for her. When there was family trouble, she pulled herself together and could fix anything. She had a good heart. Everyone respected her … your father loved her and she loved him."

That was the first time I'd heard Ma say that Pa loved anyone. At the age of 11, I had no way of knowing that *family trouble* had to do with my other grandmother. It would be years before I learned that *La Bobeh* Ana had been adamantly against my parents' marriage, and that the ceremony happened without her knowledge.

On the day of the wedding, Guillermo, my father's oldest brother, volunteered to remain at home to allay their mother's suspicions while his siblings rushed off to the morning event. Realizing her sons hadn't appeared in the kitchen for their *café con leche*, *La Bobeh* Ana began a determined search.

Whenever *La casa de la Vieja* came up in conversation, I could hear the agony in my father's voice, long after leaving his maternal home, after leaving his country, after living in Iowa for decades.

"Imagine, borrowing money, buying a lot and building a house during the Depression, when no one around her had a dime! It took all of us just to hang on to it. *El Viejo,* my brothers, all of us. We worked multiple jobs to keep that pile of shitty wood—*¡Un montón de madera de mierda!*—out of the loan shark's hands."

Marching through the *estilo chorizo* courtyard to the back garden, *La Bobeh* inspected chicken coops, lean-tos for bathing and laundry, and lifted clothes lines to peer over the stone wall separating her from neighbors. As she grumbled, perplexed, the young couple were saying 'yes … in sickness and health … for better for worse …'

Was she wearing that long bathrobe of gray flannel with the whipstitched collar and lapels? Perhaps not, she was only fifty when my parents were married. But shortly after the wedding, after the accident that took the lives of her husband and eldest son, family photographs taken on the patio of 4156 Calle Helguera regularly featured *La Bobeh* and her robe. Warm weather or cold, one photo to the next, that whipstitched collar remained pulled up around her neck—protecting against drafts—while patient, appropriately dressed relatives posed around her wicker chair.

La Bobeh's brother, *Tío David*, a professional photographer, was no longer in charge of tracking the family. He had finally thrown up his hands in exasperation after his beloved brother-in-law, Abram, died. *Tío David* had been documenting his sister's married life since the beginning, since that first nuptial recording of the attractive pair sitting across from each other at the table. The good-looking Abram and beautiful Ana dressed in their finery, the lace tablecloth, samovar and silver candlesticks brought from the old country. There is stillness over troubled waters in the steely resolve of Ana's gray eyes, a nascent abdication in Abram's face.

From February 15, 1907: THE RIFKE CHRONICLES
Losers and Keepers in Argentina
A book of fiction, published, 2001

AARON, WHO HAS BEEN LIVING with the Milekofskys, helps out with part of his weekly salary and puts away the rest. He's saved enough to finally bring over his fiancée, Sonia, and her younger brother. Peshke told me that it was made quite clear to Aaron that, if he wanted Sonia, he was to bring her little brother as well. In Vilna, they left a married sister with many children. Sonia and her brother are inseparable. I admire her for that. I still wish I'd been able to bring my younger brother with me. For the moment, they are living with an older cousin and her family on Talcahuano street, not far from our apartment building. Sonia helps the household by doing piecework embroidery.

I've met Sonia once. She is indeed as striking and formidable as her photograph promised. That evening, she was wearing a deep amber, velvet dress she'd brought from Vilna. The bodice was pleated brocade with strips of lace in the same rich color—more lace at the collar and cuffs. I haven't seen such wonderful fabrics in years. I'd almost forgotten they existed! We've gotten so used to our dark, functional cottons, our simple blouses and skirts. We wear poor versions of the 'Gibson Girl' attire. Sometimes Peshke's girls bring home fashion magazines, hoping their Mama might produce a clever reproduction on the next occasion for a new dress. Peshke is skilled with her hands, and her girls are never disappointed.

Sonia's dress seemed so incongruous in our tenement, but so beautiful. It enhanced her figure, with the full sleeves and tight waist. She looked positively regal. Her pearly skin and shiny, chestnut hair make it clear why Aaron is so smitten. She has a smooth manner and is quite articulate, but she makes me nervous, and I can't explain why. Despite her great beauty, there is something calculating, almost cold about her steel, gray eyes.

Peshke is not pleased, and she does not look forward to being Sonia's sister-in-law. A wedding is planned for a few months hence.

Family troubles continue, 1938

N O, GREAT UNCLE DAVID WOULD never have permitted my grandmother to pose in that bathrobe. Always a fastidious dresser, there was no way he would have allowed that dreary flannel garment in his photographs.

He was married by then. A bachelor most of his life, he had been devoted to his sister and her family. After all, she'd brought him with her from the old country, along with the samovar and candlesticks. They were a package deal, Ana had informed her fiancée, Abram. It was the only way she would join him in the Argentine. *Tío David* lived at his sister's beck and call, kind and willing, but the moment must have come when her self-indulgent anger was the final straw. It goes without saying that Ana did not approve of his marriage, or the woman.

That mid-December day in 1937, Guillermo, my grandmother's first born, tirelessly followed behind his mother attempting to distract her as she shooed away chickens and left no shed door unopened. Because he was the most caring, the most respectful of all her sons, the gentle Guillermo missed the courthouse ceremony, the modest wedding celebration Pilar had prepared, and most of all, he missed the satisfaction of seeing his brother so happily wed.

I was 15 or 16, old enough to understand, when Ma's *Bobeh* stories began emerging, always triggered by renewed, marital complications. After the deaths of *La Bobeh's* husband and eldest son in the Patagonia, she moved in with my parents in Córdoba, despite her disapproval of the union. Her visit occurred in the months following William's birth, a stressful moment for Emilia, a young bride and nervous new mama. Especially exhausting was her moth-er-in-law's continual superstitious nonsense about the baby's care. Under no circumstances should the infant's bathwater be thrown out in the dark, and so on and so forth. It was a challenging time for the marriage. My parents both suffered, my mother assured me, but she never forgot my father's failure to protect her—his inability to stand up to his mother.

There must have been endless pacing as he vacillated, torn. Choices involving his mother could sink him into agonizing in-decisiveness, an aberration I found hard to understand, given his self-confidence in most aspects of his life. On rare occasions, we saw signs of that residual uncertainty. After paneling our Summit Street kitchen in warm, knotty pine, the nails were never com-pletely pounded in. I don't know if Pa couldn't make up his mind or he thought he might change it.

Just as I didn't understand what *family trouble* was, I assumed arthritis was responsible for Pilar's unhappiness. Standing there in front of the Balneario Hotel, right hand resting on the fountain's basin, her beads caught the sun and her gauzy outfit, the breeze. I could see the delicate straps and tiny buttons of her fabric shoes, their squat Goyaesque heels. Even in those shoes she was taller than her husband, Luis. Why no hat? In her left hand, she held a bunch of wildflowers and feathery grasses. It must have been remarkably bright the moment the photograph was taken. Preoccupied and squinting, the *Abuelo* wore a white shirt with no collar, off-white pants and suspenders.

He wanted to take Pilar to the wooded spot he'd found on the grounds the day before, hoping to set up his easel, hoping to do a little painting while she rested beside him. Halfway there she became too exhausted to go further. He stopped to pick the bou-quet of wildflowers and grasses, hoping to cheer her. Just as they returned to the hotel, the photographer was waiting. If there was going to be a photograph, he would try to look his best. Luis placed his folded easel and small canvas at his feet. Straightening up, he reached for the small of Pilar's back.

That landscape beckoned his brushes and canvas. The distant stooks, luminous in the sun, their field's boundary stretching to meet the purple, green copse sleeping in the far shade. Close by, the fast flowing brook with steppingstones. Above him, jack pines jutted from the bluff, lifting to the sky. It reminded him of Cezanne's drawings of cliffs and pines around the Château Noir.

He missed his art books. They had to choose carefully when packing in Buenos Aires. The trunk was only so big and Pilar needed her linens and such, and they all had their wardrobes—shoes for good weather, boots and bulkier items for winter. It had been complicated, not knowing how long they would stay. That wasn't Pilar or the children's fault. He hadn't decided what his intentions were regarding their return to Buenos Aires. His old partner had plans for a new grocery emporium and wanted to regroup, but Luis wasn't sure. There was only so much failure a man could take. The cigar always helped him put on a brave face, but he wasn't courageous, not really. Perhaps this was the clean break he needed, a chance to finally be serious about his painting. Both their families were clamoring for them to stay in Castilla. There would be no shortage of accommodations, either with Pilar's family in Cardiel, or with his in Berlanga. He was hopeful that, once Pilar's pain and fatigue were eradicated, her unhappiness would vanish as well. He'd read about the Buenos Aires doctors specializing in the treatment of these disorders. Some had even gone to Europe for their studies and training with Dr. S. Freud. If the body could be healed, why not the will and the spirit?

---·•·•·•·---

EXCERPT
'Aurelio Ribera'
from *ONE APRIL AFTERNOON*
in the time of Silberman and Gould,
unpublished novel, 2010

AURELIO RIBERA HAD PERSONALLY SUPERVISED the construction of their Buenos Aires home, CASA BELLA, finally completed shortly before the wedding. He devoted many hours to the design, carefully planning the layout so southern light would embrace the rooms and patios. Isabella's depression was worst during the damp winters, and some days her body could not generate warmth. Aurelio's compassion had not faltered. He understood how essential sunshine was to his wife's wellbeing. It was the first thing she looked for in the morning, the last thing she hoped for at night, standing at a dark window, thinking of the next day.

When CASA BELLA was finished, Aurelio commissioned nine tiles, large cream slabs with a clear glaze, one for each letter. In the neighborhood ceramic factory, he undertook the lettering himself; blue script, with swirls and curls and tiny, naked angels positioned in the corners, holding the blue ribbons of each letter's configuration. Leaning over the wedging table, powdered clay grinding into his gray, serge sleeves, blue oxide glistening on the calligraphy brush, he knew moments of bliss. Since childhood he'd loved the smell of wet clay, the slick feel of fired glaze.

Aurelio wondered if this love for clay could be linked to his ancestors, a great-grandfather and his twin brothers, all sculptors. For generations, the Riberas had lived in Berlanga de Duero, Aurelio's hometown in the province of Soria. Only his great-grandfather married and raised a family. The twins remained bachelors, famous for their height and curly blond hair, both unusual in a Spanish landscape where men were short and dark. Most of all,

291

they were known for their bashful qualities and an unrivalled love of song and wine. They built a large studio at the edge of the city beside the river. In due course, they gained recognition throughout the province as the Hermanos Ribera, respected sculptors of religious art specializing in the male saints: John the Baptist, George, Jerome and Francis of Assisi and his entourage of animals. They worked mostly in clay, until the night a firing burned unattended. According to legend, the singing, drinking bachelors imbibed so much, they ended up dancing and howling at the moon. The whole kiln burnt down to a molten mess of clay and glaze.

Indifferent, or unable to cope with society's customs and rules, the twins lived in a private world. Their communication was mostly with each other—a strange combination of speech, whistling and signing. In that part of Soria where miracles flourished, and eccentrics were deemed 'magical', no one in Berlanga thought twice about the twins and their unusual habits. It was a well-known tale that in a neighboring village there'd been two sightings of the Virgin, one in this century, the other in the last, and on both occasions she was found bathing in the Duero river, nude, except for her halo.

After that infernal event, the Riberas stuck solely to wood. Turning to the forest they felled tall lindens, their faces smudged with sweat and dirt, their curls in frizzy disarray. July was their favorite month, when the fragrance of linden blossoms thickened the air and honeybees fell to the ground, intoxicated by the poisonous nectar. Sometimes, in protest or as a statement, they'd cut down an old chestnut, occasionally an olive. There was a secretive thrill in their eyes as they hauled the logs back to their studio, despite the olive's unyielding quality and the chestnut's rebellious grain, despite the dictates of a market that would ultimately have them gesso and paint their beloved sculptures.

As a small boy, Aurelio played near the remains of the family kiln. He was never able to rescue the face of a weeping John the Baptist embedded in the glazed, rocky base that had served as the structure's foundation, moss growing out of his open mouth, barnacle-like calcifications, clinging to his lips. Though John had entered the kiln a proud statue about to cross the river with the babe on his shoulders, head held high and mouth surely closed, the kiln disaster beheaded him. Aurelio understood he could not change the direction of this man's fate; yet it intensely disturbed him that he was not able to free that mournful face. For him, it became a symbol of all the world's unfortunates, trapped by their unyielding misery.

A more peaceful St. Francis, with a lamb sleeping on the hem of his cassock, was a familiar object of Aurelio's youth. His widowed mother, Juana Alegría, looked after the sculpture with the same love she bestowed on her four sons. She dusted his niche of cobwebs, inspected the painted wood for signs of cracks, and patted the lamb's head. Unlike most women of Berlanga, Juana Alegría was not religious. Nevertheless, she was discreet and respectful of her husband's family and their religious artistry. Aurelio's father, who died of a ruptured appendix at the age of thirty-five, was a teacher like his own father. Though neither of them had followed the Riberas' sculpting tradition, nor had any of their descendants, the young Aurelio believed artistic genes were in the blood.

Aurelio was 16 when his childless uncle, Roberto, traveled from Buenos Aires to Berlanga in search of an heir among his dead brother's four sons. When Roberto first immigrated to Argentina, he had been employed by two established Buenos Aires merchants, a grocer and a dry-goods supplier. Traveling house-to-house through the barrios, selling provisions from a horse-drawn wagon, Roberto proved to be an excellent salesman, and he was shrewd. As a child, it was said he could sell spots to a leopard. From the beginning, he insisted on collecting a commission from his sales rather than a salary. Tall and good looking, a throwback to his ancestors, the blond, whistling twins from Berlanga, he rapidly earned the respect of his bosses and had a list of dependable customers. He soon saved enough money to court the blue-eyed daughter of an English family, appreciative of his fresh produce.

Within a few years, he opened his own corner store and eventually the grocery, Roberto Ribera, Wholesaler. His English wife dressed in loose, white linens and enjoyed the comfort of the patio hammock to read popular novels. She was loving enough, in fact, the union was remarkably passionate, but it produced no children.

Aurelio was his uncle's choice. The following spring, he left Spain for Argentina, with little more than his mother's blessings and assurances that he would succeed and achieve. He happily adjusted to his new country, learning the grocery business from his Uncle Roberto (not well enough) and the English language (quite well) from his blue-eyed aunt. In short order, the business became Ribera & Ribera, Wholesalers.

Aurelio was grateful to his uncle, but he could not forget those artistic genes that ran in their family. The truth was, he wanted to apprentice himself to the potter down the street, but he had no idea how to tell his uncle. He was contemplating these thoughts when a tragic turn of events unexpectedly sealed his fate. His aunt and uncle's premature demise left the wholesale grocery business entirely in his inexperienced hands. He was 27 and married only a matter of weeks. In view of this catastrophe, thoughts of clay had to be put aside. Aurelio knew he did not have the nerve and strength it would take to go against the grain, to howl to the moon. He was not a rebel, he could not be a maker of art. The grocery business was now his life, the reason he was living in Buenos Aries and not Berlanga.

Iowa, April 2009

Y EARS LATER, AFTER SPAIN, MA told me the hot springs helped her mother's inflammation, but it wasn't until the family returned to Argentina and my uncle Julio was born—my grandmother's last child—that she regained her health. In 1936 Julio was a boy of eight when the Spanish Civil war broke out, when Pilar offered her help to the Republican effort. She collected clothes and funds in her Spanish community of Buenos Aires, and every free moment was spent knitting socks and sweaters for the Republican troops. A new cause, a new way to keep busy beyond caring for her family.

There's a hint of a smile in the 1912 sitting taken shortly after my grandparents' wedding, but only a hint. It's not easy finding joy in photos of my grandmother—not formal or informal, not young or old, not happily engaged with the people she loved. Was it the dour portraiture style of the period? Or were the few existing photographs taken on the wrong day, from the wrong angle. And why weren't there more? Did Pilar dodge the camera the way I do?

A lot of 'whys', and did some form of melancholia play a role in my grandmother's personality? I don't remember her. I was a toddler when we left Argentina, so I've relied on my mother's narratives, and later, my aunt Nieves' carefully chosen words during my Buenos Aires visits. Ma always emphasized Pilar's goodness of character, while Nieves spoke cautiously of her mother-in-law's disapproval. 'I know you want to write,' my aunt Nieves confided during our last conversation, 'so I'll speak openly.'

She revealed that Pilar was extremely judgmental and only warmed up to her at the very end. She was in the clinic and dying

of cancer when she remorsefully admitted she had been wrong—
that in truth, Nieves had been a wonderful wife for her son, Julio.
'Despite the fact that I was a Jewish socialist from the provinces,'
Nieves added candidly, uncertain which bothered her mother-in-
law more—*Jewish, socialist,* or *being from the provinces.*

Neither my mother nor Nieves spoke of the sadness and
dissatisfaction that seemed obvious to me. I never heard anyone
mention *depression* in connection with Pilar, but I still wonder if the
Abuelo wasn't well aware that his total devotion, and everything else
good in Pilar's life, were not enough.

My parents never wanted to hear talk of mental illness. My
father habitually dealt with it in the print room over the years, and
occasionally he referred to a student as a 'a real loon', or a 'cuckoo-
ru-loo' *sotto voce.* I know he worked hard getting them help, making
sure they found their way up the hill to Psychiatry at the University
Hospital. But it was different when it came to family—that landscape was certainly not a place to visit. I imagine that when my
parents spoke about my grandmother or her eldest son, depression
was not a topic of conversation.

And so I come to my uncle Luis, my grandparents' eldest
child, my mother's older brother, my father's art school companion.
During my trips to Buenos Aires, I found him more self-involved
and closed than those months in 1954 Madrid. He neither inherited his father's generosity of spirit, nor his mother's goodness. He
preferred his own morose company.

While not surprised by the unhappiness seeping into my generation—one of my cousins was hospitalized for depression, though
his father assured me the doctors were wrong in their diagnosis—I
was shocked seeing despondency stretch into the third generation.
Stunned by the mantle of sorrow surrounding a cousin's child, a
small, grim-faced girl, I found myself both saddened and relieved
to see she had inherited the eyes of her great grandmother, Pilar.
And finally, our son, Adam, with his entrenched disturbances. He
calls himself a prisoner of war—a war within—and rightly so. Until
the end of my father's life, he insisted there was nothing wrong with

our Adam, nothing that hard work wouldn't fix. It was the doctors who were wrong.

I've no idea what became of the Medina del Campo photo with the *Hotel Balneario de las Salinas*. Occasionally it materializes for me, and when it does, I surrender its existence to the grace of God—a shocking idea, considering my disbelief. Luis and Pilar, uncomfortably poised in the sun, almost insignificant in the grand scheme of things, and yet (here's where the grace of God comes in), the moment was captured by a poor photographer in a mended suit.

Then, the leap to Van Gogh and his vase of iris. From Saint-Rémy he wrote Theo, his brother, marveling at the harmony of colors, the alizarin crimson background, the bluish purple and greens of the iris.

It hangs now in the Metropolitan Museum in New York. Violet iris shiver against a nude background drained of that crimson, but for the hint of blush at its edges.

Where am I going with this?

Besides all else that plagued Vincent, how was he to know the fugitive nature of his alizarin crimson? How was he to know its molecular composition would program the loss of color over time?

How were Luis and Pilar to know the future magnitude of that fleeting moment beside the fountain, the impact of their hesitation and preoccupations? How were they to know of a granddaughter's need to connect, through the distance of time.

It confounds me that happiness can be as fragile as that photograph, as fugitive as Van Gogh's alizarin crimson. These truths have taken on new dimensions as I count my blessings and consider my own life, now divisible by decades. Years that have come and gone, strengths and assets, weaknesses and loses. Like plasma physics and black holes, like the age old production of power from flowing water and gigantic wooden gears, despair is one of my blind spots—another challenge, another destination I'm unable to reach.

I've been told I inherited Pilar's homemaking gifts, and my *Bobeh* Ana's fair hair and light eyes. Everything considered, I am grateful for all I didn't inherit.

EXCERPTS
'When Louisa Cheyenne Meets the Bornsteins'
from a story collection in progress,
This I Can Tell You

THE BORNSTEINS AND THEIR TWO young children arrived in Iowa on a hot, autumn day. World War II had been over less than a month and the head of the art school was away for his two weeks of holidays.

With the director gone, the studio faculty decided they ought to welcome their new colleague from Argentina. A fine idea, but in truth, the two painters, the sculptor and the potter were annoyed and threatened before they laid eyes on Saul Bornstein, and when they met, his lively personality and bright disposition only made things worse.

They were not impressed. He'd been hired to create a print-making program, but exactly who was he and why such glowing recommendations from the Guggenheim Foundation? The petulant faculty fretted and grumbled. So what if he was a fellowship recipient and studied at the New School in Manhattan? Big deal. The four art professors squabbled and speculated until one of them remembered: Dr. Tucker Holmes, president of the University, and what's-his-name, the director of the Guggenheim Foundation, had been Rhodes scholars and Oxford roommates. There you have it, the four concluded. As for Saul, Lily and the kids going from the train station directly to their accommodations at Iowa House, the Presidential Mansion, that was far more baffling and upsetting.

Students were returning to the university in hordes, many on the GI Bill, and rental possibilities were practically nonexistent. Considering the town's dire housing shortage, the practicality of Dr. Holmes' invitation and the generosity it extended to foreigners, newcomers to Iowa, was obvious, though apparently not to the studio faculty.

In a gesture springing from envy but disguised as mischievous goodwill, the two painters, the sculptor and the potter sent the art department's favorite nude model to meet the Bornsteins' train— tall, blond, Louisa 'Lulu' Cheyenne, a.k.a., The Indigo Siren.

Not a lot was known about the gentle Louisa. Her family farmed in western Iowa near the Loess Hills, and Cheyenne was not her real name. It was something like Yoder or Eby. Years later, when the Bornsteins and their growing family were comfortably settled in that rambling Victorian house on Oak Avenue, Lily had a cleaning lady named Grace Yoder. She was from Kalona, one of several Mennonite girls who carpooled into town every Wednesday. They'd park the car in the middle of the block and spread out along the street to clean those stately, old homes, polishing bubbly windows and sweeping oak leaves off compromised sidewalks.

During the winter that Louisa from the Loess Hills was sleeping with that visiting art historian from Schenectady, in a moment of trust she told him that as a teenager, she'd gone west with a group of young people to help build an Indian meetinghouse. After that, she became Louisa Cheyenne. The historian, a specialist in Sumerian art, told everyone he knew, and some he didn't.

That bit of information was of little interest to the art faculty. Many people left their past or went by other names, especially artists. It was like talk of borderline personalities, or disorders of the brain, also not of much interest, and for the same reasons. In that time after the war, university artists did not have a mental health vocabulary to draw upon. Terms such as bi-polar, schizoaffective, Asperger's, even 'syndrome' and 'episode' were not yet common. Political correctness wasn't even a speck on the mental health horizon. 'Nuts', 'crazy', and 'mad' were bandied about, 'loony' and 'Lulu', in Louisa's case—acceptable expressions in artistic circles, benign enough to describe behavior, sufficiently stimulating to endorse creative autonomy.

No one really knew what was wrong with Louisa, including the men she took to her bed. She made a valiant attempt at cheerfulness, despite the anxiety and debilitating detachment, the drifting back and forth between the world around her and her private place. Until the day Saul offered Louisa the job as his assistant, she'd never found anything that seriously engaged her, other than working on the farm in her mother's vegetable garden, and modeling for art students.

She felt good standing on the main table in the print and drawing studio, holding a pose. Grateful to have her clothes off in the heat of summer, she focused on the fans' droning sounds. On winter days, her copious figure absorbed the space heater's rosy warmth. Frost collected on the insides of the old windowpanes and she kept her kimono on the wobbly, bentwood chair stained with printer's ink. Usually the professors had her do ten-minute action poses. Louisa didn't mind, but she was happiest when they let her do what she wanted, the heroic stances. They were her favorite and she assumed them naturally: Norse goddesses with thick, blond braids over bare breasts, a yardstick for spear, Athena in her niche, the posture of Diana of the Hunt, with her bow and dog, her strength and speed. When she wasn't modeling and wore clothes (though never undergarments, as rumor had it), she dressed in purple—the Indigo Siren.

That September day Louisa waited on the station platform for the Bornsteins' train, she wore her favorite Oaxaca shift of mauve cotton—ankle length, side seams split to the knees, breasts embroidered with purple peacocks. Blond hair, released from its braids, rippled down her back and velvet petals were tucked in around her ears. Silver bracelets adorned her forearms. Her posture was commanding and she moved with the physical certainty of a dancer. Though her verbal communication came in a surge of fragmented questions, a rapid singsong of repeated, self-doubting statements, the rich resonance of her voice was a fitting match for her striking presence. Everyone agreed that the Indigo Siren could have been on the stage. Wagnerian operas would have suited her, except that Louisa couldn't sing, and if things were really bad, she could barely speak. When her disconnect became too intense, she referred to herself in third person.

"Long trip, long trip?" Leaning forward, Louisa peered anxiously at Saul, then Lily—back and forth, her perspiring brow wrinkling with concern. "Good night, Louisa! Such a thing to ask." She straightened up and looked at the sky. "Of course, long trip. But what a perfect day to arrive in Iowa, absolutely perfect!" Eyes closed as though responding to private music, she threw her head back and flung one arm up in the air, her body swaying from side to side.

At times, Louisa Cheyenne realized her momentary lapses. Abruptly pulling herself together, she addressed Saul. "You're wondering how she could ask such a silly question." She turned to Lily. "And right you are to wonder. Long trip! Beautiful day! Good night, Louisa! What a goose she is, what a goose." She reached to tousle young David Bornstein's hair. "Why would hungry children care about a perfect day with no clouds in the sky?" Louisa grabbed two suitcases and waved for them to follow.

So, this was Iowa. Puzzled, Saul guided his family across the station platform, multiple pieces of luggage in each hand. In the breeze, Louisa's dress took the shape of her hips and breasts as she moved into a cloud of dust lifting from the empty lot beside the parked cars. The girl was kind, but Saul was offended. Why hadn't someone from the art department come to meet them? His English was still shaky, but who was this gigantic girl with the sweet face and blue eyes like the sky, and what was she saying? What did a goose have to do with hungry children, and why good night in the middle of the afternoon? A blond Frieda Kahlo, but twice as big, he thought, waiting as Louisa opened the trunk of her car. He imagined her strolling into the Museum of Modern Art, flowers in her cascading hair, bangles jangling.

Lily was drawn to Louisa's gentle manner, but she was disappointed with the long, purple cotton. Was this what they wore in Iowa? She'd gotten used to New York—the short, synthetic skirts and smart haircuts. Didn't women here know about nylon? In the city, girls were no longer painting brown lines down the back of their legs. Not that she did that. She'd considered it, but Saul would never approve.

Where did he get his energy? He had to be as tired as she was. None of them had slept on the train. Yet there he was with suitcases in hand and a spring in his step, ready to take on world, and of course, already annoyed about something. That small aggravation in his eyes hadn't escaped her. Whatever it was she would hear about it in bed. Propped on his elbow facing her, he would go on about the day—and the disappointments—the lock of black hair falling over his forehead, charming her, as always. And as always, she would listen, struggling to stay awake.

A short bob would be so much more practical, Lily thought, fixing pins in her hair with one hand. It was senseless to want things Saul wouldn't permit. Shifting Mimi to her other hip and adjusting the coats and scarves on her arm, she gently nudged David, who was dragging his heels. What were other women wearing? Lily looked around the station, but there were only men, smoking and tucking newspapers under their arms as they prepared to board.

"Hot and tired? For goodness sakes … exhausted!" Louisa helped Lily and the children into her Ford sedan. Saul climbed into the front.

"We're off!" Glancing into the rear-view mirror, she pulled out of the station and started up the hill toward town. "If we're lucky, we may have an Indian Summer!"

The car swerved around a group of students crossing the street. "On your left, the Old Capitol." Louisa's long arm stretched out the car window. "Greek revival. Built while Iowa was still a territory, it served, briefly, as our state capital, before abandonment. Eventually …" Louisa abruptly stopped talking and pulled into a parking space. "She's rattling on again … good night, Louisa." She killed the engine and turned to smile at David leaning wearily against his mother. "Look Davy, a terrific view of the entire Pentacrest with its four sentinel buildings. Someday I'll take you for a walk around." She reached and patted his head. "Now, where was I? Oh yes, the old Capitol. Eventually it was re-born as the University's heart and soul. Such a goose, rattling on the way she does!"

Saul was so reassured by the building's elegance and simplicity, the white limestone and gleaming, gold cupola, his confusion and annoyance vanished—the girl's language, the faculty not coming to the train station. Everything he saw made him want. The river, the log cabin shelters sprinkling the landscape, the big sky and orange red leaves. New York was already receding, Central Park and the museums, the Village. This Iowa would be his. He turned, glancing with satisfaction at his family in the back seat. Lily looked so peaceful holding Mimi and watching the passing sites. If only she could be stronger, not so needy, especially in the way she missed her family. It took her a long time adjusting to a new place. She was calm now, but he knew very well how sad and lonely she could become. Suddenly irritated, Saul realized he would soon be worrying about Lily. Wouldn't he have enough to deal with?

Calming, cool air entered the car windows. Holding a sleeping Mimi on her lap, Lily watched the passing campus. The town's streets seemed pleasantly less congested and cleaner than New York. Enormous trees and neatly groomed green spaces accompanied the Pentacrest buildings. Hurrying students carrying books and walking in pairs, looked fresh and young. She tried not to think of everything they'd left. In the evening, she would write her parents that they'd arrived safely and the children were over their colds. David was eating better and Mimi's cough was gone. She might even tell them she'd already met her first Iowa friend, Lily thought, glancing at Louisa.

[EXCERPT]

In later years, whenever those first months came up in Bornstein family conversations, Lily spoke of Iowa House with pleasure. Describing the stately residence with its large windows and soothing arrangement rooms, she remembered everything in detail. The parlor, with its traditional pieces of upholstered furniture and matching drapes, silky lampshades beside wingback chairs, coffee tables with magazines in neat stacks and the impressive limestone fireplace. Her favorite was the sunroom—large palms, parakeets in cages and forest green wicker. That space reminded her of home, of her parents' Buenos Aires patio with plants and cages of birds.

She often referred to her friendship with Louisa Cheyenne, but never mentioned Louisa's breakdowns. Lily was of the mind that if bad things were not mentioned, they might disappear. The most devastating episode—many years after Iowa House and the Holmes—followed the suicide of Louisa's thirty-year-old daughter, Skye. Skye had inherited her mother's frailties but none of her strengths. By the time Louisa was finally released from the hospital, undoubtedly the longest of her committals, Saul had retired from teaching and the university had terminated Louisa's contract. There was no reason to keep her on.

Indignant, Saul hired her as his personal secretary. He was old and tired, no longer working in his studio. His eyes had gotten smaller and his nose larger—it dripped like a leaky faucet—his fleshy ears, sad and drooping. None of this seemed to bother Louisa. While she sat across from him taking dictation on her typewriter, his hands grasped the air for ideas. They moved by too quickly, he complained, his voice distant and hollow.

She'd show up at the Bornsteins' condo twice a week carrying her tiny Remington and occasionally a treat for her old friend, Lily. Sometimes it was organic honey, other times, heirloom flower seeds for the window boxes. Everything had faded for Louisa: the purple cotton, her hair, the everlasting, velvet flowers. The old wringer washer on her porch continued churning purple water, but the dye didn't take the way it used to. Still tall, though time had rendered her thin and ethereal, Louisa glided quietly through her days, her voice no longer resonant. She often helped Lily prepare lunch. The two old friends enjoyed being together.

Lily was pretty much lost in those last years. Nevertheless, she had unfinished business—things to babble about, things she could not forget. Louisa had heard some stories before, others were new. One day, methodically tearing up bread for lunch—they never stopped her, it was therapeutic, and could always be made into crumbs or pudding—Lily spoke of that first duplex and the awful, matte, black furniture he'd made her live with. The pieces came from the art department's design classes. Prototypes, if all went well, seconds, if not. It didn't matter if their designs were a success or failure. He brought home those inky cabinets and coffee tables, hauling them in the back of the station wagon, never once asking her if she wanted to live with them. They were contemporary, he told her, the furniture of the future. She didn't care. She should appreciate them, he'd reprimanded. Perhaps, but she didn't.

Lily had lived under Saul's shadow for so long, in the end, she hardly knew who she was or where she could look for herself. When she passed, when the undertaker and his assistant strapped her little corpse to the gurney and tilted it upright to get her into the condo's small elevator, her family watched aghast as Lily slid down through the straps, vanishing into the white sheets. Receding was nothing new for her.

Grape harvest, Ibiza, Autumn, 1965

Seeing Alan's parents in good spirits and looking well after their lengthy trip was a relief, but unlike Alan, I was drained. It was that unexpected rainfall during the night, the early morning rush to whitewash our walls, the ride to the airport in José's cart. While I'd worried about meeting the plane on time, José was surprised by his horse's excessive pooping. Laughing and leaning forward to discreetly spread the horse's tail for every call of nature, he said it was a good thing we were returning by cab. I was too stressed to respond to his humor.

Eager to please and nervous about our lack of amenities, my parents-in-law's enthusiasm for our exotic, primitive Ibiza, was quickly reassuring. Alan, happy to see his parents, was not worried. He must have known his mom would be fascinated by the ripe, black figs on our tree. She was so delighted with their tasty freshness, nothing seemed to concern her—neither our limited water supply nor the hanging box instead of a refrigerator, not even that Alan and I would be sleeping on a straw filled mattress.

I put the finishing touches on a light meal while Alan took his parents next door to *Can Chocolate*. Moe was his usual gregarious self as he exchanged cheers with Juan and sampled a shot of the local specialty, *Frígola*. He delighted Juan by learning, *salud, amor y pesetas, y tiempo para gastarlas*. Health, love and money, and time to spend it. Juan was honored to meet Alan's parents and politely refused payment for the aperitif.

The next day, we made the trek up the mountain to the Palerm farm, eager to introduce our friends. On the trip to the airport, José told us they would be making wine and suggested we come by. It was a breezy, autumn day and Alan's parents were good sports about the hike—Bess, in her tie-up walking shoes and silk scarf stylishly tied around her head, Moe's Leica swinging from his neck. Usually Moe shot rolls and rolls of film so it's odd that he didn't take photos of that climb. The white-washed tops of low stone walls meandering the terraced landscape like bleached trails, the grapevines and almond trees, olive and *algarroba*. As we climbed higher, Ibiza Town came into view, wrapping the mountain, the sea at her feet.

Thank goodness for Moe's Leica. Alan and I refused to have a camera on Ibiza. We didn't want to be taken for tourists. Neither of us wore a wristwatch, either. If we needed to keep track of the hour, we carried our small alarm clock in our Ibiza shopping basket. The same was true in Holland. When our friends, the Bolkesteins, invited us to attend an evening orchestra practice at the church in Bergen—both parents and two of the three daughters were classical musicians—the clock accompanied in our tote. The last bus back to Bergen aan Zee could not be missed.

Sitting in a high balcony of the red brick church, taking in the orchestral music and spectacular brass candelabras, we were unaware that our alarm was inexplicably set to 8 pm. Regardless of the cause, an am/pm confusion or a carelessly engaged alarm pin, the loud, clanking ring suddenly burst into the somber, old sanctuary. As Alan dove down and began fumbling though our tote, the musicians immediately stopped playing, glanced up at us, and commenced clapping and waving their bows. We were humiliated, but not enough to go out and buy a wristwatch.

I'm sorry now that we were so stubborn, especially about a camera. We weren't thinking about the future and having to rely almost completely on visual memories. The Potts took a couple snapshots of the exterior of our house, and Moe was responsible for the few photographs we have, but there was so much more. The old *fincas* we envisioned acquiring, some of the shopkeepers in Ibiza, the interior of *Can Chocolate*, the Palerm's house, our own. Everything.

We found José stomping in the barrel, wearing shorts and a new pair of rubber *alpargatas*. María and Antonia carried in basket after basket of purple grapes waiting to be pressed. Antonia was in the process of transitioning to modern dress, but she reverted to her long skirts for Moe's camera. The three of them, José, María and Antonia probably decided her traditional outfit would be far more charming. They were right. Moe captured her posed beside the wine barrel, smiling proudly. She told us the hardest thing about modern dress, was getting used to walking. With the long skirts gone, tiny, mincing steps were no longer necessary.

In honor of my parents-in-law, María and Antonia insisted on dressing me in a traditional outfit. We stand tall and straight in that perfect space of youth and radiant bliss—the cloudless sky, the mountain, the view of Ibiza behind us. Alan's white pants and shirt are cool, nylon blends. My dark blond hair is pulled tightly back, smoothed into a braid. I wear a white apron over the black skirt, a printed blouse, an embossed black and gold fringed shawl. The garments are bulky and heavy, hard to imagine in the heat of summer. A cord, tied high above my fringed belly, speaks of forthcoming fecundity and our four children, yet unborn. My hair and gold earrings are the only elements not part of the costume.

I was so fascinated by Spanish earrings, the more antique, the better, we decided to never pay more than one thousand pesetas a pair, $16. We measured everything by one month's rent. Before we left Ibiza, my modest collection had expanded to include the three styles typical to the island. From one jewelry shop to another, I stood over glass cases, explaining our desire for *pendientes antiguos*. Eventually we were directed to an older woman who lived in town above a shop. She bought and sold, had dyed black hair, garish red lipstick and silky cushions on her couch. I could see she'd been pretty in her youth, probably pleasantly plump instead of what she'd become. I felt sorry for her. Alan referred to her as the old prostitute. Perhaps, but she had exactly what I wanted.

Madrid, spring, 1954

SPRING BROUGHT UNREST. TENSIONS BETWEEN my father and uncle increased over the winter months. They could hardly speak without disagreement. One day I returned from school to find my mother studying my uncle's paintings lined up in our foyer, leaning against the walls. The pieces had accompanied them from Argentina and Luis's plan was to locate a suitable gallery and have an exhibition during the months they'd be in Madrid. That day he told Ma to select a painting as a gift. She did.

I don't recall an exhibition materializing for my uncle, but apparently a collector expressed interest in my mother's choice, and Luis sold it. He may have had his reasons for not leaving the painting with her the day she made her selection. Perhaps he was hopeful about an upcoming show and wanted to include the piece, marking it *'Not for Sale— property of artist's sister'*. That would make sense, but it wasn't what happened, and as far as Pa was concerned, the damage was done. The falling out that followed would last too long.

Mauricio took it personally. It was unforgivable to sell what had been promised as a gift only weeks before. It became a dishonorable act that demonstrated a flaw of character. I heard his rage and name calling, words not intended for my ears. I heard my mother insisting she didn't care, it didn't matter, she could pick another.

"Let him have the pleasure of selling a painting," she said in tears.

Things went from bad to worse until the situation became García Lorca's kind of 'bad blood'.

Any little thing could set off my father, any excuse for an argument. As difficulties presented that winter, he became more volatile.

Under duress, his quick temper lashed out at the nearest target. I've never forgotten his furious words about my cousin, Pablo. Who knows what made him so angry? The cocky, good-looking Pablo may have expressed opinions on subjects he knew nothing about. Or perhaps he had the gall to talk back, or he irked my dad because of his interest in nudist colonies, or because of the way he wore his beret and thought he was the cat's meow. He was, after all, a boy of 15.

"*Ese mocoso de mierda me debe la vida!*" That little shit owes me his life.

What?

Though I never asked Ma about things I wasn't to hear, she invariably found a way to weave her tribulations into our conversations, like the *Bobeh* stories. She counted on me to listen as she battled through sporadic moments of fury and self-disappointments. She rarely put up a fight and seldom stood up for what she knew was right. Listening was easy, but I wasn't equipped to help her navigate the dreaded terrain of my father's nasty moods and disparaging words, except to say it wasn't her fault. Though my mother wilted easily, if she sensed an attack on one of her sons, love swelled her heart, pride stretched her five-foot frame skyward, and pre-Inquisition Spanish conceit stepped to the frontlines, her mouth curling in indignation.

Back to Pablo. When Luis and Isabel were dating, she became pregnant. Times were tough, money was short and they couldn't afford to get married. Mauricio talked them out of an abortion and found a job for Luis at the school of Manual Skills and Arts in Córdoba, where he was teaching.

"It wasn't Pablo's fault," my mother cried. "Why does he have to torture me, throwing those terrible words in my face. He has no right!"

I seldom saw my parents fight. If they did, it was out of sight, out of earshot. I imagine that's why the window incident on Vinalhaven remains so vivid. As a teenager, I wrote a story about the day—Sea Window. It began as an ordinary morning with Pa going off to the studio and the rest of us engaging in our regular routines. It was the July of *La Bobeh*, the July of William's first time on his own, away from us. Attending university summer classes in Iowa, the sculpture studios became his second home. I missed him, and I especially missed his presence that afternoon. He might have handled it differently, better, and I've wondered if Pa would have permitted himself to lose it in front of his first born, eldest son? Occasionally we witnessed Pa's awesome respect for William—moments that made me feel my own humiliation rather than pride for my brother. Clearly I wasn't in the same league as William. His younger siblings just weren't, and that's the way the cookie crumbled when we were young. As we matured and Pa softened, I believe he wanted to include us in that league, but it took years of educations, work, marriages and grandchildren before he felt comfortable accepting our grown-up offerings of pleasure. Years, before we felt the freedom needed for our own adult independence and wholeness. So it seemed to me.

Everything was fine that morning, until lunchtime. Washing up in the bathroom, I opened the window for air and immediately noticed the crack in the glass.

Pa must have been in a foul mood returning from the studio for lunch, and the cracked glass sent him into a livid rage. Storming out of the bathroom, he positioned himself in the middle of the kitchen, demanding to know who broke the pane. Shouting, calling for the truth, he was oblivious to the terror swooping through the silent room.

"Who's lying, who broke the window?!"

The self-indulgent lashing out was relentless. His face red, his eyes tight with fury, he moved to the counter and pounded the speckled Formica. When my two youngest siblings began crying, my mother finally turned from the stove.

"Stop! No one intended to break the glass. Why can't you accept it was an accident?"

"Someone is lying and I'm going to find out who it is!" he threatened.

"Enough screaming! It's just a cracked glass. Enough, before one of your children tells you they did it, just to make you stop!"

"I will get to the bottom of this! I didn't raise my children to be liars!"

By then, we were all frozen to our spots, and even if one of us had something to say, fear had turned us inside out and tied our tongues into knots.

The ranting continued, increasing in volume, his arms waving at the lot of us. More counter pounding. My younger siblings sat at the table, large-eyed, silent with fear. We were terrified.

Finally my mother broke down, weeping. Approaching my father, she began hitting his chest with her tiny fists. He pulled back, stunned, as though he'd never seen her anger, her despair.

"Did you ask your mother if she broke it? Did you?!" my mother sobbed hysterically. "Maybe it was your mother and not one of your children!" She continued crying and pounding his chest. "See," her voice suddenly fell to a pleading whisper, "see what you make me do front of our children ..."

We were accustomed to Pa's bad moods, but my mother's falling apart occurred so rarely, it was shocking. In desperation I moved from my position next to the bay of windows toward my parents in the middle of the kitchen. Out of the corner of my eye I saw my startled *Bobeh* approaching from her bedroom. How much had she heard? I saw my siblings' pale, panicked faces. If I picked up my mother and carried her to the bedroom, she could lie down and rest where it was quiet.

"I broke the window!" I called out, bending down, trying to lift Ma's legs. "I did it! I did it!"

Everything stopped—voices, fists against chest. My words echoed in the still room, bouncing around like a ball at play.

"*Sacate!*"—take off—my father commanded firmly, regaining his authority, waving me away. He attempted to embrace my mother but she pushed away from both of us. Eyes swollen, face blotchy, she turned, crossed the big room and disappeared into their bedroom. Not a word.

I finished the lunch preparations and coaxed the kids to eat. *La Bobeh* was the only one who carried on as though nothing had happened. Rather than join the table, Pa paced about the big room fastidiously straightening rockers, scatter rugs, pictures on the wall. Finally, opening the bedroom door, he disappeared inside. When he returned to the kitchen he announced that I would accompany him to town for the shopping. I finished cleaning up and made a grocery list.

Pulling away from the house, Pa blurted out angrily that he never wanted me to do that again. I was wrong not to confess immediately, and the mess that followed was my fault, all my fault.

"I didn't break it. I said that so you would stop fighting."

We drove to town in silence.

Pa returned to the studio for the afternoon, and Ma remained sequestered in her bedroom. I made dinner and got my sister to set the table. Later, Pa sheepishly took a tray of food into the bedroom, but it was refused. After getting the kids to bed in the evening, I retreated to the wood box beside the stove with my book.

When *La Bobeh* appeared in the kitchen, slippers scuffing the wooden floorboards, I knew she was coming for her glass of warm milk before bed.

"Tell me the truth, *hijita*." Her voice quavered as she looked up from the small sauce pan. "Tell me, did they fight like this before I came?"

Momentarily considering a fib so as not to hurt her feelings, I understood we all needed the truth. Nothing more was said about the incident, and I don't remember broken glass ever again causing so much grief.

In Madrid, when my uncle Luis dropped by 77 Francisco Silvela shortly before their return date to Argentina, he came alone. My aunt Isabel, a bright, disgruntled woman with a sharp tongue, was undoubtedly angry about something. During those Madrid months, I'd seen her drift from impatience to general discontent. She tried shaking off her resentment with forced laughter and a distracted interest in what was happening. By my first visit back to Argentina in 1983, a stroke had left Isabel partially paralyzed. More miserable than ever and barely able to speak, my aunt would relay her garbled desires only to Pablo, her eldest son, ignoring her caretaker, her other sons, her husband.

They'd been living in the same flat for decades. It had seen better days, but the building's central location was convenient. Standing beside her chair in the narrow, high ceilinged kitchen—the pulley rack of laundry hanging above our heads, the glass on the small, leaded window murky from smog—I waited for my long-suffering cousin. Once again, he'd been summoned from the office to attend to his mother. It was a dismal scene.

When I returned to Iowa and reported on my visit, Ma was saddened by the news and expressed compassion for her sister-in-law. She repeated stories of how close they were in their youth, how well they'd all gotten along in Córdoba. My aunt, an excellent cook, prepared meals while Ma cared for the children, my brother and me, our cousin, Pablo. She told me that Isa was very beautiful and had modeled for *La Rosa y el Espejo*. I could see Isabel's face in the print, her eyes and mouth. Why hadn't I known that before? Always seeking connections to my parents' past, I suffered from FOMO, fear of missing out.

When had life hardened my aunt? Where had it gone, that youthful face of soft contours and dreamy eyes of *La Rosa y el Espejo*?

That afternoon Luis dropped by our apartment, he didn't take off his overcoat. Dejected, he stood at the door exchanging quiet words with Ma and the *Abuelo*, mostly about plans for his family's return to Buenos Aires. Gloom hung in the foyer as they said their goodbyes. My father was not home. I stood about awkwardly until my mother told me to kiss my uncle good-bye. That was the last time I saw him, until that first trip back to Argentina 30 years later.

Madrid, spring continues, 1954

MAURICIO WAS UNSETTLED. OUR STAY was coming to an end and he may have felt he hadn't done or seen as much as he'd would have liked. In correspondence with the Guggenheim Foundation before we left Iowa, he put in a request for a greater stipend. Wanting to visit museums in France and Italy after the months in Spain, he explained that traveling with a family was expensive. The fellowship could not be augmented. Travel plans to France and Italy ended. That disappointment, coupled with in-law troubles and my grandfather's illness, probably nudged him toward discontent and hostility.

In the midst of this anxious atmosphere, on the Monday before Ash Wednesday, I returned from school innocently announcing that my forehead would be smeared with ashes.

All hell broke loose.

"That does it! No more. Finished!"

And so, it was. I did not return to school, not even to clean out my desk. I was completely traumatized. Soon after, we received a note from my teacher, Mr. Phillips, expressing concern about my absence, inquiring if I was ill. School companions wrote as well. I was missed. Ma felt bad. Not so much about Pa's outburst—we were all accustomed to his temper—but she was sorry my school experience had to end that way. Nevertheless, I was told to write a letter explaining that we would soon be leaving Madrid and returning to the States. Distraught, the abruptness made my loss worse. I couldn't imagine what the director of the school thought, or Mr. Phillips.

Except for Nina Martí, all contact with classmates and the school was lost. I still have my textbooks, but no papers or notebooks with information on the school. It's strange that for so long I accepted its contribution to who I am without specific details: the school's exact name and address, photos of the building, of my classmates, of Mr. Phillips. When I recently asked William, he remembered the school was near the Museo Lázaro Galdiano on the Calle Serrano. The internet turned up all needed information. Under the sponsorship of the British Council, the *Colegio Británico* was located at 31 Paseo General Martinez Campos. William was correct. The Galdiano Museum is five minutes away by car. I emailed the school's administration. Yes, certainly my name was still in their files. Seeing the Google image of the patio and stone building, the ornate iron gate, I was rushed with memories. My classroom, our uniform's gray skirt and red cardigan, the kindness of my teacher.

Luis, Isabel and the boys had already returned to Argentina when our grandfather died. The morning of his second heart attack, I heard my father calling nervously from the *Abuelo's* bedroom, telling my mother to hurry. He must have been nearing the end. Ma was returning from the bathroom with the bedpan she had washed out with bleach. In her haste, a few drops splashed onto the hem of her pinwale corduroy dress, instantly leaving a white blotch on the rust color.

In the following weeks, I watched my mother's petite, seamstress cousin, Paquita, create pleats in the circular skirt, concealing the white stain. She came often in those days after the *Abuelo's* death, *para acompañar la prima Emilia*, to be supportive to her cousin Emilia. It was hard for Paquita to see our grandfather buried without a priest. Her extended family was devoutly Catholic—her pretty, younger sister, '*la monjita*', a nun. My father tried to explain my grandfather's aversion to the church, but I don't believe she wanted to hear the depth of his opposition.

I found Paquita's pious reticence mournful. It may have been the sadness of spinsterhood and not being comfortable in the presence of my dad—possibly men in general, other than her old father. Even children made her ill at ease. Whatever it was, I always felt she preferred being alone with my mother, so they might communicate in their secret childhood language.

They had last been together as youngsters playing in their grandmother's patio. It was 1925, the year of Barragáns' family visit to Spain—when Luis took Pilar to the waters at Medina del Campo, when the children, Emilia and Luis, were left in Cardiel with family. I wondered if Paquita had been reserved as a child. Over the years, letters between Buenos Aires, Iowa and Madrid kept the girls close. My parent's marriage, the residual scars of the Civil War, news of the extended families, and finally, the recent deaths of their respective mothers. Their bond was strong. Joining them on outings, I saw my mother banish her worries and Paquita lose her seriousness as they strolled together, chatting and laughing. In Iowa, I'd never seen my mother walk arm-in-arm with anyone other than my father. Stopping at outdoor cafés in the *Puerta del Sol*, they sipped their coffee and anisette liquor while I drank hot chocolate—happy for my mother, happy taking in the sights, especially the ads for *Anís del Mono* liquor whizzing by on the sides of streetcars.

Paquita had finally married by the time Alan and I arrived in Madrid from Holland. Our reunion was surprisingly enjoyable with dinner at their tiny apartment in the outskirts of Madrid, catching up on family news. I was able to report to my mother what a changed, happy woman her cousin had become with Alfonso at her side, a friendly, easygoing fellow. Paquita reminded me of my sewing projects when I was 11, and how she'd bring me remnants of fabric for my doll clothes. We laughed recalling the day my father accidently burned a cigarette hole on the front of his white, nylon shirt, and how he asked me if I could fix it. Very carefully I embroidered a five petal daisy around the burn, a perfect circle beside the third button. Pa was delighted and wore it often.

Finding ourselves quite comfortable with Paquita and Alfonso, Alan and I felt we could entrust them with some prized possessions. Not knowing how long it would take to find a place on Ibiza, how long we'd be living out of suitcases, we were nervous about carrying around our fragile antiquities—an Egyptian sarcophagus mask purchased in England and an Inca pot from Holland. Paquita and Alfonso were delighted to hold them for us until Alan's parents came through in September on route to Ibiza, and a meeting could be arranged for the transfer of our treasures.

When we knew Alan's parents' travel plans, I wrote Paquita and asked if she could meet them at the Madrid airport when they changed planes for Ibiza. For identification purposes, Paquita took along our wedding photograph that Ma had sent her the year before, while Alfonso carried our parcels of valuables.

By the time they finally located the plane for Ibiza, Moe and Bess had boarded. Remarkably, Paquita talked her way on board, thrilled to make their acquaintance. An English speaking stewardess was very helpful. (Could it have been Pan Am and one of the Martí girls?) Paquita convinced the pilot to wait a few minutes so she could find her husband holding the parcels. Regrettably, Alfonso was not to be found in the airport chaos and the plane took off without our treasures.

How could we have asked such of favor of Paquita? It was a long journey from their place to the airport—several buses and subways. What were we thinking?

Later, Bess described the encounter in detail: Paquita's elation, the well-spoken stewardess, the tall, handsome pilot. I retain an image of my mother's diminutive cousin explaining the story to the pilot towering over her, showing him the framed wedding picture, trilling with delight that she found my parents-in-law. I can imagine the perspiration of her forehead, her straight, black skirt and white, eyelet blouse, the flash of excitement in her dark eyes.

Was this the same, dour cousin accompanying my mother after her father's death? The transformation was surely a testament to love.

And to think that, after all, the Inca pot turned out to be a fake.

After the *Abuelo's* funeral, when Leo, Jimena and I returned home from the Ferrants, we were told not to speak about our grandfather. I understood the ban on his name was to avoid further pain.

But in the calculated effort to shelter our mother, we were denied a right—to talk, to remember aloud. With our parents shielding us from discussions about death, we were deprived of the inevitable process of grieving. In my family, most life cycle events were rarely spoken of. If they were considered important enough to mention, it was generally in a restrained manner, even happy occasions. As I've mentioned, celebratory moments were few and far between for my parents.

Not until adulthood did I realize something hadn't ended right about my grandfather. The 'unspeakable' that transpired became suspended in the cosmos of my small world, unable to rise or fall. It remained in unresolved limbo until I could draw it down and give it closure.

Perhaps the institutional memory of our grandfather was not unlike digital data saved to the clouds. The difference is that in the event of a crash, I'm not sure we would know how to retrieve and restore those memories. We didn't send them there as a backup. That's where they ended up.

Winter on Ibiza, 1965

AFTER A MONTH OF TRAVELING, we returned to Ibiza to find that winter had arrived on our island. It had been a packed trip with Alan's parents. Israel, Greece and Turkey, and then a rendezvous in Italy with my father and William. After weeks of exhaustive touring and museums, we were ready to settle down again. By the end of October, we had to buy a kerosene heater.

The cold months saw strong winds, another dry spell, and the *matanzas*, pig killings. It was a ritual on Ibiza, with family and neighbors arriving to help out at the event. It involved an entire day of labor that produced the family's meat supply for a year. Several meals were served during the event, elaborate preparations that included pork, chicken and rabbit. The pig, carefully guarded in its pen, was never permitted to forage for food, his diet controlled as he feasted on *algarroba* pods, acorns and kitchen scraps, even the occasional almonds and figs, to sweeten the flesh. Most of the pork was turned into *chorizo* and *sobrasada* sausages. The intestine linings, carefully washed and cleaned with orange and lemon juice, became sausage casings. Every part of the pig was used. The feet were pickled, the blood used in blood sausage (black *botifarra),* and the salted bones stored in amphoras in the dim *depósitos*, the equivalent of an above ground fruit cellar.

It was considered an honor to be invited and we didn't have the courage to refuse a neighbor of the Palerms, but the thought of a *matanza* was terrifying. We'd heard it described, and would have given anything to avoid the event. The pig was hoisted onto a low table and five men held it down, one for each leg, another for the tail. The 'butcher' inserted a long, sharp knife through the throat, aiming deep toward the heart. At first the animal squealed hysterically, but finally, his noise slowly quieted as his life ebbed away. A woman crouched under the table with a large pan, catching and stirring the blood so it wouldn't coagulate. She kept eying us, smiling with her toothless grin, her face and straw hat splattered with blood.

The whole scene was overwhelming and we had no idea how to help, so we remained observers and that was enough. I declined the offer of *hor d'oeuvres* that appeared from the kitchen. Alan accepted. Neither of us realized what he was tasting. When he learned he had ingested fried blood patties, I thought he would vomit on the spot. Everything went downhill after that. When we finally made our way home, Alan crawled into bed and ran a fever for an entire day.

Invited to more *matanzas* over the course of the winter, we found good excuses to politely decline. When it was José and María's turn to butcher their hog, we had sufficiently recovered and were prepared not to eat. Sticking to fried potatoes, we enjoyed the celebration. At the end of the day, we were able to congratulate the Palerms on the impressive sausages hanging from a wooden beam in the *depósito*.

On New Year's Eve, Anna W. invited us for dinner and an overnight at the old *finca* she was renting. It was a couple miles from *Tienda Can Chocolate* and our *casa*, so we walked. It was a typical Ibicenco December day, sunny and cool, about 60 degrees. We brought a bottle of wine and an almond and fig pound cake I'd baked in the tin camping oven. With the help of almonds and figs from José and María's farm, and Mrs. Beeton's Cookery Book that had already proven its worth the winter before in Bergen aan Zee, the cake was delicious.

Anna caught one of the chickens running around and skillfully wrung its neck. She showed me how to gut and pluck. I smile thinking of my adult daughters' aversion to handling raw chicken and their grocery stores' plastic wrapped, skinless, boneless portions presented on polystyrene foam trays. When visiting our accomplished, self-confident girls and their wonderful families, I generally cook chicken. On our last stay, I noticed my vegetarian son-in-law had given up following me around the kitchen with a bottle of spray beach and rubber gloves up to his elbows. And a week later, my daughter emailed to say she'd made the chicken tandoori recipe, and that everyone loved it. I guess we're all getting older.

Anna's plucking lesson wasn't bad, but the gutting was tough. After I recovered—Alan avoided the ordeal by going off to gather *leña*, firewood—we seasoned the bird with lemons, garlic and *frígola*. It was roasted with potatoes and onions in the old bread oven built on the stone patio. Regardless of how simple the meal, the food on Ibiza was always delicious. White beans prepared with garlic and Swiss chard, a side of cauliflower fried with croutons, a romaine salad dressed with olive oil and fresh lemon. And for the non-drinkers, like us, *gaseosa* (sweet soda water) added to the wine—our version of *sangria*.

Anna kept us entertained with stories of her life and times, yet little about her background. Born in 1900, the illegitimate child of a woman who would eventually commit suicide, she was farmed out to an uncaring peasant family, and later, to a hostile grandmother. Anna did tell us that her father—whom she never knew—was Jewish, as were both her husbands and most of her friends. She related that information because they were facts, and there were so few facts she was willing to speak about. I often felt we did not hear complete narratives.

In all her recounting, she never once mentioned loving anyone, or anyone loving her, except the painter, Leo Marchutz, who was crazy about her. She gleefully revealed it took years of living together before she finally agreed to marry him. In the end, it was neither for him nor her that they married. It was for Leo's grandfather, the Rabbi.

I saw only one photo of the young Anna. It must have been taken in her 20's or early 30's—a sunlit day in the countryside, a hazy landscape in the distance. Arms crossed, an attractive girl leans against a low stone wall, her short sleeve pullover, hand-knit. A blue-eyed blond, wisps of hair sweep her troubled face. The black and white image, slightly out of focus, echoed the actual Anna, occasionally inaccessible and needing anonymity.

At the age of 16, Anna was employed in a bookstore in Berlin when she met Albert Einstein, a frequenter of the coffee shop at the back of the store. Knowing what I do of our Anna, I have no doubt the womanizing physicist found her delightfully charming. He was still married to Mileva, though no longer living with her. Shortly after Einstein met Anna, he introduced her to another physicist, the Hungarian born, Leo Szilard. Szilard and Enrico Fermi were responsible for patenting the nuclear reactor in 1934, and in 1939, Szilard wrote—and Einstein signed—the famous Einstein-Szilard letter to President Roosevelt. Warning of Germany's work in atomic fission, the document encouraged the formation of an American nuclear program that resulted in the Manhattan Project. Anna and Szilard became lifelong friends.

We knew nothing about Anna's life between the bookstore in Berlin and early 1928, when she left Germany with Leo Marchutz, a young German artist, and they traveled to Aix-en-Provence in the south of France. An article I read about Marchutz explained that Anna Krauss paid for their trip to Aix, but we did not hear the story from her. She had apparently approached him for help in arranging the sale of a late Cezanne painting. Someone had recommended Marchutz as he was known to be seriously interested in Cezanne. The likelihood is that Anna was an intermediary, rather than owner of the painting, but again, nothing about the story is transparent or certain.

How and when Anna came across a Cezanne remains another story she never told us. The article indicated that the trip, paid for from the commission of the painting sale, was compensation for Leo's help.

Because of his early obsession with Cezanne, Anna and Leo sought out the Château Noir, not far from Aix. Leo was smitten, and they ended up renting a few rooms in the empty château. It must have been then that Leo's grandfather made the journey from Nuremberg to France, intending to convince Anna to marry his grandson. It's doubtful that Rabbi Marchutz would have been able to leave Germany much after the mid-30's. She told us she finally gave in to the old man's pleading and promised to marry Leo. They were married in 1934. By then, their marriage was on the downswing, but they remained together until 1939.

During the war, the Marchutzs managed to rent the entire Château Noir and Anna ran it as a boarding house. In addition to the *auberge* income, they tended a vegetable garden, raised poultry, and Leo occasionally sold a painting. Ends were met, more or less. In the time of Leo and Anna, the Château Noir's importance was as a gathering place, mostly for refugees fleeing Nazi Germany. Among them were artists, the art historian, John Rewald, a Scottish schoolteacher who would later become Leo Marchutz's second wife, and Konrad Wachsmann, the German Bauhaus architect, later to become Anna's second husband.

In 1940, three men began the process of sponsoring Anna and Konrad's emigration to the States. Albert Einstein—for whom Wachsmann had designed and built a vacation house in Caputh, Germany in 1929—Leo Szilard, and Walter Gropius, founder of the Bauhaus and Konrad Wachsmann's friend and later business partner in Massachusetts.

In the meantime, Wachsmann had been in touch with the Emergency Rescue Committee in Marseilles. At their suggestion, he listed Anna Krauss as his assistant on the applications, rather than his fiancée. The ERC, established in New York in 1940 when France fell to the Nazis, was based in unoccupied Marseilles and headed by the American, Varian Fry. Fry remained in France for 13 months helping more than 2,000 refugees escape the Nazis. In August of 1941 he was arrested and finally forced to leave the country in September. Fry's team had certainly been involved with Wachsmann and Anna's case, but whether or not Fry himself participated is unknown.

Wachsmann had obtained quota visas from the US consulate in Marseilles, but they were unable to leave before their visas expired. Departing ships were few and far between. It was during that wait in Marseilles that the hotel fleas set their sights on Anna, an event she would later recall in response to my story about fleas in the mattress I made from José and María's straw.

Finally, Albert Einstein applied directly to the White House and was able to procure emergency visas for Konrad and Anna.

They left Marseilles for New York in August of 1941, only weeks before Varian Fry returned to the States.

My mother loved hearing narratives about our friend, Anna Wachsmann, but I didn't dare tell her that Albert Einstein had been one of Anna's sponsors to this country. I'd be stirring up bitter ashes of another story. In the late 50's, when my parents were asked to act as sponsors for a son of Ma's cousin, Mercedes, my father refused. The young man, an architecture student in Buenos Aires, had the opportunity to study in California, but he needed an American sponsor.

In the end, Emilia was permitted to send the boy American architecture magazines, but sponsorship was out of the question. Mauricio would not get involved. As usual, my mother had no say. I can't imagine the letter she had to write her cousin, Mercedes.

Ibiza, January 1966

B Y MID-JANUARY IT FINALLY STARTED raining again. The winter months brought more activities with the Palerms, most centered around food and meals. We were not excited about their version of Christmas mincemeat—a nasty combination of ground pork, sugar, almonds and oranges, too sweet, too porky—but they liked my cookies. When José said it was time to dispose of the rooster because he was bothering the chickens, we prepared roast chicken in María's gas range, which she'd rarely used. This proved to be a new culinary understanding, as their custom was to fry or boil. There were other projects for cold days. I showed María how to knit and use her treadle sewing machine, which she'd never tried. Together we made a skirt. She was happy to circumvent the seamstress who lived on the other side of the mountain and overcharged for her sloppy work.

When the almond blossoms began bursting onto the landscape like snow, the two of us were well into our most exciting venture—reading lessons. I'm not sure how it began, but María was eager to learn, and I was willing to try teaching. The Ibiza public library on the *Paseo Vara de Rey* had old, illustrated alphabet primers dating from the 1930's. They were outdated, but served the purpose. Beside the letter **J**, Alan and I were dismayed to find a caricature of an old man with a hunch back, hooked nose and money bag. **J** for *Judío*.

Other than a passing comment or two, the only time religion came up was at Easter, when the parish priest appeared at the Ribas Palerm farm selling church indulgences. Fascinated they still existed, Alan was eager to learn more, but José dismissed it as an antiquated custom. Something of a *bubbe-meise*, as they say in Yiddish. José, María and Antonia were not religious people, rarely went to mass, and recognized the indulgences as a way of raising money for the church. Not prepared to face even a hint of anti-Semitism in our beautiful environment, we never brought up our Judaism. If they knew anything, I figured the Palerms probably thought Jews were from the time of the Bible. After all, they had refused to believe those fellows in TIME Magazine were astronauts, insisting they were deep water divers. Knowing that we were not Catholic, they may have assumed we were *Protestantes*.

The **J** beside the caricature of the *Judío* was ignored. Bright and motivated, María advanced rapidly through her lessons, and by the time we left Ibiza, she was reading simple sentences and writing rudimentary phrases.

Since Ibiza, I've read about Ibicenco building styles, roof constructions, and the historical presence of hidden Jews on the island. Most recently, I learned that **Ribas** was a typical Jewish name.

·•◦•·

EXCERPTS
'Manhattan Outreach', 1993
Losers and Keepers in Argentina,
A book of fiction, published, 2001

THE PEOPLE AT THE EAST Side Cleaning Agency call me Evalina la Argentina. It's because I'm small, more child than woman in size and shape, and because my black hair is straight and my skin brown, and my broad, flat features are like Papa's, the Indian from Jujuy. I must tell you, Reader, I've never known Papa. He walked in and out of my Cordobés mother's life, courting her with scented blossoms from the paradise tree.

The agency people are ignorant and disrespectful. In fact, they're stupid. I don't waste my energy trying to make them understand about rights, about dignity. Trying to make them understand that small, brown people can be intelligent and speak fine English, even though they have to clean houses to survive. Do I tell them that small, brown people also feel love and pain? Of course not, I just put up with them. Sometimes, even Juan Carlos Forsyth Botero calls me Evalina la Argentina. I put up with him too, because he is my husband, and because finally, I can no longer help him.

With Mr. and Mrs. Stern, it's different. They have reached their seventies in good health and good spirits, the Sterns, and they always call me Eva. They are kind and unassuming. Since they do not worry about their own importance, they have no need to make me feel lowly. At this moment, I hear their voices drifting out of the apartment kitchen. I close the library door behind myself so I can be alone with the peaceful hum of the radiator, the rain, and the muffled street noises from Park Avenue. I like being alone. I often open the window to air the room while I clean. I fix the bright, silk cushions on the couch and arm chairs, I adjust the lampshades, the magazines on the end tables. Week after week I enter this room

328

pretending it's like any other; I will clean, with my usual efficiency and leave, and nothing will happen. But it always does, and always when I climb onto my little step stool and begin dusting the bookshelves. The sudden dampness springs in the palm of my hands, the prickly sensation at the back of my neck, under my hair. My body becomes motionless, dust rag still, as my eyes move to the old photograph.

There are other pictures on the wall. New ones, more old ones, they are set among the books. The one of Mrs. Stern in her college days, smiling, holding a track trophy. The one of Mr. Stern, playing the clarinet. Photographs of children, weddings. But Reader, this is the one that draws me, that makes me save cleaning this small, quiet library for the end. This is the one that makes me remember things—Mama as a beautiful, lonely young woman, the *Abuelos,* my grandparents, the ancient stone house and windy village near Córdoba. I rarely think about my past anymore, yet in this room, it eagerly comes forward, merging with this sepia image. Together they give me peace and energy to go on into the next week. I reach to dust the ornate frame. An imposing-looking family has gathered around the patriarch, the matriarch. Single brothers flank the back row of dour, spinster aunts. The mustachioed, cocky married son and his stunning wife in the striped, satin blouse stand directly behind the two old people. They sit in the center, the old ones; young grandchildren surround them, sitting and standing in the foreground.

It's just an old photograph, I tell myself, week after week. Typical, like the family images that Mama stashed in hat boxes. But every time I stand before this photograph, the same thing happens. My palms sweat and the old man draws me in—his small, beady eyes riveted to mine, the long, white beard and dark clothes, like the *Abuelo's.* The coat is ankle-length and double-breasted, of shiny, black fabric, like the small, tight-fitting cap. The old man's relaxed hand dangles from the chair's armrest—the very way Mr. Stern's does when he watches TV—and every time I stand there, that hand beckons, and I follow.

I've learned it's not hard to enter a photograph. It's not hard leaving the present, with my doubts and frustrations, Juan Carlos, the children, the varicose veins and rough hands I've acquired cleaning these Manhattan apartments. It's a question of will. The old man beckons, and I follow. I travel the dark corridors of his small, wooden house, always calmly certain I've been here before, familiar with every slat of scrubbed floor, every doorway, every cluttered sill. I move silently past the women and children sitting around the dining room table, heads bent over consigned, piecework sewing, elbows at a kerosene lamp. Behind them, on the modest mantelpiece, a pair of silver candlesticks. I move past the iron bedsteads with babies nesting, piles of clothing, the feather ticks and chamber pots. Finally, I come out on the other side of the water-stained, cardboard mat, where the inky handwriting is blurred and the alphabet so foreign, I can read only the date, 1908.

There I am, at the very edge of my own fugitive memories. Back, through tangled time, I land in the swept patio of youth, Mama in the kitchen and the foothills of Córdoba in the distance. Every day, I, the lonely child, entertain myself in that patio space, skipping around my cocoon-like *Abuelos* sitting in the sun. *Abuela* is tightly wrapped in dark woolens. Spots of old soup stain the lapels of *Abuelo's* ancient, black coat. Still and silent, they never want to talk or play, but drift in and out of private dreamscapes, places unknown to me, the child. As the two old people feel the mantle of a shadow, their eyes open a slit, and they move to stand—more bent than straight—to drag their cane chairs across the ancient stones, in pursuit of the sun. I, the child, dance, and try to imagine them young and dressed in white, as in the photograph hanging in Mama's bedroom, taken somewhere in Russia. They pose at a small table under trees, the pattern of leaves on their faces. With a white, lace cloth, a samovar, and two candlesticks, they await the future.

I refold the dust rag and gently wipe the glass. They are dead now, the *Abuelos*. Mama has been moved to a government housing project in the city of Córdoba for the needy, the sick, the aged. How she must miss the patio, the sparse, stony landscape. Letters take so long. We've been in New York for nearly four years, and, Reader, I still haven't been able to save the airfare to send for my Mama. In the library of this Manhattan apartment, in this photograph of matriarch and patriarch and clan, there are no feather ticks or chamber pots, no women and children sewing. So from where? Why am I so certain I've been and seen? The old man, with his beard and satin cap, his eyes that will not close, not even blink, why does he insist he knows me?

A sudden draft from the window makes me shiver. Stepping down from the stool, I turn away, finally, to finish dusting the book shelves, to mop the parquet floor. As I carry the bucket, mop, and my little stool past the French doors of the kitchen, I see Mr. Stern in his stocking feet, his tall figure leaning against the refrigerator. He is talking. Mrs. Stern works at the counter, still in her slicker and rain hat, still surrounded by groceries she hasn't put away. She's stepped out of her damp, flat shoes and stands in her nylons, her brown eyes deep in concentration as she unties the butcher wrap and examines the roast. Tall like her husband, and still with the athlete's grace she had as a star runner in college, Mrs. Stern is an attractive woman. She has a pleasing, angular face and thick, wavy, white hair, cropped at the nape of her neck. I know that under the yellow slicker, recently ordered through a catalog from the state of Maine, Mrs. Stern is wearing a denim skirt and turtleneck sweater. I watch Mr. Stern still leaning against the refrigerator, and I realize they've been engaged in conversation since I began cleaning the bedrooms. Something important must have happened. Usually on Saturdays, he's left the apartment by this time.

Today, for sure, I will ask Mrs. Stern about the photograph. I've put off asking for so long, not wanting to hear or know anything, not wanting to spoil whatever it is I share with that patriarch. But today I will ask, I resolve, lugging my cleaning supplies into the small bathroom.

[Excerpt]

"Mona, isn't the world feeling a little heavy on your shoulders?" Richard Stern asks, glancing at his wife. He straightens up, turns, and pulls open the refrigerator door. He takes out the pitcher of V8 juice. "I thought we'd resolved this?"

Mona shrugs.

Disturbed, Richard pours himself a tall glass and drinks the juice quickly. "My darling, we're talking about one young man, for God's sake, one Jew! We're not dealing here with the whole past, present, and future of the Chosen People!"

Richard's words make Mona close her eyes and shake her head. She places the roast on a pan, feeling very long-suffering.

"We've been through this already," Richard says patiently, lowering his voice. "I thought we'd agreed to be realistic. Our grandson, Nathan, is on the verge of marriage, and as far as Judaism is concerned, the odds don't look good." Richard rinses out the glass and leaves it in the sink. "As my old man would have said, 'This comes as a surprise?! We have a choice in the matter?!'" Richard smiles, remembering briefly, then pulls on his sweatshirt and smooths his hair. "Listen, Mona, since when did Judaism play such a big role in Nathan's parents' 'blessed union'?" He chuckles softly.

Richard is entitled to his humor, Mona decides. Their son's marriage is on the brink of dissolution. It's nothing new. It's been a constantly recurring theme.

"For that matter, how about us? You know what I mean? O.K., so maybe religion didn't have to be a big deal because we're all Jews. Maybe that was enough. Who's to say? All I know is that with every generation, things change, it's natural law." Richard puts on his nylon jacket and zips up the front. "Aren't you going to take off your coat?"

She nods.

He opens the refrigerator again, looking for something to eat. "Your grandfather was a rabbi, my grandfather was a rabbi." He pops some grapes into his mouth and closes the door. "Would they have believed that in our house you could prepare a roast," he nods toward the meat on the pan, "to serve at the same table with cheese cake?" He pats the refrigerator. Not expecting an answer, Richard reaches for his athletic shoes and gym bag that are under the counter. "Is change for the better?" He shrugs, sitting down to put on his shoes. "You know me. I don't worry about the B Problems, the ones I can't do anything about. They're happy, aren't they? So O.K. They're gainfully employed attorneys, so O.K. Presumably they're old enough to know what they're doing, so O.K. He's a New York Jew, and she's an I-don't-know-what from Nebraska. So?"

"Born-again Christian," Mona says quietly, sticking slivers of garlic and sprigs of rosemary into the roast.

Richard looks up from his shoe laces.

"Judy's a Born-again Christian."

"I heard the first time. You sure?" he asks cautiously.

"Positive."

"I see." Richard remains silent for a few seconds, elbows on his knees, arms dangling. "Didn't I tell you the odds weren't great?" He stands up. "What's left to say?"

Mona didn't ask him to say anything in the first place. It doesn't matter though, because her silence is usually good for two, three, maybe even four of his monologue statements, as long as he can guess which topic is bothering her, and he always can, because they've been married for almost fifty years.

"Well, maybe she's not a true believer."

"Wrong." Mona says ruthlessly. "Nathan had a long talk with me last week."

She'd been choking on it, alone, ever since. But Richard is right. What's left to be said? She imagines there aren't any answers. So maybe she just feels like being sad and pouty. Doesn't the ripe old age of seventy-five entitle her to an occasional binge of self-indulgence? She'd agreed to be realistic. But she hadn't agreed to be upbeat about this, not so quickly, anyway. She isn't as accommodating as she used to be. Easy on the garlic, Mona reminds herself, looking down at the roast. By tonight, she'll shower and change into something nice, and she'll try to feel as close to 100 percent as possible. Richard's stomach has been kicking up lately. He blames it on her garlic.

"Mona, your coat!"

She hears the irritation in his voice. It isn't about her coat. She caught him off guard with the born-again Christian business. She reaches for her hat, shoving it into the large, patch pocket.

"Will you stop worrying, please?" Richard looks at her expectantly.

"I'll try." She struggles out of the yellow plastic.

He steps close, kisses her forehead, helps her with the coat.

"We're just Nathan's grandparents. Let his parents worry about something, for a change. By the way, when do the unhappy yuppies get back from their vacation?"

"Next Monday." Mona smiles, amused. Richard has never called their son and daughter-in-law yuppies. The fast trip to London was another attempt to repair their failing marriage. "Nathan told me his parents are finding London very expensive." She drapes the coat over one arm and looks at it thoughtfully for a few seconds. In the catalog it seemed so nice and bright, reminding her of the sea and ships on a stormy day. Actually, it's the most uncomfortable thing she's ever worn, Mona decides.

"London, expensive? Surprise! Did I tell them, or did I tell them?!" Richard glances at the clock. "I'm out of here!"

Mona stands at the apartment door, watching as Richard heads down the hall toward the elevator, gym bag in hand. She can tell his back hurts, but he hasn't said a word. Not bad for an old guy approaching seventy-eight, Mona thinks, opening the coat closet. She hangs up the disappointing yellow plastic and returns to kitchen. Maybe she shouldn't have told him about Judy. Has she ruined his afternoon? He returned from work, changed, and now he's off to the gym for a few hours. Even though he sold the business to his nephew three years ago, he still "gives the kid a hand," every day, all day. Saturday afternoons are his. He exercises, has a steam, and maybe plays a game of cards with the guys. When he comes back for dinner, he'll be relaxed and talkative, hopefully, joking with Nathan and Judy, as though all is right with the world.

Mona adjusts the roast on the pan and slides it into the oven. She glances over the groceries spread across the counter. What's gotten into her? It's the first time in her life she's worried about this. Has it taken the reality of Nathan's marriage? Richard is so easy about everything. Does he truly believe all is right with the world? She's always envied his ability to take command and be upbeat, positive, certain that everything that happens is for the best. He's right. There are no surprises here. Nathan called last night, eagerly announcing that he and Judy had something important to tell them. For a moment Mona's heart sank, and then she bravely pulled herself together. In her most cheery, grandmotherly voice, she invited their only grandchild and his girlfriend for Saturday night.

[EXCERPT]

Mona checks the oven temperature. Nathan eagerly accepted the dinner invitation. He and Judy have been living together for almost two years, so everyone knows very well what the important news is. There are no surprises. Mona puts the vegetables in a pot of water and turns on the element. So, if there are no surprises, what is her problem? She breaks up the head of lettuce and places the leaves in the spinner. One grandfather might have been a rabbi, but her other grandfather read the *Yiddish Forward* every day and refused to enter a synagogue, believing religion was the root of all social injustice. Her parents and most of their families were Socialists, if not Communists. So where does she get off having such doubts and hesitations, such sudden concern for Judaism? She, who's always considered herself so liberal, so accepting?

Here she is, concerned about another generation, a grandchild, when most of her friends' children haven't married Jews, and everyone around her seems to think it's best to erase any serious traces of ethnic and cultural differences. The norm has become intermarriage. Of course it's not that she disapproves; who is she to disapprove? But she allows herself to worry. It's become more than the norm, almost a movement. A movement "on a roll," the way "black is beautiful" blossomed during those early stages, and the way women ostentatiously burned their bras, and now all this business with gay rights. One might almost think a whole generation is waiting in the wings, waiting to be part of the "New Face" of Judaism that is sweeping the nation! It's true that her grandson is but one Jew. Richard has no idea how much she thinks about this! No idea at all! If he knew, he'd probably shrug and say something like "at least he's getting married!"

Mona, bearer of burdens, has become silently preoccupied with the articles and editorials that fill the Jewish magazines. *Hadassah* comes to the apartment; she reads the others at the library. "Outreach programs" have become the latest obsession for Jewish America. Outreach for mixed marriages. For Jews by choice. For gay Jews by choice with non-Jewish partners. For Christians committed to raising their biological and/or adopted, occasionally Asian children, as Jews, and so on, and so forth. A never-ending stream of outreach.

How about outreach for the Mona Sterns? The Mona Sterns, who, wittingly or unwittingly, have allowed workers in white overalls to paint over their mezuzahs, and now, in the same vein, they must accept, graciously, as though it hardly matters, the reality of probable non-Jewish descendants. Without a doubt, she, like many others, has taken her Judaism for granted. What now? Is there outreach for Jews who think their culture is on the point of dissolution because of assimilation? As she waits for the vegetables to parboil, Mona suddenly thinks of the Swede, Raoul Wallenberg. She imagines his famous trip to the train station of the frontier post of Hegyeshalom, Hungary, hurrying to save waiting Jews from the box cars and certain death. "Forgive me," he said, choosing from among them, "I want to save you all, but they will only let me take a few. So please forgive me, but I must save the young ones, because I want to save a nation." What would happen, Mona wonders, if the future of 5,000 years of this "nation" depended solely on her and Richard? She removes the pot of boiling vegetables from the stove and drains them in the sink. On one side of the scale, they had rabbi grandfathers. On the other, they will soon have a Born-again Christian. Mother to future Sterns.

Mrs. Stern?

Mona looks up from the vegetables. "Eva. All done, dear? Ready for a drink?" The girl is clearly exhausted. She works too hard, Mona hates asking if her husband has found a job yet. She seems to ask that every week, and every week it's the same answer.

"First, can I ask you about a photograph?"

"A photograph?"

"The one of the old people, the family. It's hanging on the wall in the library."

Mona wipes her hands on the dish towel. "You mean Mr. Stern's family?"

"I think so."

"Why don't you show me." Mona puts down the dish towel and starts for the library, pleased with a break from the kitchen and her thoughts.

"That one."

Mona carefully reaches out to straighten the frame. "No one's taken an interest in this for years! Except me, of course. They're in my care now, Mr. Stern's family, his parents and siblings. It was taken in the old country, in Russia, before Mr. Stern was born. That was his mother." Mona points to the woman in the back row, in the striped, satin blouse. "She was very beautiful. Those two little boys in front are his older brothers."

"Who was the old man?"

"*Zaide* Stern, the grandfather. And she was the grandma, *Bubbe* Stern."

"They remind me of my *Abuelos*, my grandparents."

"Really, Eva?"

Eva nods. "I feel I know them, as though I lived with them, the way I did with my *Abuelos*. Did lots of old men wear little satin caps?"

"The *yarmulke?*" Mona smiles. "Sure, in the old days. Now they're mostly worn in the synagogue. Except for the orthodox, they wear them all the time."

"So did my *Abuelo,* in Córdoba."

That evening, at the Stern dinner table, the roast is a tremendous success, and Nathan tells his grandmother that her cooking is delicious, as always. Then he asks her to tell Judy his favorite story of how she ran on the men's track team in college until a women's team was formed.

Mona is delighted; she loves to tell the story. After Nathan and Judy make their announcement, Judy smiles a lot and eats little, nervously saying she is saving room for the cheesecake. Mona always makes cheesecake when Nathan comes. Richard tries very hard to act upbeat and relaxed. Mona is proud of him. She even feels pretty good herself. Good enough that she tells them all about Eva and her interest in the photograph of Richard's parents, taken in Russia. She doesn't tell them, however, about Eva's grandfather and his satin cap and their discussion about *yarmulkes*. Mona realizes she doesn't want Judy to feel uncomfortable, and she doesn't want to make herself feel sad.

Ibiza, winter continues, 1966

Returning to Ibiza from our travels with Alan's parents, my letters began mentioning visits to a Barcelona doctor. A tone of anxiety hung over my correspondence. I was experiencing sharp pain in my left hip whenever I walked for long. It clearly alarmed us, because Alan typed a message to my parents asking them to convey the details to a family friend, an orthopedic surgeon. In the end, the Barcelona doctor could find nothing wrong, saying it was most likely because of the way I was built— like a dancer. I told him my sister was the dancer. He recommended vitamin B12 shots. I ignored the recommendation and tried to ignore the discomfort, but I was concerned. Because it became an increasing preoccupation in my letters, I wonder if the pain was tied to my mounting apprehension over leaving Ibiza.

Through the winter months, my aerograms home continued with detailed descriptions of more *fincas*, though we knew we were not going to stay. By the beginning of February, Alan was applying to printmaking jobs at universities in Saskatchewan and Alberta, and requesting recommendations from his MFA faculty he had studied with at Iowa, including my father and a favorite painting professor. We had one foot in our dreams and the other in reality. In March, I made orange marmalade from the tree at the back of our house, and in April, Alan accepted the job in Regina, Saskatchewan, for the fall semester.

The months moved rapidly after our decision. Inquiries to travel agents turned up information about cargo ships from the Middle East stopping in Barcelona and Palma de Mallorca, enroute to Toronto via the St. Lawrence Seaway. We were intrigued by the idea, but soon learned no ships would be leaving for Canada in July, so we arranged to fly back to New York. The thought of going home was exciting, but I cried just thinking about leaving Ibiza. It would be difficult.

Busying myself with departure plans, I ordered a pant suit from an Ibicenco tailor—well made, but overly masculine—a hand spun Ibicenco wool sweater commissioned for Alan, and fabric embroidered by Rita that I later completed into blouses for my mother and Bess. In May, a profound sadness finally took hold for all of us. The hardest thing was explaining the concept of distance to the Palerms. I showed them a world map with Saskatchewan, Toronto, Iowa, Spain and Ibiza, but it didn't help.

For several years after settling in Canada, we kept up a correspondence with Rita and María. Rita was especially gossipy and kept us informed about the goings-on in the neighborhood. A local farmhouse sold to *extranjeros Alemanes*, German foreigners, was undergoing many changes: larger windows, a terrazzo patio and the ground leveled to put in a swimming pool. Fat Esperanza, who tended goats in the field across the highway, had another baby. A loud, coarse woman, we'd been told she was not from Ibiza, but originally from Murcia. The aerograms always included news about the weather and how full the cisterns were. On December 16, 1966, Rita mentioned there had been so much rain, she and Antonia climbed the mountains to harvest mushrooms in the woods, collecting half a *cesta*, basket. Almost every letter mentioned sitting around the table at mealtimes, enjoying our Coleman lantern.

When we left Ibiza, we gave one of our lanterns to Rita, her mother and grandmother, and the other to the Palerms. They were all so excited, one would think we'd given them the gift of light.

Iowa City, winter 1947

I WAS AN ADULT BEFORE THE accident materialized for me, emerging with certain clarity, demanding my immediate and undivided attention. Until that moment, it had existed as a ghostly flicker of abandonment and denial. I thought about it carefully before relating the details—first to Leonardo, then my sister, and finally to my younger brothers.

There were occasions in our parents' final years when Leo and I would talk late into the night during his visits to Iowa. With my sister, it was an autumn day, a small café in New York where we'd met alone, without mates and children. Our conversations were about the usual things siblings speak of—childhood events and family relationships, the shapes of love, the spasms of jealousy. Leo said he'd wondered about the scars on the back of his torso and legs, but because his parents never explained, he felt he could not ask. I was saddened to hear the resignation in his voice.

My older brother probably knew and understood more than I did about the event and its consequences, but he was inclined to silence. Conceivably that's changed over the decades and he's had more 'talking opportunities'.

Just as William can be prone to few words, I talk too much, expanding on things woven into the fabric of our family, things perhaps better left undisclosed, like 'unknown fibers' in bolts of yardage. I've rarely been able to keep silent when I feel an airing is called for. In the case of the accident, I hoped to fill in gaps, certainly for myself, and possibly for my siblings. The nagging uncertainties that occasionally surfaced for me may have for my younger sister and brothers as well, especially Leonardo. As the older sister and eyewitness, I assumed the role of narrator.

As for my parents' unwillingness to speak about the accident, my guess is that Pa's instinct for self-preservation kicked in immediately. Ma, in her emotional distress, may have articulated her pain to my nine-year-old brother, her first born, surrendering to their special connection. I'm grateful that Ma had her close friend, Roberta, to turn to. She and Malcolm had not yet left for Minnesota, where he would assume a teaching appointment at the University. Silence became my parents' default way of handling difficult, painful situations. It happened over and over; some things were simply never discussed—Leo's accident, religion and death, specifically, the passing of our *Abuelo Luis*.

It was a winter morning. My father was off teaching or in his studio, my older brother at school. We were in my parents' bedroom. My three-month-old sister had a cold. We didn't have a vaporizing steamer, so Ma arranged a large pot of water on an electric element. She placed them on the floor beside the bed so the steam would benefit the baby while she nursed. Leonardo was under two. He was jumping on the bed behind my mother, playing.

One minute he was laughing and jumping, wrapping his little arms around Ma's neck. The next, he was turning a summersault in front of my mother, landing bottom first into the pot of boiling water. It happened in a flash, an instant.

Piercing shrieks as Ma spun around the bedroom, Leo in her arms. Around and around, into the hall, back to the room, back to the hall—a whirligig of color and wailing. In desperation, she sent me for clean towels. On the way to the linen closet, I paused at the mirror on the landing of our staircase. Earlier that morning Ma had braided my hair and tied in ribbons. I was just over four, momentarily staring at my reflection, too young to understand. Hurrying to retrieve the towels, I bent to pick up what appeared to be one of my father's gum erasers, but it was a glob of my little brother's skin. My mother must have danced him up and down the stairs as well.

Everything shifted into low gear after the accident. My parents sent me to stay with friends. It felt as though Leo was in the hospital for ages. When he got home, he required a great deal of attention and was unable to wear diapers. Burn ointments had to be applied continuously. I have a recollection of him standing in his crib, whimpering. Doctors made house calls and spoke in subdued voices. There was concern that he might not develop normally because of the extensive scarring—thankfully, he did. Even at that young age I recognized Ma's profound agony. I have in my head, though it may not be so, that she stopped nursing my sister and that my father took over. He bottle-fed, changed diapers, and walked her at night, while my mother obsessed over her boy.

Eventually the burns healed, but Leo had to re-learn everything that had been traumatized to a halt, especially how to laugh and play. Within the family, he was called 'Baby' and drank from a bottle. I don't remember for how long. The bond that formed between Ma and Leo was unusual for our family, and they remained tied for the rest of her life. Leonardo still speaks of his mother with great tenderness—he always felt her affection and never had occasion to doubt her love. Not outgoing by temperament, Emilia became sadder after the accident, more withdrawn. I sensed her unconscious distancing, and I sensed my sister turning to our father for nurturing and attention. They too formed a closeness, and so it remained, for the rest of his life.

I believe Leonardo's birth order as second son, third child, created a painful impasse during his youth and early manhood. This was further complicated by Mauricio having to fight his own troubled resentment. He was so exasperated with himself and Leo, he didn't know where to turn, and Leo became the brunt of his anger. Yet no amount of his flying anger and frustration could restore Emilia to her previous, unconstrained happiness.

After the accident, a great deal of my mother's emotional energy was reserved for Leo. My sister's isolation was palpable. I don't know if my family was fractured by the accident, but hairline cracks developed, and remain. How much of my brother's adult tendency to melancholia, and what I interpret as my sister's childhood alienation, can be traced to that accident? How much to my parents' silence?

Ma's feelings of guilt may have been so tremendous, she simply could not bring herself to speak about it. And maybe my father sincerely felt, as he often did, the less said, the better.

If my telling helped ease my siblings' angst, it was worth breaking that silence. I felt better. Personalities can be shaped by early events, good and bad. I consider it a miracle that we can overcome huge, negative forces and move on to productive lives. Both my brother and sister did. What happened was not their fault. They were the victims of an accident and its consequences, of the subsequent silence that never recovered its voice.

Córdoba, Argentina, 1942

F OR ANNA, IT WAS MARSEILLES before New York. For my parents, Córdoba, prior to Pa's departure for the States. He was teaching at the School of Manual Skills and Arts during the day and working on zinc dry plates at night—*La Rosa y el Espejo,* portraits of Emilia and the sculptor, Alberto Barral. Though a busy, happy period in their early marriage, my mother was troubled by lingering anemia and weight loss. Her condition perplexed several doctors. No one realized she had endured a 'missed miscarriage', also known as a 'silent miscarriage' or 'missed abortion'. When my parents finally turned to their physician friend, psychiatrist, Gregorio Bermann, the problem was quickly diagnosed. With swift, caring attention, he immediately performed the necessary dilation and curettage, narrowly averting a total hysterectomy. This event occurred between William's birth and mine. Dr. Bermann's intervention was a stroke of luck for me and my younger siblings.

I mention this anecdote in my essay, A Few Days in Córdoba: *Mauricio Lasansky and Stefan Zweig,* because of Bermann's connection to Freud, who was linked to Zweig, who crossed paths with my father. The difficult years of the Depression, followed by the Spanish Civil War and WWII, did not stop the exchange of ideas and research in Córdoba. Bermann was first a physician— the activist, humanist and socialist, following close behind. His commitment to social causes ranged from university reforms in Córdoba, to mental health in China, to the psychiatric treatment of soldiers during the Spanish Civil War. Traversing boundaries of education, cultures and class, his research and work touched many.

A committed advocate of psychoanalysis, he introduced a willing Argentine nation to Freud.

Mauricio's portrait of Sigmund Freud was part of his great men series from the mid 1980's that included Lincoln, da Vinci, Tolstoy, Einstein, Pasteur, Darwin and Goya. (More than once I suggested Virginia Woolf as a candidate, but Pa didn't bite. Marie Curie was the only woman he included, making her look distinctly masculine, despite her flowered dress.) While Pa was an admirer of Freud, I never heard him speak positively about psychiatry or psychoanalysis. Not a 'believer', his tendency was to dismiss the whole field. I've wondered if his unwillingness was disinterest, genuine skepticism, or something more ominous. When I was taking psychology courses in university and reading Ernest Jones' biography of Freud, he was reluctant to converse. The withdrawal was not like him. Discussion was second nature to him, but it seems I was entering worlds he had chosen to avoid. In the end, it's an intriguing thought that a prominent Freudian psychoanalyst was responsible for ensuring my existence.

While Mauricio was engaged with teaching and his own prints, and Emilia was busy at home with William, they enjoyed the company of fellow artists and writers. As their circle extended beyond the arts to include politicians and lawyers, physicians and educators, that phase of their lives was marked by awareness and growth. They formed many friendships. One of the closest was with the British poet, Hugo Manning, a columnist for the Buenos Aires English Herald.

Immediately before the Nazi annexation of Austria, Manning was a foreign correspondent in Vienna, writing for several British periodicals. Born Lazarus Perkoff to Polish Jewish parents, he was known as Hugh Leslie Perkoff in his bylines. (Manning became his publishing name after 1939, though it was not officially changed until April of 1943.)

Hugo arrived in Argentina in 1939, following that stint in Austria. He'd been living in Buenos Aires for about a year when he moved to Córdoba. Eager to leave the heat of the capital, he came in search of the mountain air and cultural environment the university community was known for. Actively involved with the art scene, he attended concerts, plays and art exhibitions, writing reviews for the Herald and other periodicals and focusing on his own poems. Eventually tiring of the Córdoba's exhilarating lifestyle and craving the peace necessary for his poetry, he accepted my parents' invitation to stay with them in the mountain village of Villa Rivera Indarte, where they'd rented a large, country house. William was four, my mother, eight months pregnant with me.

Days of stimulating conversation and regimens of intense work proved particularly fruitful for Manning's poetry and my father's art. I read Manning's recollections and heard my parents' narratives: Pa's account of Manning perspiring as he worked on a poem in the cold studio, 'as if laboring with a jackhammer instead of a pen'; Ma's description of Hugo's eager glances at the hens' eggs she kept piling up on the mantel. It pleased her that he appreciated her servings of *huevos con jamón*.

Mauricio believed Hugo was never truly happy away from England, especially during the war, when 'England was in trouble'. He felt that Manning's increasing anxieties '… as if he was being followed by ghosts', as well as Córdoba's stark landscape, both contributed to his departure from Argentina. Fraught with worries about the bombings of London and concerned for his family's safety, he returned to England in December of 1942 and immediately enlisted—a pacifist, a loyal Englishman. Recruited by the Intelligence Corps because of his proficiency with languages, he was sent to North Africa. Gravely wounded and nearly losing his right leg, he endured pain and limited mobility for the rest of his life. Back home in London, plagued by continual discomfort from his injury, bad health, eventual obesity, and the burden of making ends meet, Hugo experienced stretches of despair.

In 1951, eight years after both men left Argentina, a correspondence began. Writing about life in the States—Iowa's weather, the English language, his teaching—Mauricio complained of not having enough time for the studio while reminiscing about

Córdoba. In return, Hugo spoke of his own poetry demanding total attention, preventing him from marrying. He explained that he had a girlfriend, but a woman's constant companionship was not something he desired. Occasionally he felt serene, other times he was not at peace—not at all, in fact, quite surprised to still be walking the earth. The letters were frank about the present, nostalgic about the past. Another 13 years would pass before Hugo, Mauricio and Emilia were together again.

William remembers the Córdoba night Manning came to bid them farewell, having completed arrangements for returning to his bomb-stricken London. Following the good-byes, Hugo slipped into the studio, found a burin, and engraved a message on a wooden toolbox.

En veinte años, nos encontraremos en el Museo Británico. Cariñosamente, Hugo~ In 20 years, we'll meet in the British Museum. Affectionately, Hugo~

William said the prediction was eerily accurate. Their reunion occurred during my parents' trip to London in the spring of 1964.

The following fall, when Alan and I were in England, we met Hugo Manning. A huge, soft-spoken man, I was instantly drawn to his intelligent, dark eyes and sculpted face. Bushy eyebrows kept guard over his brightness and sweetness, his solitude and sadness. Falling in with his gentle angst felt as easy as joining a parade. My empathy swift and certain—we were tied, having known each other from the start. Guiding us around his flat in the soft, afternoon light, motes of dust settling on piles of books and collections of odds and ends, he explained about the Egyptian ushabti that caught our attention. Only weeks before we had begun collecting the funerary figurines, purchasing our first at the Portobello Road Market. As Hugo puffed on his pipe, limping slowly from one crowded desk to another, from crammed windowsills to overflowing shelves, he spoke quietly of his interest in parapsychology and the occult. My father may have been right-on about ghosts. Over dinner at a Greek restaurant, we listened to Hugo reminisce happily about living in Villa Rivera Indarte—the large, country house, the

discussions and meals. He told me about the evening a very pregnant Emilia slipped and fell approaching the table to serve dinner.
As the platter of gnocchi slid across the tiles toward the fireplace
with its mantel of hens' eggs, she remained on the floor, laughing
uncontrollably.

In 1975, long after Argentina and two years before Manning's
death, Mauricio contacted Hugo asking if he'd like to write something about the Córdoba period for possible inclusion in an
exhibition catalog. The piece Manning wrote was a series of mus-
ings rather than an analytical exploration of art and personality. In
the end it was not included in the catalog, but those of us who read
it were treated to a bird's eye view of our young parents.

The remarks about Emilia's 'highly seasoned' food were astonishing. I'd always thought our family meals predictably bland.
'Not *cordon bleu* stuff', Hugo wrote, 'nevertheless, tasty.' ('Highly
seasoned' may have said more about the plainness of the English
cuisine rather than my mother's cooking.) My favorite description
was of Emilia's loveliness and patience while continually pursued
by a tiny, needy, first-born-male-child—an amusing yarn about my
serious, independent older brother. The account of Mauricio and
Manning dropping into Córdoba's arts bar, *L'Aigle*, for a beer and
conversation, was a startling eye-opener. As a kid, I saw my dad
drink a beer at picnics, but I don't remember him ever going to
bars. As for gatherings with artists and writers, sadly, they became
fewer and far between. When those Córdoba days came up in conversation, Pa spoke longingly of companions—the gatherings and
discussions, how they attended openings, plays and readings, how
they supported one another's efforts.

It was different in Iowa. A disturbing encounter as a new
faculty member at the University of Iowa must have resurrected
reminders of what he'd left. When given his first raise, Mauricio
excitedly shared the good news with his colleagues in studio arts.
They in turn, complained to the head of the department. Why was a
'foreigner' given a raise, and not them? Though my father had a couple good friends during my youth, that early faculty incident may

have deterred him from forming more ties, close and long-lasting. Teaching, family, and most of all, the studio, became his focus. His work, everything. There weren't enough hours for the rest.

Córdoba, with its fertile ground for alliances, may have been his last, emotional frontier. That world was so embedded in Pa's psyche, he could not remove or replace it, nor did he want to. Ultimately, this loyalty to his past became an invisible shackling.

In 1995, Ivan Savidge, one of Manning's two biographers, approached Mauricio for a recollection of their time together. I helped pull together the few pages for Savidge's book. Listening to my father's memories, I could feel the beating wings of a brief, but tenacious friendship, the same sensation I'd experienced meeting Manning in London thirty years before. When Pa spoke of Hugo—calling him a symbol of the purest creative mind he'd ever known—it was with genuine admiration. There was none of the witty scorn that often accompanied his commentary. My interest in Stefan Zweig was for the same reason. My father was in awe of the Austrian writer, amazed by his literary and psychological powers. I needed to hear that unconditional kindness in his voice, his approval, especially of writers we both respected.

Hugo left Argentina in December and I was born in January. We just missed each other. I can't explain my gravitational pull to that enormous, pensive man. Our paths never crossed again after that short London visit, but I've kept Hugo close. Much the way I have Leonard Woolf—another Englishman, another certainty only amazement and appreciation can explain. His enduring devotion kept Virginia safe, away from the critics, away from distractions. He tried everything short of thinking for her, so she could write, so she could leave us her work. But her sanity was not within his power. When Virginia Woolf killed herself in England in 1941, Hugo Manning, still living in Argentina, wrote an obituary essay in Spanish for SUR, the Buenos Aires literary magazine. And in the 1965 letter Manning sent to my parents after Alan and I visited with him in London, he wrote of how he advised the young couple to travel to Cornwall, to St. Ives, '… if only to see a lovely part of England.'

St. Ives, Virginia's childhood summer haunt. But Hugo didn't mention that in his letter. Why would he? During our brief exchange in his dusty, Hampstead flat, neither of us knew Virginia Woolf would become a favorite writer, a mentor. Nor did we know that if it were possible, I'd travel back in time to Leonard Woolf. I would have gone to him, coping better in his era than he would have in mine. His thrifty nature could not have managed the torrents of conspicuous consumption that have marked the decades since his passing. I have an image of them together in Trafalgar Square. Bulky Hugo in his duffle coat, slim, bow-tied Leonard. Feeding pigeons they discuss the Hogarth Press, and how it simply would not do to bring out Hugo's most recent, long poem. Astute, polite Hugo understands that Leonard must be in complete control of all he can, for all he can't.

Interconnected spheres of people and places, ideas and memories, turn in our skies. That Hampstead afternoon, one of Hugo's and mine collided, forming a new attachment at their juncture. It was novel for me at my young age, but most likely not for Manning. He had many friends in the realms of literature, music and art, many circles that interlocked. New bonds were continually created, encouraging his resolve to push on, to make heard his voice.

Hugo's letters cover those moments of despair and isolation. I like to think that when his vessel lost its way, when stars were no longer visible in the darkened skies, those overlapping domains of support were there. Hopefully, he gathered courage as they reached out protectively, biding time until his mast was righted and course reset, until the light returned.

There is an end to this story. Not long ago I had the opportunity to examine a portfolio that hadn't been touched in decades. The collection came from Argentina with one of my uncles visiting Iowa—Julio, or perhaps, Marcos. I stood at a counter with an equally curious nephew flipping through early zinc drypoint proofs, the multiple stages of *La Rosa y El Espejo*, portraits of my mother, several incomplete drawings, and finally, a finished, signed, pencil sketch on manila paper.

"That's Hugo Manning!" I gasped, astonished.

"Who's Hugo Manning?" my nephew asked.

I told him, certain he could hear my galloping heart. I was overwhelmed by the drawing's urgency, the unfiltered intensity. It was a complete break from the drypoint needle on zinc plates, ink and tarlatan, soaked paper, the press. Unfettered, no dreamlike landscapes from Pa's imagination inhabiting his prints of the same period, no horses and distant castles, incomplete bridges and broken violins—nothing, just its own life force in a unique, captured moment.

Were there more drawings similar in feeling? Could it be the only one? Why was the drawing done at the Hotel Sarmiento in Los Cocos, a town more than an hour and a half from where my parents lived? Was Hugo there before he stayed at Rivera Indarte, or after? I was impatient for information. Did they all go to Los Cocos, my father and pregnant mother, my brother? When I asked William, he suggested that they may have taken a day trip up into the mountains, though he didn't remember it happening. I needed details. How had I missed this poignant declaration of attachment in my father's work?

Standing at the counter with the portfolio, taking in Hugo's chiseled countenance, I was in that surreal juncture of our interconnected spheres. I felt Hugo's presence but the window before me was unfamiliar. I reached for the green blind waiting to be raised. There was no distant view, only a foreground with an anatomical drawing of a heart—similar to botanical prints of root vegetables. Parsnips, beets, turnip, split open to reveal their inner secrets. At the bottom, in block letters: THE HEART IN FRIENDSHIP.

"Did you know him?" My nephew asked.

"A little. The artist loved his subject, don't you think?"

My nephew nodded silently.

Hugo hangs above my desk keeping watch. Left eyebrow raised, the slight frown, he waits, poet that he is, waits to hear my next sentence. I keep him close, for all he tells me, and all he doesn't.

In 1941, the Director of the Metropolitan Museum, Francis Henry Taylor, was on a South American tour when he met Mauricio and saw his prints. Impressed by his work, Taylor arranged for a 1943 Guggenheim fellowship so my father could study printmaking at the New School in New York.

Readying to depart for the new world, the preparations and farewells, the doubts and dreams, Mauricio's thoughts were probably similar to Anna W.'s as she boarded the ship in Marseilles.

After Ibiza

W HEN ALAN AND I THINK of Ibiza, we're always amazed
it was little more than a year. By following in the foot-
steps of her agrarian culture—virtually unaltered for
centuries—we experienced the pride of her people, the calm of
landscapes and dwellings, the balance of rural grace and poverty.
The ethos of that time and place has never left us.

Our departure from Ibiza marked the end of our first great
adventure. More would follow. The birth and upbringing of our
four children. Alan's university teaching in Saskatchewan, Ontario
and Texas. The early, year-round, decade on our Teeswater farm,
where painting and writing could expand like kids and gardens,
where proximity to the city gave our children their Toronto clan.
Teeswater, where we return, summer after summer.

Anna W. left the island a few years after us. She settled in
Laguna Beach, California to receive needed medical attention. We
met twice after Ibiza. She came to visit us on the farm when the
girls were little, and in 1977, we saw her in California with our first
three kids. We'd gone to Regina, Saskatchewan, for the unveiling of
Alan's Musicians Tapestry at the Centre for the Performing Arts,
and were continuing on to Cuernavaca to see my parents. It was a
difficult visit with Anna. She seemed old and distracted, unhappy
about sharing us with our small children. That was the last time we
saw her, though we kept in touch by mail.

In the mid 80's, we learned of her death in Laguna Beach. One
of our letters was returned unopened—DECEASED, stamped beside the envelope's postal cancellation.

Iowa City, fall 2009

W EEKS BEFORE MY MOTHER'S PASSING, I arrive for a visit and she asks me to tell her who she is.

Kneeling on the bed, just waking from a nap, she looks confused. Hair in disarray and arms extended as if trying to gather in her world, her eyes dart from the prints on the walls to the shelves of books, to the cold, November deck. Sweet Williams' ghostly stems droop from Pa's planters.

She lowers her arms and beckons.

"Please," she says, looking at me, "please tell me who I am ..."

I sit beside her and she leans in close, shivering.

"I don't remember ..." she whispers.

Pulling up a blanket, I tuck it around her shoulders.

"Everything," she pleads, patting my hand. "Tell me everything, from the beginning."

And so I do.

Summing-up

THE DISCUSSIONS BEGAN WHEN ALAN finished reading the first draft. He liked the three additions of fiction, two short fragments and one complete story.

"Would you consider adding more? It pulls together the life and work—rounds out the picture."

Perhaps he was right.

The boxes and boxes of stored files hadn't been opened in decades. Out came original manuscripts, inquiries, positive and negative responses, notes, the old logbook of submissions. Carrying arm loads into my study, I went back to cull for more. Standing in the storage room, I glanced through some of the really early pieces. Those typed, hand edited, cut and taped, faded yellow, newsprint-like pages. A high percentage of the serious, eager stabs were fragments—like unearthed, pottery shards that held no promise of ever coming together. They were left in their boxes. Also left behind, the bond copies of my first two unpublished novels. Genuine determination clamored from the pages of my third novel—similarly unpublished. I permitted it into my study and a few segments made their way into this book.

Continuing, I read letters—laudatory and the other kind, from editors and publishers, professional acquaintances, friends—commentary spanning the decades of my work. I flipped through piles of rejection slips and left them as well. They'd been stoically tolerated and ultimately ignored the first time around, so why would I subject myself now? Long ago, having listened carefully to Alan Gurganus, I'd learned to wear rejection like a cloak.

It's a wonder I kept it all. An inherited trait, I suppose. As mentioned in this memoir, my mother stashed away everything from bits of darning yarn to our old report cards, and my father did the same, seemingly keeping every scrap of paper he'd ever scrawled on. Reading through some of his papers, I came across a recycled envelope from the early 1950's covered in scribbled numbers—a totaling of the year's art supply expenses for the accountant who prepared my parents' taxes.

Within days and for days, my study was covered with writing: the published works, the others, languishing bravely. I found the journals and quarterlies that had been sent on the occasion of each publication—covers fading, spines cracking upon opening, typos glaring. I pulled out copies of my books, *No Peace at Versailles* and *Losers and Keepers in Argentina*. *The Egyptian Man*, the book Alan and I worked on together—inspired by our small, limestone statue—remained protected in its archival box. Alan heard me read the 1,000-word story at a writers' evening, and shortly after began working on six etchings. Eventually they joined the hand-typeset text in a large format, limited edition livre d'artiste—the layout, cover and casing, beautifully designed by the Center for the Book, at the University of Iowa.

In addition to the published pieces, close at hand were the printed pages of recent work. Some are included in this writing, others, still being worked on. Surrounded, I was amazed at how the decades passed and I kept pushing forward, rarely looking back.

But the past was evident. A couple early story folders still had labels with the title, date, address, and my name: Rocio Weinstein, (Mrs. Alan). Mrs.? Really? Astonishing. Was it me, or the times?

So what's in a name? A lot. At birth: Rocío Aitana Lasansky. In marriage: The formal Mrs. Alan, a.k.a., Rocio (Nina) Weinstein. For my writing: Nina Barragan. Often asked about Nina (my family nick name) and Barragán (my mother's maiden name), I explain that it came into existence for my first literary submission—a Canadian competition requiring anonymity through a pen name. It stayed with me so that my writing would not carry father's name, or my husband's. I wanted my own. But before I got to Nina Barragan, I considered pen names the way some women toy with lovers—in passing, no strings attached. Only the Scottish sounding Emily Hollis McIver became a *fait accompli*. Years ago, convinced Emily would fare better in Anglo Saxon Canada than any combination of my other names, one of her stories was sent off to Nova Scotia, where acceptance came on the pages of *The Antigonish Review*, in Dalhousie.

Standing in my office, too absorbed to sit, I read my first published story, 'The Subway Car'. It took me by complete surprise. Though heavily flawed, the story's relentless intensity was hard to ignore. I read eagerly, shocked that I had no recollection, that I didn't know what the next sentence would bring, yet familiar themes and preoccupations were present, even at the age of 23. I read other pieces, fascinated by obsessions that would continue through the years, re-inventing and re-purposing themselves, like the broken pieces of a kaleidoscope, pulling apart and coming together in ever-changing configurations of luminosity and shadow.

There I had it, physical proof of what I'd been doing: places visited, difficult situations, memorable characters. My fiction, and more recently, my non-fiction, lying about on the floor, the counters, desktop and coffee table. I was looking back as never before. Photos of the scene might have been smart, photos to send our kids. Remember those Teeswater babysitters, how they came faithfully three days a week, rain or shine, blizzard or calm? While they made you lunch and cookies—the artist in his studio, the writer in her writing shed—all was right in our world. You happily played with the cat, listened to stories, and the baby was fed because I'd pumped for his bottle before leaving the house. Our family routine, before you began boarding the school bus.

With the memoir's pages stacked on the counter, my life and work were coming together. It felt wonderful. I would have liked it to remain so forever. But the tidying happened, then the organizing by date, and finally the list. With the previously published fiction chosen for inclusion in this memoir, I corrected typos and made simple edits. (The older the work, the more necessary the adjustments, the more temping the clean-up.) A few needy sentences were rearranged and unnecessary words and commas removed, but with every tweaking, I thought of the story Alan tells about Claude Monet. In the early twenties, when the elderly artist visited a certain provincial museum, he carried with him a small paint case hidden under his greatcoat. The museum's guards were alerted to keep a lookout for the aging painter, known to pull out the paint case and touch up his own paintings displayed on the gallery walls.

I decided I couldn't worry about the 'ethics' of edits—it was, after all, my work. The main thing was the strategic placement of fiction, if the fusion was to succeed. The emotive drive, the need to comprehend, the empathy with lives in pain—understandings shared between fiction and memoir. In the end, it added up to one and the same.

I think of last winter and how Alan, who leads me by a few years, would come home from the studio telling me he'd come across an unbelievable drawing, breathtakingly beautiful, from a remarkable period he'd forgotten about. I was envious. I'd never had such an experience.

Now I understood—everything was falling into place. Allowing myself to glance back, be it briefly, I could see the big picture, as I hurriedly returned to our shared moment in time.

Acknowledgements

I would like to thank the following presses and publications for granting permission to reprint my work:

BOOKS

Barn Collections Press, *The Egyptian Man,* a large format, limited edition livre d'artiste, fiction and original etchings. Barn Collections Press,1988 ISBN #: 978-0-615-53468-8

New Rivers Press, *No Peace at Versailles and other stories,* Minnesota Voices Project competition in short fiction,1991 ISBN #:0-89823-123-x

University of New Mexico Press, *Losers and Keepers in Argentina,* a book of fiction, Jewish Latin America series, 2001. Introduction by Ilan Stavans, series editor. ISBN #:0-8263-2222-0

ESSAYS & STORIES

ART TIMES Journal, *"A Few Days in Córdoba: Mauricio Lasansky and Stefan Zweig",* February 2014.

North American Review/Open Spaces, *"When Fiction Becomes Memoir",* September 17, 2019.

Hyperion Books, BECOMING AMERICAN, Personal Essays by First Generation Immigrant Women, *"Doing Archaeology in My America",* 2000

Wascana Review, *"The Subway Car",* Vol.2 No.1. 1967 (Under: Weinstein, Rocio).

The Antigonish Review, *"Fur Elise Before the War",* Antigonish, Winter Issue No. 40, 1980. (Under pen name: McIver, Emily Hollis).

About the Author

NINA BARRAGAN, pen name of Rocío Lasansky Weinstein, was born in Córdoba, Argentina, raised in Iowa City, Iowa, and received a BA in English from the University of Iowa. Married to artist Alan Weinstein and mother of four grown children, home is Iowa City and Teeswater, Ontario. She has published three books of fiction. *The Egyptian Man*, 1988, Barn Collections Press, is a large format *livre d'artiste*—Nina's story and Alan's etchings. *No Peace At Versailles and Other Stories*, 1990, New Rivers Press, was a winner in the Minnesota Voices Project Competition. *Losers And Keepers In Argentina*, 2001, University of New Mexico Press, presents a fictional, historical journal with thematically related stories. Since 1967 Barragan's work has appeared in quarterlies, journals and anthologies.